SCENARIOS

SCENARIOS

The Art of Strategic Conversation

Kees van der Heijden

JOHN WILEY & SONS
Chichester • New York • Brisbane • Toronto • Singapore

National 01243 779777
International (+44) 1243 779777
e-mail (for orders and customer service enquiries): cs-books@wiley.co.uk
Visit our Home Page on http://www.wiley.co.uk
or http://www.wiley.com

Reprinted February and September 1997, March 1998

Other Wiley Editorial Offices

John Wiley & Sons, Inc., 605 Third Avenue,
New York, NY 10158-0012, USA

Jacaranda Wiley Ltd, 33 Park Road, Milton,
Queensland 4064, Australia

John Wiley & Sons (Canada) Ltd, 22 Worcester Road,
Rexdale, Ontario M9W 1L1, Canada

John Wiley & Sons (Asia) Pte Ltd, 2 Clementi Loop #02-01,
Jin Xing Distripark, Singapore 129809

Library of Congress Cataloging-in-Publication Data

Van der Heijden, Kees.
    Scenarios : the art of strategic conversation / Kees van der Heijden
        p.   cm.
    Includes bibliographical references and index.
    ISBN 0–471–96639–8 (cloth : alk. paper)
    1. Communication in management.   2. Creative thinking.
3. Strategic planning.   I. Title.
HD30.3.V36   1996
6589.4′52–dc20   96–32465
                                                            CIP

British Library Cataloguing in Publication Data

A catalogue record for this book is available from the British Library

ISBN 0-471-96639-8

Typeset in 11/13pt Bembo from the author's disks by Mackreth Media Services, Hemel
Hempstead, Herts
Printed and bound in Great Britain by Biddles Ltd, Guildford and King's Lynn
This book is printed on acid-free paper responsibly manufactured from sustainable forestation,
for which at least two trees are planted for each one used for paper production.

Contents

Preface

People often get exasperated by what they read about strategy. It's a highly dynamic area, full of fads and fashions, where ideas come and go. Yet it is interesting to see how a few texts seem to remain valid over the years. These seem to aim more at analysing underlying structures than at proposing specific strategies. The reason should be obvious: while it may seem to make sense to copy ideas that "work" for others, a lasting, winning strategy can only be based on being different from competitors.

One of the structures that has helped me a lot, making sense of what I have experienced, is what I call the three "schools of thought" in strategy:

- rationalists (finding the "optimal strategy", e.g. Michael Porter);
- evolutionists (strategy emerges, can only be understood in retrospect, e.g. Henri Mintzberg), and in between these two:
- processualists

Managers love the rationalist school, it assigns power to them to determine the destiny of the organisation. However, they also realise that it does not always work very well. For example things often turn out rather differently from planned, and there is a lot of uncertainty about implementation.

Managers hate the evolutionist school, because it disempowers them nearly altogether. They need something in between these extremes. Enter what I call the processual school, which emerges through strategic conversation. If things change rapidly and are unpredictable, today's strategy may be tomorrow's disaster. You have to stay with the issues until real world action is taken, and then you have to stay with the consequences. The less things are predictable the more attention you have to pay to the strategy **process.** Uncertainty has the effect of moving the key to success from "the optimal strategy" to the "most skilful strategy process".

The strategy process, or strategic conversation, has a formal part, designed by the managers, and an informal part, which consists of the casual conversation about the future and which emerges spontaneously in any organisation. The latter is extremely important because it determines where people's attention is focused. Managers cannot control this, but they can intervene. The issue here is to find the high leverage points. That's what this book is about.

It's important to remember that the language of organisations is rational. If managers want to intervene they need to build a solid line of strategic reasoning, around which people in the organisation can gather. Another part is to align views in the management team; if there is one thing that kills management interventions it is mixed signals from the top. Finally management needs to maintain its own strategic conversation until change champions stand up and go out to "make it happen". A significant part of this book therefore, is about how management should get its own strategic house in order.

But building solid logic is never sufficient. In the end success derives from being different. It requires an original invention. Management can contribute by creating the conditions that make it favourable for inventions to emerge. But there will always be an unfathomable part to this; how else could the invention truly be original? Blending invention into the logical language of strategy is an art, the art of strategic conversation. We can learn from the great masters who have gone before us. Having done that, we then have to make our own creation.

The question, of course, is how. It's important to remember that the strategic conversation is shaped by the way people in the organisation see their world. Mental models have been built up over time, and these are coupled through a common language that makes the strategic conversation possible. Over time people influence each other in the way they see their world.

An effective strategic conversation requires a balance between integration of mental models, to enable the organisation to come to a shared conclusion and move forward, and differentiation of mental models, to ensure that a wide range of weak signals in the environment are perceived, understood and brought into the system to enter the conversation and be acted upon.

There are two pathologies at the end of the continuum from integration to differentiation, namely "group think" in case of an excess of integration and not enough differentiation, and fragmentation in case of an excess of differentiation and not enough integration. It can be shown that organisations, if left to their own devices, will inevitably drift towards one of these extremes. A healthy balance requires active management intervention. So we see managers bring in "new blood" to move away from "group think", or engage in "team building", to move away from fragmentation. These are examples of intervention by managers in the strategic conversation.

Another powerful intervention is by creating more space for the informal conversation, by creating events and systems of events through which views can be exchanged outside the pressure of immediate decision making. This type of intervention needs to be carefully designed to ensure that it helps the balance between integration and differentiation, and doesn't drive the system into one of the two pathologies.

It is my experience that scenarios are the best available language for the strategic conversation, as it allows both differentiation in views, but also brings people together towards a shared understanding of the situation, making decision making possible when the time has arrived to take action.

Managers have been doing these things since time immemorial. It is only now, through the conceptualisation of the notion of the strategic conversation, as a sort of nervous system throughout the organisation, that we can see clearly how these activities link to the strategy of the organisation, and ultimately to its success and failure. Being aware of the strategic conversation in the organisation and the opportunities it offers, frees managers from the bind they are in between rationalism and emergence, and can help them practise more skilfully and intentionally many aspects of the job that the best managers have always done intuitively.

This book represents much of my life's experience as a planner and as a manager during my 35 years with Shell. The last 6 years, which I spent as an academic at Strathclyde University, have been a wonderful opportunity to articulate this experience and apply it (and confirm its validity) over a much wider range of organisations. During all this time I have had access to the heritage of thinking about strategy through reading and direct interaction with a number of remarkable people who stick in my memory as pivotal at crucial times in the development of my thinking. I am sure there have been others who have been equally influential, but who for some reason have moved into the background. And we all stand on the contributions of thousands, made during a long history of thinking. Trying to acknowledge contributions is always going to be a tricky and highly unfair business.

While many people were experimenting with scenarios for organisational decision making in the 1960s and early 1970s Pierre Wack, through his work in Shell since the mid-1960s, is the undisputed intellectual leader in the area of scenario-based strategic thinking. He was the first to set out the essentials of the use of scenarios as instruments for strategy development. Subsequent historical evolution has clearly shown his far-sightedness, as most other, more probabilistic approaches have fallen by the wayside. Crucial elements of this thinking include:

- The aim of changing mental models of decision makers.
- The need to understand predictability and uncertainty.
- The need to take existing mental models of the decision makers as the starting point.
- Creating a reframing of the issues involved, through the introduction of new perspectives.

From the early days of scenario planning in Shell a prominent role was given to "remarkable people", who had the power to create such a reframing. The network of remarkable people became a crucial instrument of the scenario activity, first in Group Planning in Shell and subsequently embodied in Global Business Network. Nobody understands the power of such a network better than Napier Collyns, now with GBN, who taught me the art and power of networking. The remarkable person "par excellence" for me is Peter Schwartz. I don't think I know anyone who has his ability to introduce a new perspective into just about any conversation in which he participates (Schwartz 1991).

Interestingly, while Shell as a company did not have any problems seeing the value of scenarios, planners from the early days of scenarios onwards considered it somewhat problematic that they could not always lay a clear trace from the scenarios to organisational action. In studying the work of Emery and Trist it became clear to me that scenarios become meaningful only in the context of an understanding of the "organisational self" (Emery & Trist 1965). It seemed plausible that thoughtful managers had more of an insight, albeit intuitive, into the characteristics of the organisational self than the planners and therefore had fewer problems with what became known as the "scenarios to strategy" issue. Jay Ogilvy's metaphor of scenarios as test conditions in a windtunnel for designing strategic success helps a lot to clarify this. From this it seemed to me that in order to understand the overall notion of scenario-based planning it would be useful to help people to articulate the essentials of the organisational self. This would allow them to look at the organisation and its environment in each others contexts, and in this way make both more meaningful.

Pierre Wack also led the way in thinking about the organisational self. While Pierre is well-known for his contribution to the area of scenario planning (his HBR articles are the most frequently cited in scenario related literature) few people realise that he was one of the first to articulate a resource view of strategy in general. In the late 1970s Pierre undertook a comprehensive study of strategy-making as practised at that time, with the aim of showing the strategic context of scenario planning more clearly. In the heyday of the "positioning school of strategy", articulated by Michael Porter in 1980, Pierre intuited (inspired by Richard Normann 1977) that a resource view might lead to a more stable theory of corporate success. At the end of his second HBR article (Wack 1985b) he summarises his conclusions in a simple diagram in which he introduces the notion of "Strategic Vision". He saw Strategic Vision as "the counterpart of scenarios" for coping with turbulence and uncertainty, a "complexity reducer", a common frame of reference within which information can be organised. It enables executives to know what signals to look for, against the "noisy" background of the business environment.

His basic thinking on this, dating back to the 1970s, has never been published. Internally in Shell he described his concept of Strategic Vision as follows:

- A clear and explicit rationale for achieving business success, focusing on building up "profit potential" (as distinguished from operational profit), by developing a reservoir of potentialities.

- A system for dominance, expressed as a commitment to excellence in a number of capabilities (more than two, less than ten) perceived as such critical factors of success that their importance tends to override everything else.

- Coalesced into a unique combination the above mentioned are then experienced as a strategic vision of what the company wants to be.

Note his emphasis on profit potential (not often considered in one breath with "vision"), and the systemic view of a limited number of capabilities working together to create uniqueness. At Shell we subsequently developed this concept further in what I call in this book the Business Idea. But the conceptual underpinning of the thinking in this book, including the insight that scenarios can only acquire meaning against a (tacit or explicit) understanding of the identity of the organisation – the organisational self – derives from Pierre Wack.

Arie De Geus (De Geus 1995) introduced me to the theories of William Stern. It made me realise that the search for profit potential may be related to shareholder interests, but is in the first place a manifestation of a basic characteristic of any "living system", namely the urge to survive and grow. Another major component, related to this, was the view of organisations as systems of loops. This has a long history, with contributions from Darwin, Maruyama, Bateson and many others. Through that perspective growth means "positive feedback". Michel Bougon was the first to use the concept for drawing out the essentials of the organisation's success formula. (Bougon & Komocar 1990). It became clear that a real "success formula" would always be based on a positive feedback loop.

I will argue that there is a close essential connection between this positive feedback and uniqueness. The discussion of uniqueness has a long history in economics. It is usually discussed in terms of competencies. The term Distinctive Competencies goes back at least to Selznick (1957). Today people seem to prefer to talk about "core competencies" (I find this a step backwards, contrary to distinctiveness the metaphorical notion of "core" cannot be conceptually tested). Pierre Wack introduced Dick Rumelt to Group Planning in Shell in the late 1970s, and through him I became aware of the economic literature in this area. Shortly afterwards I had the opportunity to work closely with Paul Schoemaker, who joined us for an extended sabbatical from the University of Chicago. Together we worked through the literature and experimented with ways to apply these concepts in the real world of Shell. Paul pointed out that distinctiveness could never be for ever, it would always depreciate over time, and organisations need to maintain and develop these if they want to stay ahead.

Gradually the specifics of the positive feedback loop we were looking for became clearer, with distinctive competencies leading to competitive advantage (Porter 1985), leading to profit potential, leading to resources which can be invested in maintenance and development of the Distinctive Competencies. Richard Normann helped us a great deal in clarifying the relationship between competitive advantage, customer value and distinctive competencies. I am most grateful for the many in-depth discussions with Richard and his colleague Rafael Ramirez, as part of the "Business Logics for Innovators" initiative, launched by their company SMG. I believe that their book (Normann & Ramirez 1995) will be one of those lasting contributions to the strategy literature.

In this way the concept of the Business Idea, which has proven powerful in bridging the gap between scenario analysis and strategic thinking and conversation, took shape. The underlying paradigm emphasises the ongoing process of strategy making. Don Michael was the first to make me realise that from the moment of acknowledgement of uncertainty the key to success moves from the idea of one-time development of "best strategy" to the most effective ongoing strategy process (Michael 1973). Under the influence of Colin Eden, now at Strathclyde University, I began to understand the overriding importance of the quality of the strategic conversation in the organisation (Eden 1992). The strategic conversation is partly formally embedded in various mechanisms, including the planning system, mandatory submissions and documentation, meetings and decision making processes. But a large part of it is informal, and takes place when people meet casually. It is important to understand the role of scenarios and the Business Idea in the context of this total process.

At the time of his involvement in Group Planning Arie De Geus suggested the label "Organisational Learning" for all of this (De Geus 1988). Our purpose was to try to conceptualise the notion of organisational learning beyond the metaphorical. Colin Eden suggested the crucial interaction between learning and action. The embodiment of this in the learning loop as articulated by David Kolb (Kolb & Rubin 1991) allows a direct connection with the idea of a positive feedback loop, and helped me to develop an overall framework for the argument in this book.

In writing this book it has been my intention to discuss practical things. I wish to acknowledge the contributions of many people with whom I have been working over the years in trying things out in a practical setting. I am grateful to have been able to work in a company like Shell which provides room for experimentation. And we tried things out a lot. The person I worked with most to make our theories useful in a practical setting is Jaap Leemhuis. Our partnership dates back to 1980, and in the course of the years we have worked on scenarios, strategy development, entrepreneurial innovation and organisational development. Many of the approaches suggested in this book go back to that partnership. I am also grateful to my friends in Group Planning, in particular Graham Galer, Brian Marsh and John Collman, without whom most ideas in this book would have remained stuck in theory. They suggested that the best laboratory to test approaches to strategy are the smaller companies, without extensive planning resources. As it turned out the smaller companies have forced us to become very clear about what it is we are trying to do, if any practical result is to be achieved. It proved a salutary discipline.

Introduction: Why Plan?

I have written this book for practitioners of strategic management. These are managers who believe in making a modest investment in thinking about where they want to go. Their aim is to achieve a better result through approaching daily decisions in a structured and efficient way to make the best use of their time and resources. This approach also meets psychological needs of decision makers who prefer to make thoughtful decisions. Most managers would be reluctant to rely entirely upon a "seat of the pants" approach.

With management comes the responsibility and excitement of realising the human potential in one's organisation. The intellectual challenge of this focuses the attention on the long term. This is one side of the management coin. The other side is the day-to-day practice where one operational urgency after another consumes the manager's working day. The manager is fully aware that the urgent drives out the important. When sitting back for a moment, many admit that they are dissatisfied with their own performance. It is this need that I hope to address in this book.

The approach discussed here is premised on the assumption that it is both necessary and efficient for organisations to make an investment in thinking through in advance where they want to go, and in developing policies and strategies based on this. The aim is to achieve a better structured and more efficient day-to-day management practice, so that managers at all levels can take account of longer-term aims in their daily decision making. Research shows that this leads to superior overall results (e.g. Hart & Banbury, 1994).

There are other reasons for investing in the creation of a strategic business policy:

- A modest up-front investment in planning avoids the need to think through every crisis situation from scratch. It is efficient in terms of use of time and thinking resources.
- Appropriate planning assists in making the transition from individual insights to institutional action.
- Appropriate planning creates an institutional learning and memory system; it helps an organisation avoid repeating mistakes.

Managers who are experiencing problems in their business cannot help but think about their situation and try to work out how to change things. They normally need little convincing that a bit of strategic thinking would be helpful, if only to better structure their understanding of what they are experiencing. Their problem mostly is to find the time and resources to engage in a strategic thinking process. This book is about scenario planning – an efficient approach to strategic business planning, focusing on business ideas in an uncertain world.

The need for efficient strategic thinking is most obvious in times of accelerated change when the reaction time of the organisation becomes crucial to survival and growth. All organisations experience such periods from time to time. The problem is that such periods of change alternate with periods of relative stability, when organisations often get stuck into established ways of doing things, making them ill-prepared for when the change comes.

Slow reaction to change is costly. If we want to know how quickly companies react to change it is useful to study their behaviour when they are subjected to large step-change shocks. The oil industry was subjected to a major discontinuity in 1973 with the first Energy Crisis and we will try to draw lessons from this.

The first behavioural example relates to investment decisions in refining. Figure 1 shows the total industry demand for all oil products as this developed since 1945, through the crisis in 1973 until well into the eighties. We clearly see the 1973 break in the trend for the demand for products in reaction to the crisis. Consistent exponential growth was experienced until the crisis took place, after which demand levelled out. Increases and decreases continued to be experienced from year to year, but the broad demand picture became essentially static from then onwards.

BT/annum

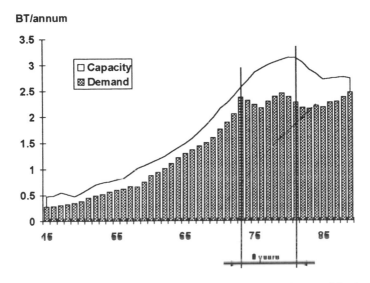

Figure 1. *World oil demand and refining capacity (Source: BP Statistical Review).*

Figure 1 also shows how the oil refining industry reacted to this dramatic change in the business environment. The line representing world-wide refinery capacity in the industry shows very little initial reaction. The industry was obviously used to exponential growth, 6 to 7 per cent per year, it obviously seemed difficult to imagine anything else. Planning new capacity in this business had become an established routine. One knew that the business would expand by six per cent next year, it was not difficult to figure out how much additional capacity was required every year. And if you got it wrong in any one year continuous growth would ensure that correction was relatively painless in the following years. However, in 1973 the crisis occurred and demand started to fall away, then came back and fell away again. For our purpose the development of capacity during this time is enlightening. For two years it continues to grow at the rate that the industry has been accustomed to, 6 per cent per year, with no apparent reaction to the crisis. From then onwards we see the growth slowing down somewhat, but continuing. It is not until the early 1980s that the industry adjusts its capacity back to the level of demand as it had actually developed since 1973.

This industry apparently needed **two years** to discover that anything at all had happened, and then required another **five or six years** to work out the real impact of the oil crisis.

Of course there are lead times of considerable length in planning and building refinery capacity, but not as long as eight years. We obviously have to subtract something from these eight years to arrive at the cognitive gestation time of the industry, but a significant reaction time remains, measured in years. Eventually the oil companies reacted, modified their construction plans, and adjusted to the new situation, but only after taking years to come to that conclusion, and losing billions in the process through the pressure of over-capacity.

The second example concerns new building orders for crude oil tankers. Figure 2 shows new tanker orders by the industry from 1973 into the eighties. Even though demand flattened in 1973 it was only in 1977 that new building orders started to drop off. The effect on the industry was dramatic. Huge over-capacity resulted in large numbers of tankers laid up in various anchorages around the world, and freight rates stayed at absolute rock-bottom for many years.

The difference between the seven years' delay in refining and the four years' delay in tanker orders may have to be explained by the difference in lead times. In both cases, however, substantial delays, measured in years, were experienced before the industry caught up with what was actually going on in its business environment.

The oil crisis example is one of the clearest illustrations of how long it can take for organisations to react to change in the environment. But most of us have similar stories about events in a whole range of other industries (steel, motor cars, IBM, etc.) in which response times are clearly measured in years rather than months.

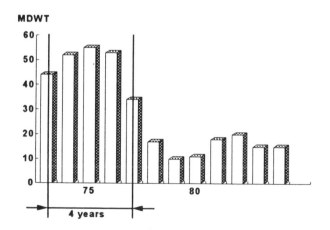

Figure 2. *Demand for new tanker capacity. (Source: BP Statistical Review).*

Imagine a company that would have required only one year, rather than three years, to reorient its business. Imagine the competitive advantage that would result from moving two years earlier than one's competition. Significant competitive advantage does not require perfect and total foresight and prescience. But it does require enhancing the institutional skill in perception and adaptation to produce the fastest most accurate possible response to environmental change.

A DEFINITIONAL POINT

The word scenario is not very well defined in strategy literature. It is used for many different approaches and tools. In the context of this book we need to make a distinction between what we will call external and internal scenarios.

External scenarios are derived from shared and agreed upon mental models of the external world. They are created as internally consistent and challenging descriptions of possible futures. They are intended to be representative of the ranges of possible future developments and outcomes in the external world. What happens in them is essentially outside our own control.

Internal scenarios belong to a person and relate to his/her anticipation of future states of the interactional world, as it relates to the "self". They are less complete but are almost by definition internally consistent. An internal scenario is a causal line of argument, linking an action option with a goal ("if I do this then this will happen which will lead to that and so on until I achieve my objective of A"). The person will play a role in his/her own internal scenario. It can be seen as one path through a person's cognitive map.

For the individual it is quite natural to play a role in his/her own internal scenario – this is part of our everyday-life thinking process. Internal scenarios tend to be normative, with some outcomes preferred over others, reflecting our goal system. This is the world of good and bad scenarios. They involve ourselves.

For the purpose of the strategic conversation in the organisation it is preferable to stay with value-neutral external scenarios. Herman Kahn (see page 16) saw as the great value of the scenario approach that it allowed the observer to engage in value-free exploration. It allows executives to see the world through different lenses, stretching beyond their conventional mental map. Value-free scenarios can help them see things they were not looking for. (Some will argue that a scenario can never be value-free. Even if it cannot, there is considerable value in reducing its emotional charge, simply through the expedient of being only one of "multiple futures".) We should retain this advantage by projecting them clearly in the part of the business environment that we will call contextual (where things are described primarily in terms of "factors" rather than "actors"), and keeping them away from the daily "playing field".

We must distinguish the organisation itself, where the strategist has control, from its *transactional* environment, the world of actors over which the strategist has influence. This world is in turn part of the *contextual* environment, over which the strategist has no influence but which he needs to appreciate as it affects him crucially. Identifying the boundaries between these three areas is a crucial part of the strategic task.

Following Emery and Trist (1965), we define the two environment categories as follows:

- The contextual environment is that part of the environment which has important repercussions for the organisation but in which it has limited influence. Actors in the contextual environment are known as "referees", i.e. those who set the boundaries of what we do, without being subject to our influence. While the organisation does not have power to influence the contextual environment its major task is to arrange its own affairs, such that it remains an effective player whatever may happen there.

- The transactional environment is that part of the environment in which the organisation is a significant player, influencing outcomes as much as being influenced by them. This is sometimes called the "playing field" for which the organisation develops its strategy in order to turn the game to its advantage.

External scenarios play in the contextual environment. An (implicit or explicit) aim of the scenario planning exercise is to consider strategy against the external scenarios as test conditions, in order to assess strength and robustness. This objective requires the distinction between contextual and transactional environments. The test conditions need to be descriptions of the contextual environment, against which characteristics of the behaviour of the organisation, in interaction with its transactional environment, can be judged.

Throughout this book I intend to use the word scenario only in the "external" sense, where it describes the contextual environment. These scenarios will not be good or bad, they are conceived as worlds that may well develop independent from what we do, and in which the organisation will need to be a skilful operator. As individuals we may have a value judgement about these scenarios, but the organisation as a whole cannot think in those terms. It can only take the position that, being unable to significantly change the external contextual world, it will be successful in whatever future comes around.

SCENARIO PLANNING IS ORGANISATIONAL LEARNING

The organisation needs a good fit with its environment if its aims are to be achieved. The purpose of strategy is to develop policies guiding personal behaviour of individuals in the organisation such that the total system achieves a good fit. Traditional "common sense" requires good strategy to be based on the following elements:

- Acknowledgement of aims, either through an external mandate, or the organismic purpose of survival and self-development.
- Assessment of the organisation's characteristics, including its capability to change.
- Assessment of the environment, current and future.
- Assessment of the fit between the two.
- Development of policies and, following from this, decisions and action to improve the fit

Although scenarios in a narrow sense of the word are stories describing the current and future states of the business environment, scenario planning is normally understood to be an approach towards dealing with all five steps.

Scenario planning distinguishes itself from other more traditional approaches to strategic planning through its explicit approach towards ambiguity and uncertainty in the strategic question. The most fundamental aspect of introducing uncertainty in the strategic equation is that it turns planning for the future from a once-off episodic activity into an ongoing learning proposition. In a situation of uncertainty planning becomes learning, which never stops. We have an in-built urge to try to pin down situations, and to try to reach a point where we have got it sorted out in our mind. If uncertainty is acknowledged it is not any longer possible to take this position of "we have done the planning, we can now get on with making it happen". The idea of continuous learning is less comfortable as it does not give us this feeling of problem closure.

However, strategy is about the future, and therefore involves uncertainty. The traditional approach tries to eliminate uncertainty from the strategic equation, by the assumption of the existence of "experts" who have privileged knowledge about "the most likely future", and who can assess the probabilities of specific outcomes. Scenario planning assumes that there is irreducible uncertainty and ambiguity in any situation faced by the strategist, and that successful strategy can only be developed in full view of this.

The study of scenario planning is the study of organisational learning. Organisational learning involves the total system, assuming that characteristics of the whole system become apparent through its interaction with its environment, based on empirical observation. Another aspect of the learning system are the individuals who make up the organisation and influence the whole. However, institutional cognition and behaviour have emergent characteristics which are not immediately apparent from the cognitive characteristics of the members making up the institution. The total is different from the sum of the parts. Understanding comes from pursuing both perspectives.

A number of assumptions underlie the reasoning in this book:

- Organisations are made up of people who approach their organisational actions in a thinking way.
- The organisation does not simply behave as the sum of the behaviour of individuals. Through their interactions unique institutional behaviour emerges.
- Individual strategies need to take account of the systemic properties of the institution as a whole, if they are to lead to their intended results.

The managers I particularly want to reach are those running successful organisations. They may be more in need of a disciplined approach towards strategic management than their colleagues facing serious problems, and they are often not aware of it. There is something pernicious in business success. An observation I have made over many years of practice is that management teams in charge of successful organisations show significantly more consensus on strategy than teams in trouble. They often ascribe their success to this clear and shared vision. In my view it is equally true that the causal relation is the other way around, and that success leads to focusing in the team. Miller (1993) argues that most successful organisations lapse into decline because they have developed too sharp an edge. They narrow the focus of their attention to a reducing set of strengths and functions, while neglecting others. The organisation will become a more and more efficient machine, doing fewer things increasingly well.

The problem is known as the "Icarus" effect. Initially the organisation may experience considerable success with this focusing strategy. This will lead to strong re-inforcement of the "success formula" through cognitive, cultural and structural mechanisms. The problem arises when societal change reduces interest in that one activity. The organisation then finds that it does not have the "requisite variety" (Ashby 1983) to take cognisance of, and adjust to, evolving needs.

Such organisations and their management teams need to take on board a disciplined way of looking outside their daily business. In order to improve their perceptual capabilities they need to become more nuanced in their understanding of the business environment. The traditional rationalistic approach to strategic management with its emphasis on the organisation as a unitary actor is of limited help here. What is needed is a more complete philosophy mobilising the cognition, culture, structure and process throughout the organisation. Only in this way can the company as a whole acquire the perceptual skills needed to see, understand and act on important changes in the business environment across a wide front. This book approaches strategic management with such an integrated focus.

HOW TO USE THIS BOOK

The book has four parts which cover the subject in the following way. In Part One we will first of all discuss a number of the underlying assumptions of traditional ways of thinking about strategy. Specifically we will discuss three paradigms, based on views of the world characterised by rationalism, evolution and systemic process. Consideration of uncertainty and ambiguity will allow us to see that all three are valid perspectives on a situation which is too complex to be packaged in only one of these views. We will then argue that a synthesis can be achieved by the introduction of the notion of institutional learning. We will show how all three traditional views of strategy have a logical place in the organisational learning loop. Finally we will argue that scenario planning can be seen as a form of such integrative institutional learning. Using that as a basis we discuss what this means in terms of shaping the approach with the objective of creating a practical tool, using all modes of thinking about strategy.

In Part Two we will discuss the theory of scenario thinking. This is based on articulation of the characteristics of the organisation itself, and consideration of the environment in which it exists. The organisational "self" is the starting point of skilful strategy. We will introduce the concept of the "Business Idea" as a way of making explicit those aspects of the organisation which are crucially tied up with the question of survival and development. In the environment we will be particularly interested in ambiguity and uncertainty, which will lead to a characterisation in the form of multiple, equally plausible futures. We will then bring these two together and address the question of how to judge the robustness of the Business Idea in the future business environment. Answering this will lead us towards an understanding of strategic direction.

Part Three introduces the practice of the scenario planning process. Specifically we will discuss how a management team can go about engaging in a thinking and discussion process to surface the understanding of the executives in a form which allows rational discussion leading to strategic conclusions. We will also discuss how external perspectives can be introduced into the process, to avoid "institutional myopia". Although there are many ways in which this can be achieved we will suggest specific approaches that can be adopted by the inexperienced. Following this approach a management team will articulate its shared Business Idea, analyse its business environment in all its uncertainty, analyse its competitive position, and then discuss its strategic fit in the world. On the basis of the conclusions reached it will articulate options available for strategies to either improve the fit, or develop its position by exploiting an already strong situation.

After Part Three has taken the management team through a rational thinking process to articulate its position, Part Four introduces the wider institutional behaviour context. The institutional learning model which underpins this book argues that strategy development does not happen only within the management team of an organisation, but involves almost all layers of decision making. A management team which tries to develop strategy in isolation will quickly find that there is not much relation with the actual behaviour the organisation as a whole displays in the world. If the ultimate aim is to make the organisation more adaptable in a changing world, strategy processes must pervade the organisation. Therefore we will need to address both the formal planning and decision processes, and we will discuss steps that can be undertaken to move the whole organisation into a more skilful behavioural pattern. We will also reach the conclusion that the introduction of skilful scenario planning is not only a deliberate decision by management, but also involves the culture in the organisation. An organisation that wishes to move from a traditional rationalist approach towards a corporate learning approach will need to work towards changing the culture. This is a time consuming process that will require not only a conscious decision, but also persistence and consistency from the part of management. They need to realise that they have embarked on a road that will be demanding. On the other hand, we are discussing questions of life and death for the organisation; it would be unrealistic to expect survival to come for free.

Part One

The Context

OVERVIEW

In this part we consider scenario planning in the wider general management context. We will base this discussion on the premise that the ultimate purpose of the scenario planner is to create a more adaptive organisation which recognises change and uncertainty, and uses it to its advantage.

Traditionally this has been the subject of a discipline known as "strategic management", and we review the various schools of thought that have developed over the years under this heading. We will argue that three main directions can be distinguished which tend to be put forward by protagonists as competing explanations of what happens in real-world organisations.

We will then develop a framework for integrating these schools of thought by means of the concept of organisations as learning organisms. We will move beyond the metaphor and develop a model for organisational learning, based on a general learning model developed by David Kolb.

This unified theory of strategic management will put us in a position to discuss the contribution that scenario planning can make. We will argue that, properly institutionalised, the effect of scenario planning can be all-pervasive in an organisation's ability to adapt in a continuously changing world.

Chapter One

1965 to 1990: Five Discoveries at Shell

Scenario planning has a long history emerging from its use by the military in war games. It moved to the civil domain through the RAND corporation during and after World War Two, and was subsequently developed by the Hudson Institute, set up by Herman Kahn after he resigned from RAND. Kahn's most quoted scenario publication was his book *The Year 2000* published in 1967 (Kahn 1967). From the late 1960s onwards scenario planning took off in the corporate world. Scenario analysis has evolved quite considerably. A short history of this evolution will help in understanding the basic principles involved.

In the beginning, scenario analysis was essentially an extension of the traditional "predict-and-control" approach to planning, except that a single line forecast was replaced by a probabilistic assessment of different futures, leading to a "most likely" projection. It did not offer a fundamental advance over other forecasting approaches. By the end of the 1970s, the flaws in this approach were widely known. It is important to understand that the scenario planning process described in this book has at its heart an entirely different central idea. This type of scenario planning relies not on probability but on qualitative causal thinking. As such it appeals more to the intuitive needs of the typical decision makers in their search for enhanced understanding of the changing structures in society. Shell, one of the pioneers of scenario analysis, can probably claim to be one of the first and most consistent users of the methodology.

In Shell, interest in scenarios at a more flexible conceptual level arose with the increasing failures of planning based on forecasts in the mid-1960s. Scenarios were initially introduced as a way to plan without having to predict things that everyone knew were unpredictable. Through Pierre Wack, who introduced scenarios in Shell, the early attempts were based on the Kahn philosophy. Planning must be based on the assumption that something is predictable. If the future is 100 per cent uncertain planning is obviously a waste of time. The problem therefore is to separate what is predictable from what is fundamentally uncertain. The predictable elements became known as the predetermineds. The idea of the Kahn scenario approach was that predetermineds would be reflected in all scenarios in the same predictable way. Uncertainties, on the other hand, would play out differently in the various scenarios.

ROBUST DECISION MAKING

These multiple, but equally plausible futures served the purpose of a test-bed for policies and plans. In Shell, as in most engineering-dominated companies, big future-related decisions are project related. Each project is evaluated against a set of, say, two or three scenarios, so two or three outcomes are generated, one for each scenario. And a decision on whether to go ahead with the project is made on the basis of these multiple possible outcomes, instead of one go/no-go number. The aim is to develop projects which are likely to have positive returns under any of the scenarios. The scenarios themselves are not the decision calculus indicating whether or not to go ahead with a project, they are a mechanism for producing information that is relevant to the decision. Decisions are never based on one scenario being more likely than another; project developers optimise simultaneously against a number of different futures which are all considered equally plausible, and treated with equal weight. In this way both the value and the risk of the project is assessed.

Similarly if a particular strategy or plan needs to be evaluated this is done against each scenario. This produces multiple assessed outcomes, which are considered by the decision makers. Instead of one picture they look at, for example, three. After more than 25 years of scenario analysis top management in Shell would not want to make do with anything less. They are fully aware that if the quality of a strategic decision has been whittled down to one single indicator, important knowledge about the fundamental risk factors in the project have been filtered out. **In this way the first objective of scenario planning became the generation of projects and decisions that are more robust under a variety of alternative futures.**

STRETCHING MENTAL MODELS LEADS TO DISCOVERIES

One of the early findings of the scenario planners was that the search for predetermined elements required them to consider driving forces in the business environment in some depth. The need to separate predetermineds from uncertainties cannot be done without a considerable degree of fundamental analysis of causal relationships

The earliest examples of scenarios created by Wack's team are a good example. The main item on the scenario agenda in the early 1970s was the price of oil. So planners had to consider what was predictable and what was fundamentally uncertain in the price of oil. That meant they had to examine what drives oil price, and, therefore, the whole question of supply and demand.

Interestingly, in those days the outlook for demand world–wide was hardly problematic. It was regarded as predictable, growing around six per cent every year. This had been a consistent pattern since World War Two and was not questioned. So attention turned to supply. To what extent was this predetermined or uncertain? This involved the question of where the supply would be coming from. Of course the Middle East loomed large in this.

Shell's technical people had concluded that supply was predetermined, the resource in the ground was plentiful, and the necessary number of wells could be drilled. But Pierre Wack was not satisfied with that answer. He looked behind it, considering the people who controlled the reserves and would be making the actual production decisions. In the late 1960s these were still the major oil companies, but the producing governments had already established their authority. It was one of Pierre's great contributions to the scenario process that he insisted in looking at the people behind decisions, not just at the technical or macro phenomena. The planners started to wonder whether it would make sense, from the point of view of the producing governments, to continue to supply the increasing quantities required by the oil companies. They had to conclude that this was sufficiently uncertain to make it worth developing a new scenario. This scenario (one out of six initially) became known as the crisis scenario, in which producing countries would refuse to continue to increase production beyond what made sense from their perspective.

When the oil crisis actually occurred in 1973 it became clear that the scenario analysis had put the company on a thinking track where traditional forecasting would never have taken it. Mental models had been stretched well beyond what traditional forecasting would have achieved. Forecasting produces answers, but scenario planning had made people ask the crucial questions. Scenario planning allowed the company to override the domination of the credible, popular but very wrong imagined future. As Shell's managing director André Bénard commented: "Experience has taught us that the scenario technique is much more conducive to forcing people to think about the future than the forecasting techniques we formerly used" (Bénard 1980). **Better thinking about the future became the second objective of scenario planning.**

ENHANCING CORPORATE PERCEPTION

Not much later a third powerful effect was observed resulting from using scenario techniques in an institutional context: People who practised scenario planning found themselves interpreting information from the environment differently from others around them.

For example, against the background discussed earlier of a crisis scenario in the oil industry, the actions of a group of Shell executives stand out. This group recognised in developments in the Middle East the elements of the energy crisis scenario they had been discussing. They interpreted persistent signals from that part of the world as an indication of the accuracy of the crisis scenario, and so they made a number of critical strategic decisions. The most important decision was a change in refining investment policies to allow for the possibility that the crisis scenario was in fact playing out. They interpreted the October 1973 events in the Middle East as the unfolding of this scenario, and were able to quickly shift their investments. While most of the refining industry needed years to decide that something really fundamental had happened in the industry, Shell moved immediately, switching investments from expansion of primary capacity to upgrading the output of the refineries, well ahead of the "pack". As a consequence of industry inertia, refining capacity in the industry ran into considerable oversupply, with disastrous consequences for profitability, but due to Shell's early adaptation of alternative policies they suffered much less from overcapacity and outperformed the industry by a long margin. This later was shown to have had a fundamental impact on the way the company as a whole came through the turbulent 1970s and early 1980s.

Other parts of the company, such as the marine transport sector, which had not worked with the scenarios, did not appreciate the depth of the changes underway and so did not adjust effectively. They continued putting money into more and more tanker investments until much later, and that part of the business never recovered fully from the losses it incurred as a consequence.

What the scenarios did was to enable Shell's manufacturing people to be more perceptive, recognise events for what they were, a part of a pattern, and on this basis realise their implications. As a result of this they were able to respond quickly to events in a way that would have been impossible without the mental preparation of the scenario analysis. This became the first objective of scenario planning.

Important in all this is the institutional aspect. Decisions of the type described here are not made by any individual in isolation, but require a considerable degree of institutional consensus. The ability to read signals must be institutional: enough people must have jointly acquired the mental model if any action is to result. Only if scenario analysis has become an institutionalised planning tool, embedding the insights in the institutional conversational process, do we see the development of consensus necessary for action. When a company commits to this process, scenarios quickly become part of the institutional language. This is due to the effective way in which a story line is capable of representing and transferring a complex reality to a listener in a relatively simple and effortless way.

ENERGISING MANAGEMENT

A fourth aspect of scenario planning emerged later, when top management began to use it as a way of influencing decision making down the line through context setting, rather than direct intervention.

Most organisations have formal "rules of the game" concerning how important decisions are made, involving top management's approval for significant outlays. A simple change in the rules made at Shell in the early 1980s required the justification of any proposed major project against the set of going scenarios. This replaced the usual procedure in which such justification was made against a single line forecast of the environment for the project. The result of this was significant. Since the scenarios now provided the context for making key strategic decisions project champions needed to pay attention.

For example, assume that project developers, matching a project against scenario A, find an attractive pay-out, but against scenario B they find a poor return. In such a case they will be reluctant to submit the proposal, as it may be rejected due to the possibility of this poor outcome. The effect of this will be that people will try to modify the project such that the performance under scenario B is improved, even if that means a slight reduction in the performance under scenario A. The result of this will be a much more robust project, one that is likely to be successful under a wider range of circumstances.

What we see here is that project development work will be influenced by the scenarios even before the project is submitted to top management. The scenarios make an impact when the detailed project decisions are made. **This early influence by top management is not exercised by means of direct instructions, but by using scenarios to set the context within which decisions are made down the line.**

SCENARIOS AS A LEADERSHIP TOOL

A further consequence of this is that the interest of top management in the scenario process is re-inforced. They will become more involved in the generation of scenarios when these become a powerful contextual tool for influencing the development of projects down the line.

Interestingly, in the day to day practice it quickly became apparent that this can work only if scenario planners are fully conscious of their role as intermediaries. When scenario planners start following their own agendas the resulting scenarios are quickly experienced as less relevant in the organisation. This in turn leads to reduced interest from the top, a signal which is quickly perceived in the organisation, isolating the scenario planning effort even more. In this dangerous vicious circle a point is reached quickly where the context setting role of scenarios becomes ineffective.

In Shell, top management use scenarios to provide leadership to the organisation. For example, in 1989 (Kahane 1992) top management became concerned that the company as a whole needed to renew their approach towards environmental issues. They considered the general attitude too defensive, and felt it was important that the company should rethink this. As a consequence one of the 1989 scenarios described a world in which environmental factors developed in such a way that only companies responding positively could survive. As a consequence this issue was on the agenda whenever a project with significant environmental aspects was considered.

Scenario thinking now underpins the established way of making decisions at Shell. It has become a part of the culture, such that people throughout the company, dealing with significant decisions normally will think in terms of multiple, but equally plausible futures to provide a context for decision making. This is known as focused scenario thinking. Focused scenarios are not directly related to the global scenarios used by top management to establish the overall strategic framework. They are of a more ad hoc nature, developed by departments to aid in lower level decision making. The company is satisfied to let scenario analysis take place at different levels in this way without trying to connect these efforts formally. What matters at Shell is the thinking process rather than the bureaucracy of planning.

The distinguishing feature of the scenario culture is that it has invested in assumptions, values and mental models. Tools and techniques are secondary. However sophisticated the tools, if there is no significant effect on assumptions, values and mental models, people will quickly fall back into the old habit of asking "Tell me what will happen". In contrast in a true scenario-culture people will understand both deep structure as well as fundamental uncertainty, and deal with the day-to-day accordingly. Strategic thinking and strategic tools (scenario analysis) in Shell have co-evolved in the company. Better tools have created more effective thinking, and enhanced conceptualisation has created room and demand for superior tools, such as scenario analysis.

The account of Shell's experience illustrates the fundamental point that scenario planning is vital to the normal day-to-day management task. It is not a new management fad, an episodic special activity, a disruption of the normal flow of activities, but a way of thinking which penetrates the institutional mind and eventually affects all activity. It is based on a number of basic assumptions which the Shell experience shows are just common sense:

- Possessing sound strategies reduces the complexity of the management task rather than adding to it.
- Discussing strategy is a natural part of any management task, and not the exclusive domain of specialists.
- There is nothing unusually difficult in good strategy, based as it is on common sense thinking.
- Investing time in structuring the strategic debate will pay off many times over in increased efficiency of dealing with the day-to-day issues managers face.

Chapter Two

Three Competing Paradigms in Strategic Management

The management task in general is one of the most observed activities and academic thinkers have tried to interpret and understand what is going on in the institutional context. The thinking that evolved over the years can be categorised as schools of thought that gradually developed in this area. It is useful to consider this background briefly in order to place scenario planning in context.

Over the years, three schools of thought have arisen to interpret the way managers and entrepreneurs think about their daily business. These can be characterised as rationalist, evolutionary and processual. Other taxonomies have been proposed (see, for example, Whittington 1993 or Mintzberg 1990) but it is not difficult to map these on to the three paradigms suggested here.

The rationalist school codifies thought and action separately. The tacit underlying assumption is that there is one best solution, and the job of the strategist is to get as close to this as possible, within the limited resources available. The strategist thinks on behalf of the entire organisation, and works out optimal strategy as a process of searching for maximum utility among a number of options. Having decided the optimal way forward, the question of action (known as the "implementation issue") is addressed. Mintzberg (1990) lists the (somewhat unlikely?) assumptions underlying the rationalist school:

- Predictability, no interference from outside
- Clear intentions

- Implementation follows formulation (thought independent of action)
- Full understanding throughout the organisation
- Reasonable people will do reasonable things

The rationalistic strategy school is alive and well, in fact by far the largest part of the strategy literature and reporting reflects this viewpoint.

The evolutionary school emphasises the complex nature of organisational behaviour, beyond the realms of rational thinking (Lindblom 1959, Mintzberg & Waters 1985). Strategy is a perspective on emergent behaviour, a winning strategy can only be articulated in retrospect. In this context evolution refers to the phenomena of emergent properties of systems which have a discriminating and transmissible memory of successful strategies. Discrimination may be self-applied or it may be imposed from outside, but it ensures that the strategies which survive are those which are best fitted to do so. In this school of thought strategy is a process of random experimentation and filtering out of the unsuccessful.

The problem with this theory is that, in common with most other evolutionary theories, it has rather little predictive power. Most managers believe that they have some power to influence things, and therefore that strategic thinking is useful. Proactive managers do not often subscribe to the evolutionary view, because it relegates them to insignificant pawns, played by circumstances.

The processual school takes a middle position. It suggests that while it is not possible to work out optimal strategies through a rational thinking process alone, managers can create processes in organisations that will make it more flexible and adaptable, and capable of learning from its mistakes. It looks for successful evolutionary behaviour of the organisation as the ultimate test of a successful process. But it believes that this can be influenced, for which it draws on the "management of change" literature.

The three schools differ in the way organisations are perceived. Morgan argues that people understand their organisations metaphorically, by comparing these with well-known analogues in nature. For example:

- The rationalistic paradigm suggests a machine metaphor for the organisation.
- The evolutionary paradigm suggests an ecology.
- The processual paradigm suggests a living organism.

While much energy has been invested in arguing the relative merits of the three perspectives, strategy making in the real world manifests elements of all three. Rather than preferring one school of thought over another it is more productive for the purpose of creating skilful and adaptive organisations, to see these as three aspects of the same complex phenomenon. The approach to strategy in this book attempts to integrate these three schools of thought in strategy. Before we attempt to do so we need to discuss each in some detail.

THE RATIONALISTIC PARADIGM

In the 1950s and 1960s planning for the future was mostly based on the "predict and control" principle, based on the rationalistic paradigm (Mintzberg 1990). This works well when the questions for the future are well-defined. It requires that we know in principle what we need to do, reducing the question of our actions to one of degree rather than nature. It requires relatively stable interfaces between actors in society. If the value systems of the players on both sides of an interface are relatively stable both parties can assume that things between them are well-defined and get on with optimising their own part of the transaction activities. Businesses will use the fixed elements in the interface to define themselves in terms of the products they produce (e.g. "we are in the textile business") They concentrate on being effective and competitive in putting their well-understood products on the market. The nature of what needs to be done is clear, the problem is to design and optimise the detailed blue-print. This is where predict-and-control planning, based on the rationalistic paradigm, works well.

The Rationalistic Approach To Strategy

The rationalistic perspective starts with the concept that there is one answer and the task is to find it. The purpose of strategy is to get as close as possible to that one right answer. For the rationalist, the perspective of the strategist himself is not important. If there is only one right answer, then anyone, given the right resources, will ultimately discover it. It may be the chief executive, but (s)he may legitimately delegate this job to an intelligent subordinate if this brings more rational thinking power to bear.

Table 1 shows the rationalist approach in terms of a number of steps, which translate the purpose of the organisation in terms of strategies chosen to pursue the purpose as effectively as possible.

Rationalist strategy making starts with the definition of a purpose of the organisation. This is often called a "mission". The outside "owner" of the organisation determines this purpose, or the CEO does this on behalf of the real or imagined outside owner. This view goes back to the military origin of the concept of "strategy". The military organisation does not decide whether or not a war will be fought. An outside political entity decides their mission and the military organisation develops its strategy on that basis. Similarly, rationalist business strategists work from a given mission statement. Interestingly, few strategy textbooks say anything about where the mission comes from. They provide examples from a variety of companies, from IBM's Thomas Watson to the present, and invite the student to crib from their examples. What seems to happen in reality is that the founders of the firm imprint their personal vision on the activity, and when the company has grown up and operates successfully people feel at home with the business they know and there is no need to question the basic mission.

Table 1. *Steps in strategy development*

- Defining the mission
    - Defining utility
    - Defining strategic objectives
- SWOT analysis
    - Internal analysis
    - Environment prediction
    - Identifying strategic options
- Selecting maximum utility option
- Implementation
- Appraisal and control

The next task for the rationalist business strategist is to derive a set of strategic objectives based on the mission. These link the mission of the organisation with the operational scene, and translate its purpose into a series of operational goals. For example if the mission is "to maximise returns on investments" then an objective might be to achieve an improvement in profitability of two points next year. In order to translate this in operational terms the internal situation must be analysed, including the organisational capabilities and limitations. Then the attention moves to the contextual and transactional environments. Out of this analysis feasible objectives are formulated.

Strategies are designed to achieve the objectives. Normally there are a number of options to be considered and the rationalist strategist needs to select the most effective. In order to do this a forecast must be made of the future business environment against which various strategic options can be evaluated. After deciding what the future will look like, the utility of each option is calculated. The one with the highest utility is the preferred strategy. Having accepted the mission, and chosen the preferred strategic option on the basis of maximum utility, then there is no longer room for argument.

That is the theory. In reality the rationalist planner faces a number of limitations. How to identify the options in the first place? Rationalist strategists always face the nagging problem that their intellectual and computing power is limited and the best option may be the one that is still eluding them. They are never finished searching. There is a constant doubt about how close they are to the "real" optimum. Scenarios of the future may help them discover a wider range of options.

Types of Forecasts

In the rationalistic paradigm the strategist, thinking on behalf of the entire organisation, works out an optimal strategy as we described above. In order to do so he needs to predict the future, forecasting a "most likely" picture of the future against which plans can be judged. Everyone is of course aware that there is considerable uncertainty in the future, and that it is not possible to predict things precisely. However, the assumption underlying forecasting is that some people can be more expert than others in predicting what will happen, and the best we can do is ask them for their considered opinion of what might be in store, either as individuals or as a group (e.g. Delphi technique). Our rationalist strategist's final result describes one future world, specifying his best guess of the conditions in which the organisation will find itself. Although this prediction will probably not be exactly correct (in 1971 a Delphi conducted among experts within Shell on future oil price did not come up with any number higher than $2 per barrel!), it is as close as we can get.

All forecasts are based on the assumption that the past can be extended into the future. At the simplest level this means a statistical extrapolation of variables. When radical change occurs, this mode of forecasting fails first. A more sophisticated kind of forecasting involves the development of a simulation model, which allows for the possibility of inter-relationships between variables to be taken into account. Examples range from macro-economic models to war-games. However, simulation models are also based on the assumption of projecting the past into the future, in this case not of variables but of relationships. They are based on the assumption of a stable underlying structure. However when basic structures seem to be shifting simulation models may not deliver at the crucial moment.

Although it is convenient for the decision maker to consider strategic options against one future only, there is a cost to pay. What will happen if the future turns out differently (almost inevitably)? Will the organisation still survive? Forecasts do not communicate uncertainty. They do not help the decision maker where it really matters for the future.

Sensitivities

One way of dealing with this is to consider sensitivities. The decision maker studies what would happen if an important variable in the environment turns out to be somewhat different from the forecast. For example we could consider what would happen to profitability if sales were to be lower by 10 per cent. However, this begs the question whether sales could be down by that amount. And if so, whether it is reasonable to assume that sales would be down in isolation. Or should we assume that lower sales would be due to increased competition, accompanied by lower prices? Or could the drop in volume be due to higher prices? Sensitivities give us very limited information indeed, because they do not deal with these interlinkages of variables in the situation under consideration. They are not internally consistent futures, and therefore misleading decision making tools.

Probabilistic approach to scenario planning belongs in the rationalist school

In the literature the term scenario planning is sometimes used to indicate a method of traditional decision analysis, involving probabilistic assessment of different futures. The aim is consistent with the rationalistic paradigm, to develop a single criterion against which options can be considered and to build a line of reasoning at the end of which the one optimal decision falls out. A typical example of this approach is the development of high and low lines of sales, judged to be possible developments at specific levels of probability. The outcomes of various policy options can then be assessed against the scenarios (typically three: high, low and most likely), and weighted according to the probability of these futures materialising. In this way one overall quality measure is produced for each option, and the one with the best result is selected.

This is not the way in which the term scenario planning will be used here. Scenarios are not seen as quasi-forecasts but as perception devices. A high/low line approach does not enhance perception as it does not add new concepts to the "forecasting" frame of mind. Creating three futures along a single dimension, with subjective probabilities attached, is conceptually the same activity as forecasting. It does not cause us to explore conceptually different ways the future could pan out. In this book, **scenarios are a set of reasonably plausible, but structurally different futures.** These are conceived through a process of causal, rather than probabilistic thinking, reflecting different interpretations of the phenomena that drive the underlying structure of the business environment. Scenarios are used as a means of thinking through strategy against a number of structurally quite different, but plausible future models of the world. Once the set of scenarios has been decided upon they will be treated as equally likely. All must be given equal weight whenever strategic decisions are being made.

WHEN PREDICT AND CONTROL FAILS

Risk, inherent in every business, varies over time. Sometimes things suddenly seem to change direction. Every business encounters periods of accelerated change when old assumptions suddenly become irrelevant. Typically new actors do not play the game according to the understood rules. They start reconfiguring the interfaces between actors in society (often made possible by new-found power, possibly based on a new technology) and the established community feels undermined. Predict-and-control no longer works.

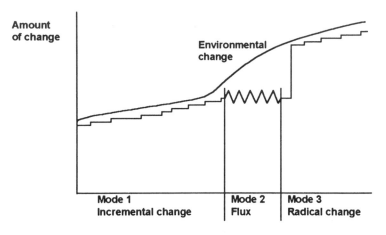

Figure 3. *Periods of turbulence*

Relative calm comes from predictability, but it doesn't mean "no change". In the oil industry before the 1973 crisis, relative calm meant exponential growth, 6 per cent every year. Because this was predicted year in and year out, capacity expansion was planned accordingly. A high growth situation is particularly benign. Competition is less severe and an error leading to over expansion is corrected quickly.

But most companies have in their history periods of extraordinary turbulence, illustrated in Figure 3 (derived from G. Johnson). Something fundamental shifts, the basic rules of the game are overthrown. In that situation, the company isn't quite sure where to go; lessons learned from history are no longer a good guide. New ways of doing things need to be found. Experimentation is the new game. Many experiments fail and then something else must be tried.

IBM is an example of a company which went through such a state of flux. Through its dominant position in the mainframe computer market IBM lived in a predictable and well organised industry where small adjustments in business policy kept the business nicely on track. Then fundamental technological change crept up on it, throwing it seriously off course at the end of the 1980s. Once again we see a well-established industry needing a period of time, measured in years, to come to realise what is happening to it. IBM spent a number of years in the turbulent zone, doing experiments to find the new way forward (e.g. decentralise, centralise again, single/double branding etc.). While these experiments were going on the company did not seem to progress. With the market and business environment moving on, the gap seemed to widen. The company got into more and more difficulty.

Inevitably the gap between business environment and organisational understanding gets reflected in terms of the bottom line, profitability goes down and the company moves into the red. At that stage, the company is in crisis. Management realises that the experiments aren't working. At this point, one of two things may happen. Many companies collapse. Or, just in time, the company makes a radical step change, something that would have been culturally impossible in an earlier era. Often this is associated with bringing in new people, including a new chief executive. The new team institutionalises a new way of doing things. If the diagnosis is right the company may come back from the brink.

The problem is often seen as one of forecasting, but the question is more fundamental than that. "Predict-and-control" cannot deal with structural change. It does not generate the right questions. It is clear that if we wish to make some headway we need to move on from forecasting to a more flexible way of looking at the future. Scenario analysis, contrary to forecasting, can react flexibly to structural change.

THE PROBLEM OF BUSINESS SUCCESS

There are a lot of very successful organisations. Without being aware of it they may be more in need of a strategic management rethink than those who are struggling. Pierre Wack in his well-known HBR article (1985) on scenario planning suggested that in times of rapid change the large, well-run companies are in particular danger of suffering from strategic failure, caused by a crisis of perception. He defines this as the inability to see an emergent novel reality by being locked inside obsolete assumptions. As we saw earlier, Miller argues that most outstanding organisations lapse into decline because they have developed too sharp an edge. They narrow the focus of their attention to a reducing set of strengths and functions, while neglecting others. The organisation will become a more and more efficient machine, doing fewer things increasingly well. Considerable initial success with a focusing strategy leads to strong re-inforcement of the "success formula" through cognitive, cultural and structural mechanisms.

Large organisations get set in their ways more firmly than small ones.

They need to organise things in more detail. Procedures and methods, once in place, become more and more difficult to change. Underlying premises get forgotten, and are impossible to question. Change is not welcome, it is "difficult to argue with success". Often assumptions get embedded in strong cultures, determining also informal and non-verbal ways in which people communicate with each other. The system reinforces the mental models, and these become more and more rooted.

Contrary observation in the business environment is explained away or denied. Or signals received are considered "inconsistent" and therefore insufficiently reliable to act on. In times of sudden change the crisis of perception has become almost unavoidable. The problem comes to the surface when societal change reduces interest in the organisation's main activity. The organisation then finds that it does not have a rich enough mental model to observe and adjust to signals of evolving needs from the outside environment. If a system cannot account for seemingly contradictory and inconsistent signals, its model of the world is not detailed enough. If an organisation finds inconsistent signals overwhelming, it should consider that its model of reality may be too simplistic. In order to survive organic systems need a degree of complexity, equivalent to the complexity of the environment with which they interact (Ashby's law of requisite variety, Ashby 1983). Organisations that have come through an extended period of success almost invariably lack this requisite variety. In those circumstances it is advisable to heed Weick's (1979) advice to companies to "complicate yourself". In these circumstances it is more than ever important that the scenario planner brings in new perspectives from the outside.

Crisis of the rationalistic approach

The rationalistic paradigm is based on a number of tacit assumptions, which are fundamental to its capability to deliver. As we saw the basic tenets are the following:

- It is useful to think of the organisation as a unitary actor in its environment.
- There is only one best answer to the strategy question.
- Everyone thinking rationally on behalf of the organisation will arrive at the same conclusion.
- Implementation follows discovery of the strategy.

It can work only if things are clear and predictable, and people understand and act reasonably.

Rationalist strategic management has allowed people over the years to successfully express their strategic situation, helping them to move forward. But there have also been major failures. Observers such as Mintzberg (*The Rise and Fall of Strategic Planning*, 1994) describe the symptoms of many of these. But surfacing the fundamental underlying premises of the rationalist paradigm raises the question whether rationality can ever explain the whole picture of organisational behaviour. This has given raise to alternative views on strategy.

EVOLUTIONARY PARADIGM

The traditional approach to the discipline of business policy and strategic management has gradually become less and less capable of modelling strategic thinking, due to:

- Logical problems with the notion of sustainable prescriptions for business success in a competitive world.
- Growing insights in complexity that make us realise better the fundamental limitations to prescience.

In reaction the evolutionary school of thinking has come to the fore.

All along there have been people saying, "Real strategy doesn't work as the rationalists make it out". Researchers have been studying organisational decision making and analysed what the decision makers did on a day-by-day basis. They observed that decision making is not only a rationalistic process. For example, Charles Lindblom studied managers in organisations in the 1950s (Lindblom 1959). He observed that they aren't goal-seeking, but "ills-avoiding" - aiming constantly at strategies for avoiding pain, harm, or constraint.

Stewart Brand suggests that nature evolves away from constraints, not toward goals (Brand 1994). Lindblom saw the same thing happening in management. Moreover, different people are moving away from different constraints, there are many different "ills" they are trying to avoid. The organisational decision-making process is polycentric. Therefore it requires the mutual adjustments and bargaining which are necessary if the organisation is to do anything coherent at all. "Nobody's happy, but if everybody's equally unhappy then we probably have a reasonable compromise."

That means high value is placed on consensus-seeking behaviour. Without agreement, an organisation will be paralysed. On the whole, organisations don't like mavericks. People are needed who are prepared to make the effort to come to a common conclusion. When differences exist, they are often held back and not articulated clearly, as people fear that it would make the negotiation process more difficult. Policy decisions are created in a serial process. There is no grand strategy, only "just one thing after another". Lindblom called this "the approach of muddling through."

A more recent analyst in this school is Brian Quinn. Based on his experience in General Electric and other large mainstream corporations, Quinn writes:

> The full strategy is rarely written in any one place. The processes used to arrive at the total strategy are typically fragmented, evolutionary, and largely intuitive. . . . Although one can frequently find embedded in these fragments some very refined pieces of formal strategy analysis, the real strategy tends to evolve as internal decisions and external events flow together, to create a new, widely shared consensus for action among key members of the top management team. (Quinn 1980)

Mintzberg observed that executives going about their job:

- Prefer verbal over numeric information.
- Prefer conversation over reading.
- Gather information on an anecdotal basis.
- Are highly mistrustful of other's general theories.
- Avoid the "grand design" sort of decisions.
- Prefer to make smaller incremental decisions.
- Let the overall strategy emerge.

He coined the term "emergent strategy" to indicate that when people talk about their strategy they will normally talk about something that has taken place in the past, a series of events that have retroactively been interpreted as a pattern, recognised as "our strategy".

Lately chaos theory has impressed on the world the view that many phenomena taking place in nature are unpredictable not just because we lack the analytical knowledge and capacity, but are unpredictable in principle. This is related to complexity and non-linear characteristics of systems, which can be shown to result in behaviour, which is intrinsically unknowable in its detail. Terms such as "the butterfly effect" (a flutter of the butterfly's wing here causing a storm on another continent next week) are stock in trade.

A picture emerges of strategies existing primarily to satisfy the psychological needs of the managers, in particular the need to feel in control. In reality, random mutations take place, and only the fittest survive. Apple survived, while Kaypro (how many remember this once well-known computer manufacturer?) did not. But if you look for some mistake in Kaypro's argument or reasoning versus Apple's, the evolutionary theorists argue you won't find it. You will merely find that some systems have had a random mutation that helped them, whilst others were not so lucky and went under. A strategy textbook written entirely from this perspective would have to come to the conclusion: "Sorry, students, we've studied chaos theory and we have come to the conclusion that we cannot help you". The evolutionary perspective whilst intellectually appealing cannot be popular with business people. They are not prepared to accept that thinking about the future is done only to satisfy inner needs, to create order in the mind. Managers believe they ought to be able to accomplish something in the real world. The pure evolutionary paradigm has little or no forum in the organisational world.

Yet, in times of unusual turbulence the business environment may seem chaotic. Change seems to accelerate and managers have difficulty in continuously redeveloping theories-in-use which organise observations. There may be a feeling of information overload, and loss of grip on the situation. In such circumstances the view takes hold that there is not a lot of sense in spending time trying to think through strategy, the world is too complex to try to get a handle on it. The best we can do is react as things come at us, and hope that serendipity makes us choose the mutations which will make us into the winning species on the competitive battlefield. Most managers have an acute awareness of a considerable element of randomness in what happens. As Mintzberg observed, most managers do not believe in the one grand "strategic answer" that will solve everything. Lindblom saw a lot of ambivalence among managers about declaring a position. They know that they operate in a system driven by negotiation and compromise, so it is better not to be too up front, and to keep things fluid, so that there is room for manoeuvre. Whilst consultants and academics work on reports on: "this strategy is the way forward", managers maintain a healthy dose of scepticism. They need the reports; they pay considerable fees for them, but the reports have some other function than telling them what to do.

PROCESSUAL PARADIGM

The evolutionists tell us that the idea that we can change and improve our corporate survival chances by thinking through our situation and trying to develop an adequate strategy is based on an illusion. Mintzberg suggests that people are discovering this and we are witnessing "the fall of strategic planning".

The processual view starts from the premise that business success cannot be codified, but requires an original invention from the people involved. This implies that the resource the company needs to mobilise is the brain power of its people and their networking and observational skills. The organisation needs to engage in a process to make room for ideas. Any inventive idea directed towards improving the match between the organisational competencies and the business environment needs to be surfaced and considered, wherever these may originate in the organisation.

The strategist looks at evolution not so much in terms of the survival of actual organisations, but the survival of ideas. This makes them interested in what happens inside organisations. Rationalists and evolutionists worry less about how the organisational process works; why bother, if there's only one right answer, or alternatively if there is no answer at all? The processualist on the other hand is keenly interested in internal processes.

Studying the processes taking place inside organisations leads to the fundamental starting point of the processual paradigm, namely the interwovenness of action and thinking. Nobel Laureate Albert Szent-Gyorgi (as relayed by Weick, 1990) tells a story of a group of soldiers lost in the mountains:

> A small Hungarian detachment was on military manoeuvres in the Alps. Their young lieutenant sent a reconnaissance unit out into the icy wilderness just as it began to snow. It snowed for two days, and the unit did not return. The lieutenant feared that he had dispatched his men to their death, but the third day the unit returned. Where had they been? How had they found their way? "Yes," they said, "we considered ourselves lost and waited for the end, but then one of us found a map in his pocket. That calmed us down. We pitched camp, lasted out the snow storm, and then with the map we found our bearings. And here we are." The lieutenant took a good look at the map and discovered, to his astonishment, that it was a map of the Pyrenees.

Weick suggests the following moral: "If you are lost any old map is better than nothing". The map enabled the soldiers to get into action.

They had been disabled; but now the map, believed to represent the surroundings, gave them a reason to act. Accuracy did not come in to it. By taking some action, the soldiers started to obtain new feedback about their environment, and they entered a new "learning loop" which gradually built up their own understanding and mental map. The map got them out of the paralysed state that they were in.

The processualists agree with the evolutionists that most organisational situations are too complex to analyse in its entirety. Whether the strategic "answer" is right or wrong is initially beside the point. The processualists hold that we need to get into a loop linking action, perception and thinking towards continual learning. An effective strategy is one which triggers our entry into that learning loop.

THE LEARNING LOOP

The "learning loop" is an integrative learning model, developed by David Kolb, who synthesised it from the theories of Kurt Lewin, John Dewey, Jean Piaget, and others. Figure 4 shows a diagrammatic representation. Starting at the top:

- We have experiences, some of which are important to us. These include, for example, what we perceive as the results of our previous actions.

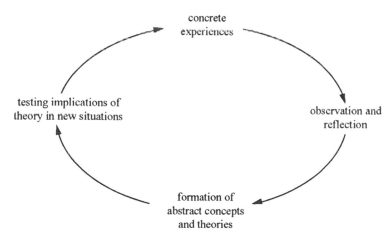

Figure 4. *Kolb's "learning loop"*

- We reflect upon these experiences, looking at what our action has created in relation to other events. The product of this reflection is the awareness of new patterns and trends in events we did not perceive before. Reflection is related to our ability to differentiate between our existing mental model and perception of a different reality.
- Through "cues of causality" we develop new theories on how our ideas about the world need to change as a result of these observations and reflections. The old mental model and the new reality are integrated in a new theory.
- Then we use these theories to plan new steps, and effectively test the implications of our theory in new situations by taking new actions.
- This brings us back to the top. We obtain new experiences resulting from our actions, which only partly overlap with our expectation.

And so we learn! Our new reflection shows us that our theory needs developing again. And the process continues.

The learning loop describes the strategy development process in its integration of experience, sense-making and action into one holistic phenomenon. It illustrates the difference between the rationalist and the processualist. The model is based on the idea of continuous step by step development, rather than "the one right answer". Therefore the process view requires less emphasis on forecasts. Instead uncertainty and ambiguity are faced head on.

The application of the learning loop in an organisational context is discussed further below. However, we first need to consider the basic force which drives an organisation to act as a learning organism. This is related to the organisation's perception of its purpose in the world.

Organisation as Organism

The processual paradigm sees the organisation as a complex adaptive system. It is open to the outside world, and adjusts its activities according to what it discovers there. However, the behaviour of complex adaptive systems is not simply a direct function of impinging external forces, like the behaviour of a ping-pong ball. Rather, as open systems become more complex, they tend to develop within themselves more and more complex mediating processes that intervene between external forces and behaviour. At higher levels of complexity these mediating processes become more independent and autonomous and more determinative of behaviour.

The total organisation behaves differently from what would happen if all units in it were independent from each other. This difference, which determines its identity, leads to the emergent behaviour of the total system. **Emergent behaviour is the outside behavioural manifestation of the internal mediating processes.** In systems terms it implies a hierarchical organisation, with the upper level guiding and constraining the actions of the lower. It is the constraints on the lower level members that creates the emergent behaviour at the higher level (Checkland 1981). Schein (1992) suggests that the constraints operate at three levels. At the deepest level are the basic assumptions, mostly shared but also imposed by the organisation. This gives rise to the next level which takes the form of shared values, indicating what is good, bad or indifferent. At the third most visible level we find the artefacts the values give rise to. At each of these levels the behaviour of the members of the organisation is being influenced, they are not any longer free to act. If such constraints did not exist, lower level members would carry on as if they were independent, and there would be no emergent behaviour, and therefore no identity for the larger system. By imposing the appropriate "rules of the game" (either formal or informal) the upper level steers the emergent behaviour in a desirable direction.

The purpose of these processes is to perform essentially three functions (Checkland 1981):

- Adjusting the system's behaviour to deal with external contingencies.
- Directing the system towards more favourable environments to improve survival chances.
- Reorganising aspects of the system structure to make it more effective in these two tasks.

Stern calls this a "living system", which he defines as a system which is continuously directed towards dual objectives of:

- Survival in a hostile environment
- Self-development in a benevolent environment (Stern 1906).

There are organisations that do not aim to survive, but that have been created to do a specific limited job, after which everyone involved fully intends to liquidate it. However, most organisations develop a way of acting in the world aimed at their own survival and development. These organisations therefore can be seen as living organisms in "Stern" terms.

Learning As Growth

Many organisations subscribe to a "progress or regress" view, lack of growth being taken as an indication of erosion and lack of health. The objective of growth, however expressed, is a natural characteristic of a living organisation. This implies the existence of a positive feedback loop. Later on we will call this positive feedback loop the Business Idea of the organisation. Organisations with strong Business Ideas often develop resistance to change. While busy with the business of development it will attempt to keep disturbances outside the system, by operating smaller subsidiary negative feedback loops (single loop learning). This systemic behaviour can persist only as long as the environmental disturbances are small.

In turbulent environments this mode can not function, and the positive feedback loop, as the basis of growth, will need to be adjusted to the changing situation in the environment (compare Figure 3. Periods of turbulence, page 30). Rather than resist change the organisation will try to create it, in what is sometimes called double loop learning. In double loop learning the system does not only attempt to make adjustment such that a predetermined preferred condition can be maintained, but also modifies its preferred condition in line with the fit with the environment (see Argyris & Schon 1978).

The processual view suggests that organismic organisations need to adopt the idea of the learning loop and build up related capabilities for perception, reflection, the development of theories about the environment, and joint action. We need to consider these points explicitly in an organisational context. Learning in institutions is not the same as learning by individuals, it has additional group aspects that need to be considered.

Scenario Planning As Adaptive Mechanism

The processual approach to strategy is concerned with improving the fitness of organisations by creating processes that can tap the resources available. Scenario planning is such a process. It looks at multiple futures, which are treated as equally plausible, reflecting the inherent uncertainty. It is non-prescriptive. It recognises that successful competitive strategies must be original inventions by organisations. It therefore concentrates on developing processes that enhance the capability of the organisation to mobilise resources towards greater inventiveness and innovation. Part of this is developing concepts and language that are prerequisites for such organisational processes to take place. Scenario planning contributes to this in a number of ways:

- It creates a structure in the events/ patterns in the environment.
- It identifies irreducible uncertainty.
- It does this through creating a process of dialectic conversation in which diverse views are confronted with each other.
- It taps into knowledge available in the individual members of the organisation.
- It brings in external perspectives.
- It puts all this in a form suitable for corporate strategic considerations.

Scenario planning is therefore a natural thinking tool for use in a strategic conversation. In this way it improves the fitness of organisations at two levels:

- In the longer term development of a more robust organisational system, better able to withstand the unexpected shocks that will come its way.
- In the shorter term increased adaptability by more skilful observation of the business environment.

Strategic conversation

The crux of the institutional aspects of the processual paradigm is conversation. The learning loop model shows the interwovenness of thinking and action. If action is based on planning on the basis of a mental model, then institutional action must be based on a shared mental model. Only through a process of conversation can elements of observation and thought be structured and embedded in the accepted and shared organisational theories-in-use. Similarly new perceptions of opportunities and threats, based on the reflection on experiences obtained in the environment can only become institutional property through conversation. An effective strategic conversation must incorporate a wide range of initially unstructured thoughts and views, and out of this create shared interpretations of the world in which the majority of the individual insights can find a logical place. And it is only through such embedding that joint action can result leading to new joint experiences and reinforcement of the shared theories-in-use.

Such a strategic conversation process requires a language and a structure. The first step in creating a language is identifying the underlying concepts. These come from observing events in the environment and recognising/creating patterns and a structure that captures the underlying truth of these events. This can go wrong in a number of ways. We can distinguish two forms of pathologies relating to institutional conversation:

- Confusion due to overload of change. When beset by too much information and data and too much uncertainty, people lose track and don't know what to pay attention to.
- Lack of diligence and attention, due to a high level of comfort in the way "our world of business" has been simplified. This leaves us with a business language which is impoverished and not adequate for the challenges faced.

Both lead to institutions paying less attention to what is happening than is needed to create the appropriate organisational response. The issue of "requisite variety" (see page 32) is a fundamental aspect of creating an appropriate strategic conversation in the organisation.

The scenario planner as process facilitator

During the late 1980s I was responsible for the Scenario Planning Department in the Shell Group's corporate centre. My responsibility was to produce global scenarios that Shell could use in the context of running their global business. These were targeted both at top management and management teams around the world in the various operating companies. When I took on this job in the mid-1980s Shell already had a history of some 15 years of scenario planning behind it. I decided to see if I could learn anything from that experience that might usefully be applied.

I found that scenarios had not always worked well. Some had been controversial, some had disappeared without trace. On the other hand there were scenario exercises that everybody seemed to remember. These key stories had become part of the company language. I analysed why certain exercises were so much more successful than others. I found a large number of differences, but one factor seemed to correlate with success or failure consistently. I discovered that most failures had been produced by scenario planners who had come to the job with a clear preconceived idea of the particular story they wanted to tell. These were people who thought they knew what this company needed. On the other hand, scenario planners who were more interested in working in a client-oriented, consultant frame of mind approached the job from the perspective of helping management solve their problems. They tried to find out what really mattered to management, including their priorities and their frustrations. They would then try to create their scenarios in areas relevant to the needs of management. The latter were much more successful than the former. People who came in with their own agenda tended to produce scenarios which were prone to disappear without trace in the organisation. The most successful scenarios were produced by original thinkers who nevertheless had an acute awareness of the concerns of top management.

This experience illustrates the natural fit between scenario planning and the processual paradigm. Only if scenarios are grown from the platform of the ongoing strategic conversation do they take off in the organisation.

Role of invention

A successful competitive strategy must be an original invention. It cannot be otherwise. One should not be misled by "gurus" peddling general-purpose success formulas. Firms live in a competitive environment, and are surrounded by competitors who are ready to copy anything that seems to lead to success. Competitive success requires finding barriers to such emulation. Therefore successful strategies must belong uniquely to the organisation, and cannot possibly be available to the rest of the world. If there were a codified way to work out the one right answer, this would be available to all competitors in the market, and would for this reason alone quickly become the wrong answer. In the final analysis this is the overwhelming philosophical problem with the rationalistic paradigm in the context of organisational strategy.

The scenario process therefore concentrates on developing processes that enhance the capability of the organisation to mobilise the resources available towards greater inventiveness and innovation. We will now turn our attention towards this issue.

THE GROUP LEARNING MODEL

The reason for the existence of the different paradigms in strategic management is uncertainty in the business situation. In most domains of long-term strategy uncertainty dominates and the evolutionary view comes to the fore. The nearer-term one looks the more predictable the future seems to become, and in the very short term most people are inclined to forecast in the rationalist paradigm. How else would one cross the street in the face of oncoming traffic?

However, uncertainty exists not only in the environment but within organisations as well. As Mintzberg points out, the rationalistic paradigm is based on the assumption that intentions in the organisation are clear and that reasonable people, having full understanding of the strategy, do reasonable things. No manager can be entirely confident on these scores. The institutional aspects of organisational behaviour are ambiguous. This is the domain of processual thinking.

The perspective of "organisational learning" provides a viewpoint which allows the three models (rationalistic, evolutionary and processual) to be holistically incorporated. This can be demonstrated by the application of the model of learning developed by Kolb.

Kolb's theory of learning

As we saw, Kolb suggests that learning is not an incidental or episodic mental activity, but a process that goes on continuously. We described his model in Figure 4. Kolb's "learning loop", showing the four elements of obtaining experience, reflection, mental model building and action.

Kolb describes the cycle as a process of individual learning, with individuals often having particular skills in one of the four activities indicated. He then applies the theory to improve decision making by suggesting a blend of individuals in the decision making team, such that all four skills in the loop are represented. The assumption is that a combination of people with these diverse aptitudes will improve the learning capability of a group as a whole.

We use the model in a different direction. Our interest is in comparing how a team of people goes through this learning loop, and what aspects have to be considered, with how an individual goes through the loop. The important point to pick out of the loop in this context is the need for action to create experiences and learning (compare with Weick's "how do I know what I think until . . . I see how I act?", Weick 1979). This aspect introduces the specific institutional learning problematique which will be the subject we now turn to.

Institutional learning

As Lindblom suggested, in the world of organisations it is only when people align their ideas that the organisation starts exhibiting specific institutional behaviour. The learning loop can only work in an institutional sense if people participate together, share ideas about new patterns resulting from reflection on experience, build a common theory, plan and act together. If they do all that, they have a joint experience without which organisational learning is impossible. We extend the theory from its base of individual learning to institutional learning by introducing the notion of institutional action. We define this as "a coherent set of individual actions which are supported as a set by a self sustaining critical mass of opinion in the organisation". We suggest that one can speak of institutional action only if a "critical mass" of sense-making and response planning is shared. Below the critical mass there are only unrelated individual actions, which lead to individual rather than organisational learning. Without consensus or shared meaning individual actions will not cohere and the organisation will fragment and, if left in this stage, ultimately disintegrate. However, if a critical level of alignment of mental models has taken place within the organisation, planning becomes effectively a joint activity, and experiences will be common, leading to joint reflection in the group and reinforcement of a shared mental model.

Therefore the institutional version of the learning loop introduces the additional factor of the degree of alignment on theories of meaning in the organisation. With an initial "critical mass" of it, consensus can feed on itself through the learning loop by feedback from joint action and experience. In this context the learning loop works as a positive feedback loop. With alignment above a minimum critical level it spirals upwards towards increasing consensus, and stronger action. For this to function institutional learning requires an effective process of conversation, through which strategic cognitions can be compared, challenged and negotiated. Through this participants learn to understand each other's world views and line of argumentation, creating a joint understanding of the situation at hand, so that a collective experience results.

What is required to create an effective institutional conversation? Obviously any conversation requires first of all a language in which the objects of our attention can be expressed. Some of the language of strategy is codified in public domain language, and can be learned from strategic management text books. In addition most organisations over time build up their own language, based on their own responses to specific breakdown situations. The existence and proliferation of labels and jargon are manifestations of this process of language building, essential for organisational learning to take place. However, elements of language can only represent yesterday's problems. Specific strategic management concepts were generated in the past as categorisation of particular historical patterns of events, and used in coping with those specific breakdown situations. It is inevitable that any new situation will at first be described in terms of past categorisations. This will almost by definition stop short of completely describing new reality. Yet the search for an original response to a new situation is facilitated by the conversational process. Yesterday's concepts lead to tomorrow's unique invention!

The conversational process needs to lead to increased alignment of ideas in order to make the organisational learning cycle active. The language of organisations is rational. In business people talk with each other by trying to convince each other. "I argue my case until you are convinced, and you do the same to me. Eventually we come to a negotiated solution in which I am convinced by some points made by you and you see some arguments my way". This is achieved by starting from certain basic shared principles. It requires a process of rational argument, measuring and comparing the utility of competing ideas by reference to the shared world view, from which the organisation derives its purpose. This shared world view (based on the dual purpose of survival and growth of the organisation, as suggested by Stern, see page 39), provides the platform on which a line of logical argumentation will be built to compare views on the specific situation in the strategic conversation process, leading to a preferred view. Rationality may not be the way in which strategy is created but it is an essential shaping force in the strategic conversation process.

So far we see the contributions to the institutional learning process from rationality (conversation based on rational argument) and process (the creation of alignment and joint plans and actions). However, the model is not complete without evolution. Learning can take place only if experience deviates from plan in an unexpected way. If everything happens according to expectation there is no learning. This aspect highlights the contribution of the evolutionary perspective, not so much evolution of organisations, as the evolution of ideas inside organisations. If we define evolution as a process that works through (1) a source of variation, (2) a weeding-out mechanism which rejects the less effective ideas and (3) a source of constancy – so that the lesson that has been learned can be retained for the future – then every learning process is a process of evolution of ideas, their generation, testing and embedding.

Members of the team know that there is no one answer. Different views must be legitimate. As a result the institutional "theory of the world" mutates, with a consequent adjustment in action. The group observes the consequences of this in their experiences, and learns the effectiveness of the mutation. Depending on the result it will be retained or filtered out.

Learning Pathologies

There are two potential pathologies in this institutional learning process. The first one manifests itself if the "critical mass" of consensus is not reached. This divergence of view can become a self-enforcing process, with lack of consensus leading to divergent action, divergent experiences, and a further erosion of the common view. The positive feedback loop spirals downwards. When an organisation drops below the critical mass of consensus, it will not overcome the problem without conscious management action to move the team back over the minimum consensus threshold. Management action needs to be directed towards increasing cohesion, recreating the "critical mass" of shared views, such that joint action can resume.

However, at the opposite extreme there is the pathology which relates to a lack of diversity of thought, sometimes referred to as 'group-think'. If consensus is strong enough it starts feeding on itself through the learning loop. The feedback loop spirals upwards out of control. More cohesion in theories of action leads to an increase in commonality of action, leading to more shared experiences and a reinforcement of theories about the world. The ideas focus and impoverish more and more, and the organisation's stock of reactions to environmental disturbance reduces. An effective learning system requires enough variety in its mental model to interlink signals, received from the outside world, with each other. Without this these signals will be experienced as inconsistent or incoherent, not understood and therefore not leading to any useful learning and adaptive action.

An interesting example was presented by a very senior executive from the US automobile industry, who, when put under considerable pressure by environmentalists, suggested that "Detroit would play ball, if only the market would provide consistent signals". This raises the interesting question whether it is the market that reacts "chaotically" to the environmental challenge, or whether the Detroit mental model is inadequate, and could be made to see pattern and consistency in market signals if its variety were developed to the requisite level. A system that lacks requisite variety will not complete the learning loop for signals that fall outside its focused coherence model. Its vision is blinkered.

The two pathologies generate the managerial dilemma between team cohesion and innovative divergence. Management of organisational learning involves a continuous attention to the balance between the two.

Summarising the above we see the following three crucial points:

- Alignment of ideas and mental models (integration) is crucial to make the institutional learning loop take off.
- The learning process acts as a positive feedback loop, it will spiral upwards or downwards, depending on the level of alignment. It requires active management.
- Too much alignment leads to a lack of requisite variety (differentiation), leading to a reduced ability to observe deviations of experience from expectation.

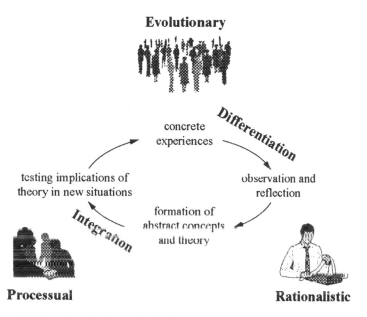

Figure 5. *Integrating the three schools of strategy.*

The deviation of emergent strategy from intended strategy is the driving force of the institutional learning loop. Such deviation initially creates differentiation in views in the organisation, with different people interpreting the situation in their own way. The alignment process then needs to bring these views together and arbitrate on the basis of rationality. In this way all three schools of thought in strategy have their role in the organisational learning process, see Figure 5. It seems that in a situation of this complexity three perspectives is not a luxury. Organisational learning represents a way in which we can integrate these three perspectives, all three playing a key role in describing reality, and therefore demanding consideration.

Speed of organisational learning

Wherever we find power to act in the organisation a learning loop is at work. Therefore the organisation is not just one loop but many, working through individuals and groups throughout the organisation. The faster learning takes place, the shorter the loop. For this reason individuals learn faster than groups, and groups learn faster than whole organisations. Communication in organisations is a time-consuming business, as each level needs to internalise observations, reflect on these and adjust mental models before the message can be transferred to the next level. This is the reason why large hierarchical organisations react so slowly, as we saw in the example of the oil industry at the time of the energy crisis.

De Geus has suggested that speed of organisational learning is the ultimate competitive weapon (De Geus 1988). What can organisations do to increase it? Unblocking communication channels is obviously a first essential condition. If information does not flow up and down the hierarchical ladder the overall learning loop cannot function. But even if communication is effective, delays due to personal information gestation times at the various levels in the loop will limit overall reaction time. As there is not a lot that can be done to reduce the time an individual requires to reflect on incoming information, the only alternative left to increase speed of learning is to reduce the length of the loop itself, by reducing the number of individuals in it. **Short learning loops means delegation of decision making, locating the power-to-act organisationally close to the point of experience and perception.** Organisations in fast changing environments tend to decentralise, with top management acting more in the nature of a co-ordinating body than as a setter of strategy. The learning organisation does not have one all-embracing strategy, but many more or less co-ordinated strategies. Such organisations can be highly flexible and adaptive, but there is a price to pay.

Breaking up the organisation in small units reduces economies of scale advantages. In relatively stable situations, where cost leadership is often the name of the game, power tends to be centralised with the purpose of creating a finely tuned organisational machine, capable of exploiting economies of scale to the maximum. If competition is based on cost such organisations have the advantage. The price here is reduced adaptability.

The situation is a typical managerial dilemma. Managers need to balance economies of scale with adaptability. Extremes on both sides are dangerous. The finely tuned machine goes under with the product it was designed to produce. The ultimate learning organisation goes under due to its high cost. There is no perfect answer here. The situation is a dynamic one, which needs constant attention from top management.

Scenarios and institutional learning

Scenarios contribute to the learning process in a number of important ways:

At the individual level

- As a cognitive device: A set of scenarios is a highly efficient data organisation tool. Stories are efficient for giving many different bits of information a mutual context, thereby making the cognitive aspects of any situation more manageable to deal with (see also Part Two, refer to "memories of the future").
- As a perception device: As individuals, people see certain things and overlook others, based on their existing mental models and resulting expectations. The scenario process increases the range of what participants see and expands their mental models.
- As a cognitive reflection tool: The scenario process helps people think through ideas generated in the strategic conversation more effectively.

At the group level

- As a ready-made language provider, assisting the strategic conversation across a wide range of partly conflicting views.
- As a conversational facilitation vehicle: Scenario planning provides an organised way of discussing relevant aspects of the business in an organisational context.
- As a vehicle for mental model alignment, which in turn permits coherent strategic action.

Scenarios play a role in all important aspects of the learning loop. They help a management team to avoid the worst aspects of the two pathological opposites of group-think and fragmentation. For an inward-looking cohesive group moving along a single mental track scenarios inject an element of caution, like a lawyer who asks "What could go wrong?". For a fragmented confused group on the other hand scenarios open up new possibilities for joint action by "creating order in chaos" and increasing understanding.

In Part Two we will first organise the discussion of the role of scenario planning in organisational learning by reference to its fundamental role vis à vis the learning loop, namely perception, theory building, and creating joint action. We will then develop this into ideas for the practice of scenario planning, cognitively, in a management team in Part Three, and behaviourally in the organisation in Part Four.

Part Two

The Principles of
Scenario Planning

OVERVIEW

So far we have discussed the history and philosophical development of the three paradigms of strategy, and the potential for integration of the three perspectives through the concept of institutional learning. In this part we will turn our attention to developing an organisational learning framework, based on scenario planning, which will make this work in a normal every-day organisation.

Scenario planning succeeds when an organisation manages to adapt itself such that it "gains the high ground", i.e. maximises its chances of achieving its purpose, in whatever environment it finds itself, through a process of organisational learning.

As discussed in Part One the basic organisational purpose is the double objective of survival and self-development. In order to make the right decisions the organisation needs to understand itself, as well as its environment.

In the context of its purpose of survival and self-development we develop a definition of the "organisational self" which we call the Business Idea. This expresses its ability to survive and develop itself in terms of organisational characteristics which can be articulated and tested against environmental assumptions.

When we discuss the chances of gaining the high ground we consider the future business environment. This is in large measure uncertain and ambiguous. Scenario planning does not attempt to predict what is unpredictable, and for this reason considers multiple, equally plausible futures. These become the testbed for the vision of the Business Idea that the organisation has for itself. Resulting from this test options for improvement will emerge.

The three fundamental steps of learning – perception, theory building and joint action – all benefit from scenario planning. Sharing multiple stories about the future makes the organisation more perceptive about its environment, and forces reflection on experience and adjustment of mental theories. Institutional testing of the Business Idea creates options for joint action.

STRATEGY DEVELOPMENT AND LEARNING

We saw that strategy development always has the following steps:

- Acknowledgement of aims, either through an externally imposed mandate, or the internal organismic dual purpose of survival and self-development.
- Assessment of the organisational factors for success, including its capability to change.
- Assessment of the environment, current and future, in all its uncertainty and ambiguity.
- Assessment of the fit between the two.
- Development of policies to improve the fit.

The link of strategy with organisational learning can be mapped schematically as follows:

STRATEGY	ORGANISATIONAL LEARNING
Aims	Learning loop driving force
Organisational success formula	Mental model, theories of the world
Environmental scenarios	Perception, differentiation, reflection on experience, seeing new patterns
Assessment of strategic fit	Integration of reflection into mental model
Development of policy to increase fit	Planning future steps
Implement	Act

The strategy approach adopted here is based on the model of the organisation as a living and learning organism, with its inherent ultimate purpose of survival and self-development. We take this as the starting point and ultimate driving force of everything that is being done organisationally, including perceiving the environment through scenario planning.

RELEVANCE FILTERS

The concept of organisational learning integrates action and experience in the strategy development activity. **Human beings and organisations do not act in response to reality but to an internally constructed version of reality** We will need to pay particular attention to the relationship between reality and the internal model of it. This will lead us to consider how signals from the outside world are filtered in the cognitive system. The most obvious filters are the senses which allow us to perceive only a part of reality. But beyond that signals are cognitively filtered through limited attention span and sense of relevance. Only events that catch the attention and are considered relevant will enter awareness, and become the raw material from which mental models are constructed, on the basis of which action is decided.

Relevance filters have various dimensions. One is time: the threat of immediate impact holds our attention more strongly than the threat of long-term impact. This is a problem that many managers struggle with, often expressed as "the urgent crowding out the important". Another relevance filter is proximity to system boundaries. We tend to be more interested in what is happening to those whose welfare is important for our welfare than in events far away which do not seem to touch us. In addition strength of signal will make a difference, weak signals are more easily overlooked.

On 20 March 1995 a cult sect carried out a sarin (poison gas) attack on the public in a Tokyo railway station, killing 11 people and injuring more than 5500. In retrospect it transpired that there were at least seven warning signals that could have been interpreted as signposts of impending danger. Each of the events in isolation was too small to lead to significant action. Only the "big bang" Tokyo event was important enough to focus attention on the underlying structural situation. Had the earlier events been perceived as a pattern, action could have been taken to prevent the attack.

THE STRATEGIC AGENDA

The notion of relevance filters relates to the aims of the person or organisation. As Bateson (1972) pointed out, a stronger sense of conscious purpose reduces an organism's adaptiveness, because it reduces the area of relevance through which events are filtered. An organisation focused single-mindedly on a struggle for survival will pay less attention to the longer term and wider boundaries than an organisation that can afford to experiment.

In order to understand organisational perception we need to understand and articulate specific organisational aims. The questions of survival and growth need to be addressed with reference to the specifics of the organisation under consideration. In order to operationalise this we will introduce the concept of the "Business Idea". We will argue that underlying every successful organisation lies an idea acting as the driving force for success. We will see that this idea is specific to the organisation, and no two organisations can have the same Business Idea.

Strategy development can be interpreted as considering this Business Idea against the outlook for the environment. How can scenario thinking contribute to this process? Figure 6 gives a schematic overview of the approach which we will develop. The scenarios can be seen as the test conditions for the Business Idea. They are used as a means to think through future policies and decisions. They are "laboratories" in which different models of future policy can be tested. And by using more than one, robustness is tested specifically.

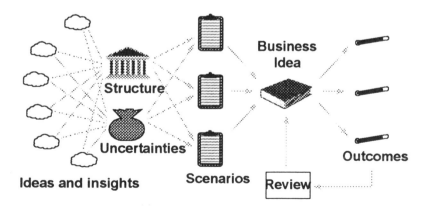

Figure 6. *Scenarios test the Business Idea.*

This requires understanding of the key environmental variables and their interlinkages. The business environment is infinitely large, and the organisation selects what is worth considering by reference to its Business Idea. In practical terms, scenario development requires understanding of the nature of the Business Idea in order to decide what are suitable "test conditions". By using the scenarios as a strategy testbed the managers are forced to articulate what they consider really important in the environment.

Sometimes the purpose of the scenario activity may be to make a final decision, but more normally the manager uses the scenarios to test strategy proposals in order to find ways to improve them, i.e. make them more appropriate and robust against the futures which might arise (Figure 6). While forecasts are decision making devices scenarios are policy development tools. Rather than a clear cut yes/no situation they present the organisation with the means to iteratively build/develop better policy. They need to stretch the range of the organisation's vision beyond what is traditionally seen as relevant. The scenario planner will need to widen the area of relevance. So scenarios can also be seen as perception tools, which can be used to develop "peripheral vision" beyond the current focus of attention in the organisation.

Scenario planning is a customised activity. The process can be compared with using a windtunnel to test the model of an aircraft. A supersonic fighter design requires different conditions in the windtunnel than a hang-glider. Generic scenarios are generally not very helpful.

We will see that in most organisations the Business Idea is tacit, and taken for granted while people get on with the day-to-day tasks. For this reason a strategy project needs to start with bringing the Business Idea to the surface. We will discuss processes for doing this and expressing the result of this activity in a manageable form. The purpose is twofold:

- To generate a basis from which the scenario agenda can be formulated.
- To generate an agreed understanding of the basic success drivers of the organisation, which can subsequently be assessed against the scenarios generated to discuss organisational implications.

Chapter Three

The Business Idea of an Organisation

In this chapter we define the notion of a Business Idea, discuss the main underlying principles and work through their implications. As we saw, the Business Idea is the organisation's mental model of the forces behind its current and future success. The scenario planner, aiming to accelerate organisational learning, needs to articulate the Business Idea. Only when articulated can it be studied, discussed, modified and improved.

As an organisational device, the articulated Business Idea is embedded in the language of the organisation. Organisational language is rational. Therefore, in order to work effectively in the organisation, the articulated Business Idea must be a rational explanation of why the organisation has been successful in the past, and how it will be successful in the future. This implies that the Business Idea needs to be built up from first principles.

FIRST PRINCIPLES: PROFIT POTENTIAL

Firms mostly represent success by establishing value. This can be done in two ways:

- They create a surplus for stakeholders, which the latter can use for their own purposes or (totally or in part) for protecting and developing the strength of the enterprise.
- They create the expectation among existing or potential stakeholders that they will be able to create a surplus and grow in the future.

One of the main purposes of strategy development is to feed this expectation, by indicating how circumstances will be created in the longer term which are considered favourable for corporate value generation. The aim can be defined as creating profit potential. This is not the same as profit. Management cannot rely on strategy alone for profitability. Strategy facilitates, but the actual profit is earned in day-to-day hands-on operations. Because of this there cannot be a one-to-one relationship between strategy and profit. The typical business situation manifests a high level of complexity, so the time period over which the system is predictable is short – days or weeks rather than months or years. On the other hand many management decisions have long term repercussions. They affect future profit potential, and need to be considered in that light. Quality of execution is the other part of the profit equation.

To understand the concept of profit potential, consider the thought process of the new entrepreneur. This focuses first of all on an idea of a possible activity, believed to create value for a customer group, for which they consequently will be prepared to pay a price. The idea specifies how this value can be created through bringing together a number of factors and competencies in a new distinctive combination that has not been thought of before. Entrepreneurial success results from a combination of three ideas:

- Discovering a new way of creating value for customers.
- Bringing together a combination of competencies, which creates this value.
- Creating uniqueness in this formula in order to appropriate part of the value created.

The "offering" is the vehicle by which the seller and customer systems are linked together to exploit the supplier competencies in the customer value system. The offering includes all aspects of the supplier/customer interface, including the physical product, but also intangible aspects such as service, risk management, information, etc. As Richard Normann points out, each product represents a division of work between the supplier and the customer (Normann 1984). Therefore the creation of a successful product is the result of a process of optimisation, aiming for the maximum effect of the supplier competencies in the total customer value creation potential. In the process the supplier incurs costs translating the idea into a product. The customer derives value from its use. The overall optimum relates to

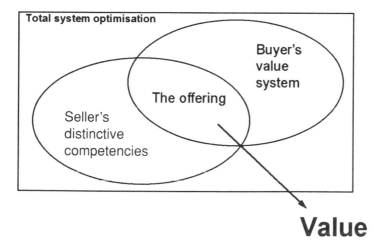

Figure 7. *Overlap between competencies and value creation.*

configuring the product so as to maximise the difference between customer value and supplier cost. The product which represents this optimum will normally incorporate both tangible and service elements. In some aspects of the product the cost/benefit balance indicates work by the supplier (e.g. performance guarantees), sometimes the balance shifts to the buyer (e.g. self-service, Normann & Ramirez 1994). In this way consideration is given to the best bundling of tangible product and service elements in an overall offering, such that supplier competencies are exploited to the maximum effect in the customer value system.

This surplus of value over cost is shared between the two parties. The degree to which it accrues to the customer or to the supplier depends on the relative bargaining power of each party (see below).

We define structural profit potential as an attribute of a system capable of creating value for customers in a unique way that others find difficult to emulate. A specification of these two elements together (value creation and making a unique contribution) constitutes what is defined here as the Business Idea of the firm.

DISTINCTIVE COMPETENCIES

Sometimes the entrepreneur finds that the new combination can be easily emulated by others. In that case cost of entry is relatively modest, new competitors flock in and success is short-lived. Alternatively, there may be something distinct or unique about the combination of competencies, making it difficult for others to copy. In this way a powerful Business Idea appropriates part of the value created. The degree to which this can be done depends on the relative power of the firm vis-à-vis the customers in the bargaining process. Customer power is determined by possible alternatives open to them. If customers have no alternatives offered by competitors they have no power and the entrepreneur is in a position to appropriate a larger part of the value created. Therefore a Business Idea needs to address the relative position vis-à-vis potential competition.

In addition the entrepreneur has to consider the power of other stakeholders in the battle for the value created. These include among others (Freeman 1984):

- Suppliers
- Employees
- Competitors
- Money providers
- Government

Ultimately the power of the supplying firm to appropriate value relates to the degree of uniqueness of the competencies brought to bear in generating the product. Appropriation requires that the competencies individually, or the system of competencies with their interactions, are difficult to imitate by potential competitors.

The word "distinctive" in the concept Distinctive Competency needs some further elaboration. Company "strengths" are not the same thing as Distinctive Competencies. Many strengths companies believe they have are not very unique and can be easily copied by existing or new competitors. If a strength can be bought, e.g. by acquisition or alliance, it cannot be a Distinctive Competency. If a Business Idea consists only of such components long-term profit potential is vulnerable, and therefore the Business Idea weak. A strong Business Idea contains elements that have been created in the organisation over time, and which uniquely belong to that organisation.

Therefore, in considering the Business Idea one needs to ask the Devil's Advocate question: "What is unique about this particular formula, and why are others unable to emulate it?".

Teece (1986) investigated the reasons why Distinctive Competencies might arise, and why competitors would be restrained from copying any successful formula. Based on his and Rumelt's work mapping out "Barriers To Entry", we can derive a list of five fundamental sources of distinctiveness in two main categories (Rumelt 1987, Rumelt et al. 1991):

- Uncodified institutional knowledge
    In networked people
    In embedded processes
- Sunk costs/irreversible investments
    Investments in reputation
    In legal protection
    In specialised assets

If the competency is based on tacit uncodified institutional knowledge it cannot be copied. In this area unique knowledge in itself is not enough. The competencies must also belong to the firm as an institution, and not exclusively to its members individually. If the company relies only on an individual expert for its business success profits will eventually be appropriated by him personally. In those circumstance it is unlikely that the firm will find it possible to translate these strengths into profit potential for the company on a sustainable basis. However, if a Business Idea is based on institutional knowledge profit potential can be sustained. Therefore a distinction needs to be made between Personal Knowledge and Institutional Knowledge. Often the individual can exploit personal strengths only when supported by the strengths of the organisation. This support may be tangible (e.g. in the form of computing facilities) or intangible (e.g. in the complementary knowledge and "sounding board" function provided by colleagues in the organisation). An institution's knowledge base is created through people networking with each other, and through processes embedded in the organisation.

The second source of distinctiveness relates to competitors having to incur costs in order to be able to compete for the profit potential. For example, a new competitor might have to make investments that existing companies have already made. If these investments are in marketable assets, then on this score there is no competitive distinction between existing and new players. Existing players have to consider their option of realising their assets in the same way as new players have to consider their acquisition, i.e. not selling the asset creates the same sacrifice and barrier for the existing players as making the investment in the first place for the newcomers ("opportunity cost").

However, many investments are irreversible, at least to some extent, and in relation to that the existing players do not face the hurdle of the economic decision facing the newcomers. Their opportunity cost is lower.

Examples of Distinctive Competencies

The following examples of Distinctive Competencies illustrate these principles over a range of real life cases:

Institutional knowledge

- Institutional R&D capability
- Company know-how
- Functional knowledge pools
- Knowledge of customer value systems
- Shared assumptions and values

Embedded processes

- Leadership style and commitment
- Links into (institutional understanding for) the world of the consumer
- Access to distribution channels
- Institutional relationships with government
- Internal communication, systems/culture
- Staff identification and commitment

Reputation and trust

- Brand
- Dominant size and presence
- Installed base
- Financial clout

Legal protection

- Concession agreements
- Patents
- Ownership of prime sites

Activity specific assets

- Investments in dominant size, market share and image
- Sunk investment in sites, exploration, experimentation, specialised equipment etc.
- Investments in economies of scale, e.g. in distribution (e.g. low unit stock levels, low unit delivery cost)
- First mover investments in production capacity

Uniqueness can derive from Distinctive Competencies individually or from their combination. It may be that some aspects of specific Distinctive Competencies are difficult to emulate. However, the strongest Business Ideas derive from a set of Competencies which are unique because of the way they are combined systemically. Most strong Business Ideas contain Distinctive Competencies which feed on each other. Synergy between even a handful creates distinctiveness at a wholly superior level of strength. The overall Business Idea is particularly strong and difficult to emulate if the set of underlying Distinctive Competencies reinforce each other. This is why drawing a causal loop diagram (a way of showing such mutual causal interaction) provides a powerful level of insight into the driving forces for success (see below).

Distinctive Competencies depreciate over time. Business is fundamentally dynamic, change is an essential part of organisational life. In an evolving world survival implies continuous updating of the organisation's Business Idea. This is necessary for two reasons:

- Eventually a competitor finds a way to emulate the essence of the competency, or
- The overlap between the competency and the customer value system reduces, because of evolving customer values.

As a consequence a Business Idea is not valid for ever. It needs to be kept up to date. Existing Distinctive Competencies need to be strengthened, and new ones created. Although entrepreneurial invention and luck may present the perceptive organisation with potential new Distinctive Competencies, normally new Distinctive Competencies must be created out of the exploitation of old ones. The organisation does not have another source of distinctiveness.

Schoemaker (1992) has analysed the nature of Distinctive Competencies. His suggestions for hallmarks of real distinctiveness summarise the points made:

- Investments are largely irreversible.
- Distinctive Competencies cannot be transferred (sold) to other firms.
- There is a limit to which development can be speeded up by ever-increasing investments.
- Development is a process of gradual evolution through collective learning and information sharing.
- Strong Business Ideas exploit multiple Distinctive Competencies reinforcing each other in a synergetic way.
- Distinctive Competencies create competitive advantage in the eyes of customers.

Competitive Advantage

If the Business Idea and its Distinctive Competencies are effective it creates Competitive Advantage. Competitive Advantage translates into profit potential in two ways (Porter 1985):

- The Distinctive Competencies are used to create a differentiated product, the characteristics of which cannot be matched by the competition and for which the customer is prepared to pay a superior price compared to what they would pay the competition. Profit potential derives from a premium price.
- The Distinctive Competencies are used to create a unique low-cost way of creating or making available a non-differentiated product. This allows the supplier to make available a competitively priced alternative, with some additional margin left to create a profitable operation. Profit potential derives from cost leadership.

Differentiation

A firm producing a product that is distinguished in its characteristics from others on the market in a way that results in additional customer value enjoys a competitive advantage. If competitors cannot match the distinctive element, part of the additional customer value can be appropriated by the supplier.

In considering how to create such a product it is helpful to distinguish two categories of sources of differentiation (Normann 1994):

- Generational, i.e. a capability to produce offerings with unique attributes, including quality, design, cost, availability and support.
- Relational, i.e. a dynamic capability to produce a uniquely fitting product, based on a superior relationship between supplier and customer, including aspects such as image and access, resulting from effective communication and understanding.

Differentiation requires a deep understanding of what creates value for customers. A Distinctive Competency of the supplier may be based on an ability to "read the customer's mind" better than competitors. Researching customer needs is not enough. Customers cannot articulate their needs if they are not aware of the supplier's competencies. The unique differentiated product can be created only out of the optimisation of the total customer/supplier system. It must be a joint conceptual project. Product research is not enough, the differentiated product company also needs to engage in continuous concept research.

Cost leadership

Sometimes customer value is relatively easy to determine. This happens when products have become "commodities", i.e. when open market trading has created standardised and clearly defined products for which there is a continuing market. In that case the value an individual supplier contributes to the customer is equal to the established market price of the product (as the customer has plenty of alternative opportunities to acquire the product at that price). In a commodity market it may still be possible to create significant long-term profit potential, by means of a uniquely superior cost performance.

Most businesses believe that it ought to be possible to develop some unique customer value, and companies for this reason try to distinguish themselves by creating a differentiated offering. But some companies accept the commodity market as their strategic starting point and concentrate on creating a uniquely favourable cost position.

SYSTEMIC STRUCTURE OF THE BUSINESS IDEA

Generic strategies cannot be freely selected. They result from a set of Distinctive Competencies which through their interaction in a Business Idea create the differentiated product or the cost leadership. The Business Idea is prime; the Competitive Advantage is its manifestation.

The process of articulating the Business Idea usefully starts with identifying the Competitive Advantage that the firm exploits (differentiation, cost leadership, or both). Starting from there the analysis then searches for underlying causes of this Competitive Advantage until characteristics are uncovered that pass the test of "distinctiveness".

As we discussed above, Distinctive Competencies depreciate so a firm needs to spend resources in maintaining and renewing its Business Idea. These resources are generated from the exploitation of the Business Idea itself. A Business Idea contains a "Positive Feedback Loop", which can create a self-reinforcing system. In such a system, activities generate resources which are used to strengthen the competencies driving the activities. But a positive feedback loop can also create collapse (less surplus leading to fewer resources, leading to weaker competencies, leading to less surplus, etc.). The primary concern of the entrepreneur is to keep the loop working in the upward direction.

Bateson (1967) suggested that the fundamental nature of organisations can only be understood by conceptualising them as a cybernetic system of loops in a network of relationships, both internal as well as external. In such networks people influence each other. Influence does not only cascade downwards. Alleged inferiors have influence over alleged superiors. As we saw, suppliers influence clients as much as clients influence suppliers. While hierarchy identifies formal relationships, informal influences can loop around through long pathways, that include indirect effects. Social systems tend to be heavily influenced by such influence loops, which are often more determining of behaviour than hierarchies. Loops tend to create the behaviour, and therefore the identity, of organisations. If you focus only on physical or legal representations of organisations you will miss entirely the fundamental forces driving organisations and change!

Firms can be interpreted as systems of negative feedback loops, designed to maintain favourable conditions for one dominant positive feedback loop, based on its Business Idea, which creates the growth of the enterprise.

Summarising the above we see that the following four elements need to be specified in order to define a complete Business Idea:

1. The societal/customer value created.
2. The nature of the Competitive Advantage exploited.
3. The Distinctive Competencies which, in their mutually reinforcing interaction, create Competitive Advantage.

Then, these three elements must be configured into the fourth element:

4. A positive feedback loop, in which resources generated drive growth.

Due to its systemic nature a Business Idea is best represented as an influence diagram. Figure 8 shows this in its generic form, containing the elements listed above in context, as well as the role of entrepreneurial invention in creating the idea in the first place.

An influence diagram shows the cause–effect relationships between key variables in the situation under consideration, expressed by arrows.

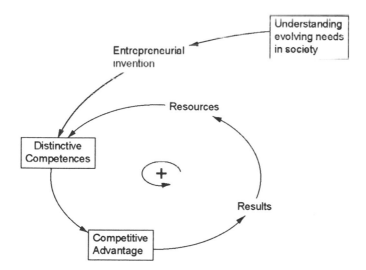

Figure 8. *The generic Business Idea.*

The head of the arrow points towards the effect, caused by the variable, indicated by the tail of the arrow. If an arrow is annotated by a plus sign, or if no sign is shown (as in Figure 8) both variables change in the same direction, an increase in the causing variable leading to an increase in the effect, or a decrease in the causing variable leading to a decrease in the effect. If a minus sign is shown the movement is in the opposite direction, an increase in cause leading to a decrease in effect, and the other way around. In Figure 8 increasing competitive advantage leads to increasing results, which cause increasing resources to be available for investment in enhancing distinctive competencies, which in turn lead to increased competitive advantage, producing the positive feedback loop discussed. As shown distinctive competencies can also be enhanced or added to by increasing entrepreneurial invention, based on enhanced understanding of evolving needs in society.

A useful Business Idea diagram contains the elements of the generic diagram, made specific in its elements and their interrelationships for the situation under consideration. This can best be explained by means of a few examples.

EXAMPLES OF BUSINESS IDEAS

Kinder-Care

Our first example is the Business Idea concept for Kinder-Care, the largest private provider of day-care in the US. The description given here is based on the entrepreneur's own account (Smith et al. 1986, Bougon et al. 1990).

Kinder-Care was started by Perry Mendel who perceived a need for innovative child care. He reasoned that many mothers and fathers experience a feeling of guilt when they provide their children with simple custodial child-care. His entrepreneurial idea was to create centres where children would not only be cared for but would also be provided with a learning environment similar to pre-schools, thus creating a positive image in the minds of the parents. In an early attempt to franchise the centres Mendel found that the type of individual attracted to a franchise was typically an ex-schoolteacher. While having professional expertise, these individuals did not have the management and financial expertise (or interest) required for running a franchise. If the learning centres were to be financially successful they would have to be kept by Kinder-Care management.

The strategy based on these observations created a set of inter-dependencies in a system of loops. Figure 9 is derived from the diagram developed by Bougon from Mendel's report (Bougon et al. 1990).

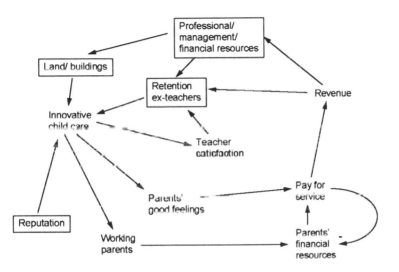

Figure 9. *The Kinder-Care Business Idea.*

The Kinder-Care system can be understood by reference to the four elements making up its Business Idea:

1. The societal/customer value created

The creation of customer value starts with the recognition of parent's guilt feelings associated with custodial day-care for their children. The ability to overcome this by the provision of a learning environment makes parents feel better and allows some to seek employment where this was considered inappropriate before. The entrepreneurial invention creates value for customers, inducing reallocation of resources, or in the latter case generation of additional income.

2. The nature of the competitive advantage exploited

The purpose of the Kinder-Care operation is to offer a new enhanced product, which creates value for customers through its differentiated nature. Kinder-Care does not aim to be a cost leader.

3. The Distinctive Competencies exploited, in their mutually reinforcing configuration

Kinder-Care has developed a number of competencies allowing the realisation of the entrepreneurial idea, including:

- Knowledge of characteristics required in personnel
- Knowledge on facilities
- Management system and expertise
- Access to specialised facilities
- Reputation, resulting in parent's trust.

These competencies reinforce each other as shown in the diagram. Note that having hired the appropriate personnel (a scarce resource) does not as such create a Distinctive Competency for the firm, as any value resulting from that alone would eventually be appropriated by the individuals with the requisite characteristics.

4. The positive feedback loop, driving growth

The system contains a number of loops. For example, more innovative child care leads to more teacher satisfaction, which leads to more retention of motivated ex-schoolteachers, which leads to more innovative child care. Or, innovative child care allows a parent to feel better about going to frequent or full-time work, increasing willingness and ability to pay for the use of more innovative child care.

We see that the main strategic loop is a positive feedback loop. This explains the successful growth of Kinder-Care – innovative child care induces customers to pay for a service which creates increased management and financial capability, which causes an increase in the amount and quality of innovative child care offered.

It does not seem very difficult to emulate the individual competencies that Kinder-Care incorporates in its Business Idea. The reason why the company nevertheless has been successful lies in the idea's dynamic nature, and the relatively slow response of its competitors. By growing fast, well ahead of the ability of the competition to catch up, the company has exploited scale effects to the maximum. It has built up and strengthened both its management system and its reputation, associated with the name Kinder-Care, well before others could catch up, thus creating barriers to entry for newcomers. The company needs to consider whether these are high enough for sustainable competitive advantage.

The Business Idea of a construction company

Figure 10 shows the diagrammatic representation of the Business Idea of a construction company. In the market where this company operates, a building project tends to be a relatively significant investment for most customers which needs to serve them for a long time to come. As a consequence, customers in this industry tend to be risk averse. As the product cannot be inspected before the sale, the reputation of construction companies for the quality of the work they typically deliver is important. Construction companies need to be able to demonstrate the quality of their products by reference to the "installed base". Therefore existing, well-established companies are protected by the positive feedback loop, from the installed base to reputation for quality work to new contracts which add to the installed base. This creates a considerable barrier to entry for newcomers, and is a fundamental part of the Business Idea of every established construction company. However, a company cannot entirely rely on this loop for its success. There is potential competition from other

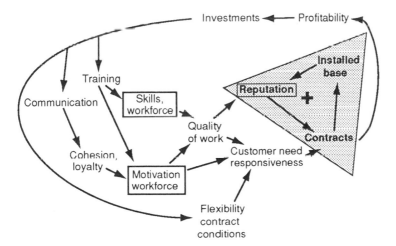

Figure 10. *The Business Idea of a construction company.*

established companies in the industry, and from time to time new entrants make the investment to break in. Therefore the Business Idea needs to be strengthened by company specific Distinctive Competencies. In the example in Figure 10 a construction company tries to distinguish itself by creating an internal culture which differentiates the company in the eyes of the clients as a flexible collaborative business partner in contrast to the traditional legalistic and sometimes adversarial customer-contractor relationship. Such collaborative customer relationships require:

- An internal culture based on collaborative relationships. The company portrayed in Figure 10 develops and stimulates this culture by organisational measures and investments in people.
- A flexible approach to developing customised contract conditions. The company has invested heavily in an ability to customise every contract to the needs of the individual client.
- Financial strength to deal with the specific financing requirements of every contract.

In this way the company stays ahead in its chosen market niche where clients are prepared to pay a premium price for the security of proven quality as well as non-adversarial co-operative relationships.

The strength of the Business Idea of Figure 10 lies in its cultural embeddedness. Companies setting out to change their corporate culture are embarking on a long term project that must be measured in years rather than months. Companies that have made such investments in the past are generally well-protected, provided that there is a good match between the resulting behavioural characteristics and customer needs.

Limits to Growth

The Kinder-Care example contains a negative feedback loop which will eventually limit the growth created by the positive feedback loop as explained. This negative feedback loop indicates that growth of the activity will lead to a reduction of demand, based on saturation in customer value creation and willingness to pay. Michael Porter's Five-Force competitive model (Porter 1980) provides a useful framework to consider the limits to growth in a Business Idea:

- Demand limits
- Supply limits

- Competition limits
- Limits imposed by the possibility of new entrants
- Limits imposed by possible alternatives and substitutes.

The Kinder-Care example demonstrates a demand limited Business Idea. Examples of limitations in the other categories include:

- Supply limits. The Business Idea of a mining company may be largely based on "legal protection" through a concession agreement. The company may not be able to extend this beyond what it already enjoys. In this case the exploitation of the Business Idea is limited on the supply side, dictated by the potential in the available reserve.
- Competition limits. In an oligopolistic market situation the growing company must expect retaliation from its competitors when the exploitation of its Business Idea leads to unacceptable dominance.
- As we have seen all Distinctive Competencies depreciate. At a cost most Business Ideas can be emulated. Any firm working a successful Business Idea will reach a point in the growth curve where it has become attractive for new entrants to incur the emulation cost, and enter the market as alternative suppliers.
- The same applies to substitute products.

In each of these examples we see a mechanism at work which, at some point in the growth process, introduces a negative feedback loop in the Business Idea, which first diminishes, and then negates its surplus creation potential. At that point growth stops.

If the Business Idea creates its own compensating negative feedback loop it need not be invalidated, as the two tend to remain in balance. If compensating negative feedback emanates from an independent source the situation may be more dangerous, as there is a possibility that balance will not be maintained. For this reason negative feedback loops introduced through existing or new competition are more dangerous than those resulting from supply or demand constraints.

LEVELS OF BUSINESS IDEAS

Wherever a management team pursues a business purpose, a Business Idea will emerge. Management teams can be found at various levels in the organisation, e.g. at the level of the corporation and the business unit. Business Ideas can be found at all these levels.

The Business Unit has external customers. At this level it is easier to define the contribution made to customer value. Taking this as a starting point the Business Idea can be articulated by considering what specific Distinctive Competencies in the company are brought to bear to create value. At the business unit level the problem around defining the Business Idea for the future revolves primarily around the question of what will be considered value creation by future customers. This is a creative task. The customers themselves cannot be aware of how their value systems will evolve in the future because the potential contribution of suppliers is unknown to them.

Articulating a corporate Business Idea is complicated by the fact that the external customer is one step removed. The corporate unit does not interact with external customers; this takes place via the Business Units. Business logic at the corporate level is based on developing shared resources, visible or invisible, that exploit synergy between Business Units and the Corporate Units. This can take place in a number of different ways:

- Business Units may include in their Business Idea the Distinctive Competencies of other Business Units. For example, marketing may rely on manufacturing flexibility to approach their customers with customised offerings. Manufacturing flexibility then becomes a Corporate Distinctive Competency.
- More than one Business Unit may pursue the same Distinctive Competencies, which then may become Corporate Distinctive Competencies, e.g. an open culture through participative management.
- Some features of the company are corporate in a fundamental way, and any distinctiveness in those can only be developed at the corporate level, e.g. financial strength, risk spreading, corporate reputation etc.
- The corporate parent may develop a Business Idea around value creation in the interaction between the parent and the Business Units ("parenting advantage", Goold, Campbell & Alexander 1994).

The Corporate Business Idea needs to be based on the Business Unit Business Ideas, concentrating on Distinctive Competencies which operate across business boundaries.

Segmentation

This raises the issue of what can be considered a Business Unit for the purpose of articulating a Business Idea. Many schemes have been invented to segment an organisation for the purpose of analysing its underlying characteristics. For the purpose of developing a Business Idea most of these schemes can be short-circuited. The Business Idea is in the first place a cognitive device. It is a vision that lives in the minds of individuals, managers and others in the unit being considered. It is they who determine the identity of their operation, and who develop the vision for its future. Therefore the single criterion whether it is worthwhile to attempt to surface a Business Idea is the question whether people, mostly in a management team, are aware of its separate identity.

Mapping out and comparing the Business Ideas of a number of Business Units, making up a corporation, may lead to reconsideration of the segmentation of the business within the organisation. Putting the lower level maps next to each other quickly reveals possible ways in which the same business can be reorganised more coherently, leading to more concise Business Ideas with more clear-cut overlap and interdependence, and simplified inter-unit interfaces.

The holistic nature of a Business Idea

A Business Idea becomes a powerful driving force in the organisation if it can be held in the mind as one holistic concept. Its essential nature follows from the way that the elements work together. The positive feedback loop cannot be understood in terms of its elements in isolation. Only the overview makes the important point. If complex systems cannot be understood holistically, the mind will break down the system into parts. In the case of a Business Idea this fragmentation destroys the essential holistic meaning of the idea.

The human mind can retain only a limited number of concepts at the same time. (Miller suggests a number of seven concepts, plus or minus two (Miller 1956)). Our experience has shown that the most effective Business Idea diagrams indeed do not contain many more than (say) ten elements. A representation much beyond that seems to reduce its power as a direction indicating device. Therefore it is advisable to draw up the diagram at this level of granularity. If further detail is required this can be included as an expansion of individual elements in the Business Idea in separate diagrams. The art of Business Idea articulation lies in defining the major elements of the system at the appropriate resolution level and maintaining consistency of this across the diagram.

This seems in the first place a point of good practice. But it is worth considering other more fundamental aspects of the human inability to overview large systems. Pursuing an entrepreneurial Business Idea requires a high degree of consistency and persistence across the organisation and over time. Staying on course requires a clear unambiguous compass. Activities that are not a crucial part of the Business Idea can be, and often are, contracted out to another firm.

Management Teams find it cognitively difficult to simultaneously pursue more than one Business Idea. Financial markets tend to discount management's ability to pursue more than one Business Idea, as manifest from the frequent phenomenon of enhanced market value resulting from de-mergers.

The fact that a management team pursues only one Business Idea does not mean that the company is in only one business. For example the management of a conglomerate company may be pursuing the overarching corporate Business Idea of providing parenting advantages to its subsidiaries, without getting involved in the detail of the subsidiaries' Business Ideas (Goold & Quinn 1990)

The concept of the Business Idea throws a new light on the notion of synergy as a precondition for success in acquisitions. The overarching Business Idea is important not only because of the "shared resources" aspect, but also because of its function as complexity reducer. It creates one holistic gestalt around the businesses, enabling management to manage the set as one.

The issue comes into focus clearly where companies consider mergers of different businesses. The above reasoning argues that the invention of one overall synergetic Business Idea is a prerequisite for a successful acquisition.

CONSIDERING THE BUSINESS IDEA IN THE MANAGEMENT TEAM

As discussed, a positive feedback loop can spiral upwards or downwards. Near the switch-over point it takes only a small nudge to flip-flop from growth into decline. Company managers are generally intuitively aware of this danger-point and try to maintain a margin of safety. The purpose of a company is defined as maximising profit for the shareholders. But the urge to be profitable is often related less to shareholder considerations, than to the need to keep the positive feedback loop away from the precipice.

Sometimes companies find themselves exploiting a successful Business Idea, based on a strong set of Distinctive Competencies, built up in the past. The unique Business Idea is not always well articulated. Although initially the underlying entrepreneurial idea was clearly understood it often happens in successful organisations that attention moves to the product and the efficiency of its production system. Companies that have been in business for a while often lose sight of the complex reasons why customers buy their particular products or services. While things are going well, many managers get on with the day-to-day business, implicitly relying on the ongoing tacit Business Idea to protect them from competitive onslaught. As time goes on, people in the business often come to take customer value for granted and managers in the company may gradually diverge in their intuitive interpretation of the Business Idea. There are considerable dangers lurking here because, as we saw, Distinctive Competencies depreciate over time.

If the Business Idea is not any longer clearly and jointly understood the danger of the positive feedback loop slipping unnoticed into its declining mode is particularly strong. Considering the long lead times required to build most Distinctive Competencies the company may run into serious difficulties trying to turn things around once profitability has started to decline. There may not be time or resources to adjust the Business Idea to the current market.

To avoid this situation arising the management team needs to jointly articulate and understand the basis of a company's success. Divergent notions of the Business Idea in the management team need to be confronted in open debate. The Business Idea concept assists the team in managing this process more explicitly, through the introduction of a thinking framework and language, allowing joint rational consideration in terms of:

- The current Business Idea.
- The strengths/weaknesses of the current Distinctive Competencies in their systemic interaction.
- The outlook for the strength of the Distinctive Competencies against the ever changing values in society.

Once a Business Idea has been articulated, strategic priorities need to be determined to maintain its health. Selection of strategic options for the future needs to be guided by their relevance to maintaining and enhancing the Business Idea. How this can be done operationally is discussed in Part Three.

SUMMARY OF MAIN POINTS OF THE BUSINESS IDEA CONCEPT

We have introduced the concept of the "Business Idea" and suggested that it should drive the strategy of organisations. This is not presented as a new tool that managers are urged to use to increase their success. We believe that the Business Idea already exists in the mental models used by managers to make sense of the world. We are suggesting that managers should try to articulate their implicit Business Idea, to focus the dialogue which needs to take place in each organisation on the emerging strategic direction.

Strategy has as its main aim the continuation and growth of the organisation. For this purpose a surplus of resources needs to be created in its day-to-day operations. The conditions required for this to happen are specified by the Business Idea. The basic motor of the Business Idea is the system of Distinctive Competencies created and exploited by the organisation. Understanding the nature of this leads to an awareness of the intrinsic constraints in the scope of their deliberate development.

As we saw there is evidence to suggest that a successful organisation concentrates on one Business Idea only. This is not the same as concentrating on only one business, sometimes called the Core Business. A Business Idea may encompass more than one **business**. It is a more dynamic concept than a core business. A successful Business Idea implies continuous renewal of the business concept. Entrepreneurial invention continues to be a pre-condition for survival and success. The concept of the Business Idea puts entrepreneurial invention back on to the agenda.

In entrepreneurship, invention goes together with risk. The entrepreneur needs to think about his Business Idea against an uncertain future. The same applies for organisations. In the next chapter we discuss various ways of thinking about uncertainty in the future business environment. This will lead to a discussion of scenario planning in comparison with other ways of describing the future world.

Chapter Four

Dealing with Uncertainty

Business is about taking risks. The Business Idea characterises the underlying principles on which success of the organisation is being built. But how does management know that its ideas are sound and a strong basis for the future? The success or failure of a Business Idea must be related to its business environment. There must be a good fit between the organisation and its surrounding world. Developing a sound and healthy organisation requires understanding the environment as much as understanding the organisation. We only have to look around to know that this is not a trivial task. Why is it that attempts to explain what goes on in thousands of organisations across the world can give rise to such different explanations? What is the source of the ambiguity we are obviously struggling with?

The basis of the problem is related to the fact that strategic management takes place within a context of uncertainty about the future. It is uncertainty that raises the question whether anything useful can be done, and if so, what and how. Uncertainty is at the root of what we are discussing here, and we therefore now turn to a discussion of risk and risk perception.

FORMS OF UNCERTAINTY

We do not know what will happen in the future, but our ignorance is not total. The degree to which we can make useful statements about the future differs from case to case. In this context we identify three categories of uncertainty:

1. Risks, where there is enough historical precedent, in the form of

similar events, to enable us to estimate probabilities (even if only judgementally) for various possible outcomes.

2. Structural uncertainties, where we are looking at the possibility of an event which is unique enough not to provide us with an indication of likelihood. The possibility of the event presents itself by means of a cause/effect chain of reasoning, but we have no evidence for judging how likely it could be.

3. Unknowables, where we cannot even imagine the event. Looking back in history we know that there have been many of these, and we must assume that this will continue in the future. But we have no clue what these events could be.

Uncertainty has to be assessed before business decisions can be made. Risk can be calculated on the basis of probabilities. However, in strategy most uncertainties are in the structure of the situation. This type of uncertainty often arises when patterns in events can be interpreted in various different ways. Based on these different structures different futures will emerge. In such deep structural questions we will find ourselves mostly in entirely new and uncharted territory, with no history to base probability estimates on.

Scenario planning can help managers to get on top of what might happen, and to develop a better judgement of what this could mean, by working through the consequences of the different ways the business environment may change. It obviously cannot take away the uncertainty in these situations, but it will help managers to come to a reasonable judgement on whether a specific decision will be robust across a range of possible futures. In this way managers can come to a conclusion on whether the uncertainty facing them is acceptable or not.

Finally, in the area of unknowables, we appreciate that prescience is not possible. The only thing we can try to do in relation to unknowables is to become more skilful in reacting to the unexpected. We can do that by developing our perception skills (see below). Scenarios can provide powerful help here. Indeed, many would argue that this is the most important use of scenarios.

The predictable risk

If there was no risk, there would be no business returns and no profitability. Chances have to be taken in the light of irreducible uncertainty. These are risks that are inherent in the business situation and have to be taken if the organisation is to continue to exist. On the other hand, taking extraordinary unwarranted levels of risk causes major problems. The art of the game is finding the appropriate balance, where risk is acceptable and calculated. Risk assessment, recognising what is going on, thinking about the future, and then being more skilful in adapting yourself in advance to possible future situations is a major business competency.

Not all uncertainty is uncomfortable. Many companies have learned to live in a situation of considerable risk. In oil exploration, for example, companies live with making significant commitments of money in conditions of high risk. This is not problematic for them as they have developed a readily available conceptual framework and analytical toolbox to deal with this. These allow them to consider individual decisions in the context of an ongoing flow of many similar decisions, which on average will produce positive results. One individual decision which misfires is not seen as "error", requiring direct managerial intervention. Performance is judged over a longer time period. There is acceptance that "you cannot win them all". The approach is basically probabilistic.

There are many ways in which risks can be managed in this way. For example, in the area of business finance the management of risk is a well-developed skill, based on the principles of "predictable uncertainty". Instruments of insurance have been developed to cope with many different situations which may arise. Companies can take out insurance against the political risk in export and foreign investments. Hedging instruments have the same basic function.

If managers do not feel they have such a ready-made framework, decision making and risk taking become conservative. In those circumstances survival may require that the organisation urgently reconceptualises the environmental conditions. Creating understanding of the possible conditions as part of an ongoing stream of similar or comparable events enables managers to start judging probabilities, making risk assessment more realistic.

Structural uncertainty

These conditions do not apply where organisations are faced with new and uncharted challenges, posed by structural uncertainty. There is no theory to fall back on and it is unclear how individual decisions are part of an ongoing flow of decision making. It is not possible to see events as an ongoing stream of decision events. Each decision is an isolated event. Big strategic questions often fall in this category. It is in this area that scenario planning becomes particularly important.

An interesting example concerns Lloyds Names and their insurance underwriters who have over the last few years been hit by losses due to a number of large-scale natural catastrophes leading to increased insurance claims. The system that operated in Lloyds put a lot of risk on their shoulders. Names were suing the firm of underwriters who they claim have put them in this unenviable position. The court concluded that Names faced almost certain disaster. They should have figured out that it was inevitable that a disaster of such proportions would happen one day, and that they would not be able to cope financially with the consequences of such an event. The possible events were not hidden from anyone. If Names had considered multiple possible futures, then catastrophes of the magnitude experienced would have been on the agenda. Essentially it was an accident waiting to happen. "The underwriters were blindly writing business without bothering to estimate the major impact. They just went into it blind".

In a situation like this, scenarios can help in dealing with uncertainty in three ways. In the first place they help the organisation in understanding the environment better, allowing many decisions to be seen not as isolated events but as part of a process of "swings and roundabouts". In this way scenario planning helps managers to avoid undue conservatism, by allowing "calculated" risk taking. Secondly scenarios put structural uncertainty on the agenda, driving home to the organisation what sort of "accidents are waiting to happen." In this way scenario planning helps managers to avoid undue risk. Thirdly scenarios help the organisation to become more adaptable by expanding their mental models and thereby enhancing the perceptual capabilities needed to recognise unexpected events.

PREDICTABILITY

We argued that the scenario methodology is a general approach towards risk management. Any such approach depends on the existence of elements which are (to an extent) predictable. Because some things *can* be predicted, an activity such as scenario planning (and, indeed, all planning) makes sense. The fact that we make the effort to manage our risks at all means that we recognise that even although there are large uncertainties out there some elements are predictable. These elements are sometimes called "predetermined elements".

An example is demography. In the sort of time frames that business planners tend to think (five years, ten years, sometimes even twenty years) population is a predictable phenomenon. It is predictable that the school children of today will be the parents of tomorrow. However, over the very long term birth rates are just as unpredictable as anything else. The point here is that in the time frame the business planner works the system exhibits enough inertia to allow making predictions. Technological innovation is another example. While invention is probably the most unpredictable phenomenon of all, innovation concerns the application of existing inventions. It is a time consuming process that therefore exhibits an element of predictability over the planners' time frame. Growth rate of production capacity is another example of a predetermined element. People can build and expand capacity at various rates but there is a maximum beyond which even the most energetic company would find it difficult to move. In some very large engineering construction projects the lead times can be very considerable, indicating that we can predict predetermined elements in this area. There is inertia in softer domains as well. For example, political power shifts take time and exhibit an element of momentum allowing an element of prediction. Cultural shift are even slower. And some human characteristics are permanent, such as the desire to survive, develop and "be connected".

The more precisely we try to pin things down the more difficult prediction becomes. While the overall direction of movement may be predetermined the specific outcomes may be highly uncertain. Culture is often predetermined to a considerable extent. Basic beliefs and values that people develop in communities are slow to change, but predicting the attitude of a smaller group of people is problematic. Similarly economic development moves within fairly narrow bands, but economists continue to have problems making detailed macro-economic predictions. Looking at the same phenomenon we may conclude that while the overall structure has a high level of predictability, the details of the possible outcome may be highly uncertain. We may decide that a particular event is predetermined, but its timing may be unpredictable. For example, we may be resigned to the fact that a policy will lead to confrontation with the trade union. But we cannot predict the timing of the strike. Or the overall political trend may be predetermined, but who will win the next election is still undetermined. While the climate may be predetermined the weather remains uncertain. The agriculturist finds climate more interesting than the weather, while the holiday maker may think the other way around.

Certain kinds of constraints allow us to predict particular environmental developments:

- Time delays, developments which are "in the pipeline" and will emerge, e.g. demographics.
- System constraints, e.g. limits to growth.
- Generic behaviour of structural feedback loops in a system, e.g. the arms race.
- Actor logic and motivation, e.g. Labour or Tory politics in the UK.
- The inertia of the system (including societal inertia), e.g. economic development, culture.
- Laws of nature.

This means that certain developments in the future are to some extent "predetermined". Scenario planning needs to be able to deal with both predetermined elements and uncertainty, in order to combine its planning function with its risk assessment function. To illustrate how this integration can be made to work we contrast it with traditional forecasting.

The need for forecasting

Forecasting is obviously necessary; we cannot live without it. In our personal lives we avoid a lot of trouble by forecasting. For example if we cross a street we forecast the movements of the approaching cars, before we decide that there is enough time to get to the other side without getting hit. In most cases this is done successfully. We are forecasting all the time, we could not do much without it.

When an industry is in a state of relatively slow incremental change forecasting is an effective way of planning. It projects the future on the basis of what was seen in the past. If demand has been increasing consistently at 6 per cent per year we can plan next year accordingly.

The problem with forecasting is that people start to believe that this situation will continue for ever. But there is always a point in time where behaviour changes structurally. Forecasts may work very well for a while, but forecasters need to be aware of the variables which could suddenly break the relationship with the past and create a trend break.

We are all familiar with stories of forecasters getting it wrong. Figure 11 shows forecasts of demand for world shipbuilding, made by the Association of West European Shipbuilders. This thorough exercise is done once every four years. Figure 11 shows forecasts made over a period of time compared with what actually happened. What this example illustrates is the power of history over the mental models of forecasters, even if the detailed predictions are made by sophisticated computer simulation. "What has come down must go up again" is one of these tacit assumptions. If not this year than maybe next.

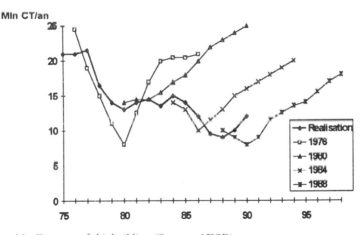

Figure 11. *Forecasts of shipbuilding (Source: AESB).*

Figure 12 shows projections made for power requirements in the Netherlands. A similar situation to that described in Figure 11.

So why do we continue to try to predict the unpredictable? For example, why does the law require the British Treasury to produce a forecast of the British economy, even if their record is so unimpressive? Or why is the government of California required to produce a forecast of oil prices, which can only be wrong?

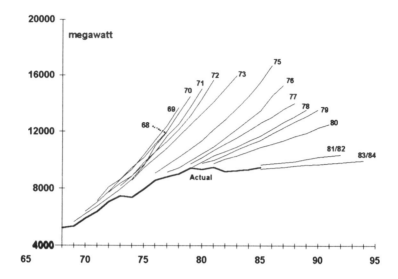

Figure 12. *Forecast of power consumption in The Netherlands (Source: SEP).*

Limits to forecasting

Albert Olensak of Sun Oil suggested the following metaphor to illustrate the situation. Forecasting can be thought of as analogous to the illumination by the headlights of a car driving through a snow storm at night. A bit of what lies ahead is revealed, not very clearly. The driver merely tries to avoid danger and pick out enough detail to arrive at his destination intact. He needs to be prepared for sudden major obstacles, be aware of his limited view and try to adjust his speed accordingly. Obstacles will appear suddenly, and then it may be too late to adjust. The obstacles the driver must be prepared for are outside the limited view that he has. The reaction required adjusts speed in response to limits in perception. We have to forecast. We couldn't drive the car with the lights switched off altogether. The important thing is to realise the limits of our view. Making predictions beyond our capability to forecast lies at the bottom of the crises of perception discussed above.

If we accept the utility of forecasting in the short term, but its diminishing usefulness further into the future, and if we have adjusted our speed accordingly, is there anything else we need to do about the longer term, where our headlights become dim?

Planning time frame and rate of change

There is a lot in the business environment that exhibits an element of predictability. In slow changing business environments planning can be long-term, and policies can involve a high level of commitment.

However, in fast changing business environments planning becomes shorter-term, and policies must exhibit a higher degree of flexibility. The comprehensiveness of the strategy should depend on the degree of uncertainty in the environment. The complexity in the business situation faced by most organisations suggests that the time horizon within which a business system can act as a predictable "machine" is short, months rather than years. Marketing positioning strategy, concerned with policies aimed at positioning the organisation through interplay with its competitors, is normally seen in a relatively short time-frame. This must be subject to frequent updating, driven by continuous unanticipated change and opportunity.

Some phenomena exhibit more inertia and momentum than others. For example energy use shows strong momentum, so oil companies plan a long way out. On the other hand, construction companies seldom plan ahead more than 3 years. Beyond that they experience little that is predetermined and they tend to adjust their business policy accordingly. The time span that business plans for tends to be chosen on the basis of a reasonable balance between predetermineds and uncertainties.

However, even in the most volatile industries organisations are involved in issues with long-term implications. Examples in this area include such activities as capital investment, staff training and creating a competent organisational culture. An example of this was illustrated in Figure 10. The construction industry is notorious for its volatility, and it is extremely difficult to make any reliable plans even a few years out. However, the company in the example had built an institutional capability over many years, and enjoyed the fruits of the resulting strong protection of a client-oriented culture. When confronted with such capability, management can consider a longer time horizon, as there is more predictability in the phenomena considered, even in the construction industry. The planning horizon depends not only on the nature of the industry, but also on the issue under consideration.

Seeing further is not always the same as seeing better. An interesting analogy is offered by chess players. Contrary to the expectations of computer scientists, neither Deep Thought (the top chess playing computer program) nor human grandmasters need to look very far ahead to play excellent games. Generally grandmasters survey the chess board and forecast all the pieces only one move ahead. Then they select the most plausible play or two and investigate its consequences more deeply. At every move ahead the number of choices to consider explodes exponentially, yet the masters will concentrate only on a few of the most probable countermoves at each rehearsed turn. Occasionally they search far ahead when they spot familiar situations they know from experience to be valuable or dangerous. But in general, grandmasters (and now Deep Thought) work from rules of thumb, relating to developing generic strengths. For instance: Favour moves that increase options; shy away from moves that end well but require cutting off choices; work from strong positions that have many adjoining strong positions. Balance looking ahead with paying attention to what is happening now on the whole board (Kelly 1994).

Similarly it is the balance between momentum and volatility in the business environment that determines how far a business plans into the future. Figure 13 shows these elements in context. Looking into the future the degree of predictability gradually goes down the further we look, and uncertainty goes up. In the very short term predictability is high and (frequent) forecasting is the planning mode

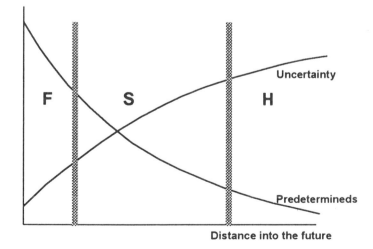

Figure 13. *The balance of predictability and uncertainty in the business environment.*

of choice (F → forecasting). In the very long term everything is uncertain and attempts to planning demonstrate diminishing returns (H → hope). In the middle zone where there is a level of predictability but also considerable uncertainty scenarios are the indicated way forward (S → scenarios).

Following the contingency strategy theory (comprehensiveness of the strategy should depend on degree of uncertainty in the environment) it is dangerous to plan strategically without being fully aware of the level of uncertainty facing the business. Specifically forecasting (instead of scenario planning) in the S region of Figure 13 leads to over-planning and false security due to a discrepancy between the level of real uncertainty and perception of uncertainty. Similarly scenario planning in the F region leads to under-planning.

Short-termism in the markets

Business leaders often feel that financial markets take too short-term an attitude vis-à-vis investment opportunities. While management wants to develop the business by making long-term investments the money providers are pressing hard for immediate returns, frustrating management's ability to build for the future. Companies in the Anglo-Saxon world often look enviously at what they perceive to be a much more long-term attitude in Germany or Japan. As a consequence financial markets are holding back long term development. How is this possible?

As we saw on page 59 value is created in two ways, in the form of a current surplus for stakeholders, or in the form of an expectation among stakeholders that a surplus will be generated in the future. Short-termism is the result of a low expectation of future value generation. If the promise of future profits are high enough markets are prepared to wait, as is demonstrated by numerous new businesses financed by venture capital on the basis of promise of future returns. If management complains about short-termism it means that they have a different perception of the possibility of future value creation from that of the markets. This can be due to two reasons:

- A difference in perception of the level of commercial risk involved.
- An inability on the part of management to convince the market that they are the party most capable to realise the value perceived.

In both cases it seems that management is not getting its message across. The task management faces is twofold. Firstly, to convince the markets that its inside assessment of the risk involved is superior to the market's assessment. And secondly, that it has the capability to realise the project. These tasks may be easier in countries where traditionally links between companies and financiers have been closer, which may explain the higher weight given to longer-term considerations in Germany and Japan.

It is interesting to note that most cases where the ostensibly short-term markets are prepared to wait involve young entrepreneurial companies, with a clear-cut communicable understanding of the Business Idea they are pursuing. Older companies often have difficulties projecting their Business Idea with the same degree of clarity. An intuitive understanding of the underlying success formula is obviously not so easy to communicate. The message from the markets is that the relative level of uncertainty businesses are facing can be favourably affected by clarifying their Business Idea.

BUSINESS ENVIRONMENT COMPLEXITY

The main problem in business environment analysis is dealing with complexity. There is a lot to consider. The world is large indeed and there is room for ever more interpretation of the events we observe. Another complication is that we will be considering the future, with its inherent uncertainties. How do we decide what is predictable, and how do we deal with the remaining irreducible uncertainty? We will need to find a way to decide what is worthwhile spending our limited resources on. Which elements do we wish to consider in planning our business? We have to make a decision about what is really important.

The area where we concentrate our limited resources is driven by the question what would really make a difference for our business. For example IBM was not caught out by economic performance, but by technological development. In the early 1980s scenario planning for IBM would have meant thinking through different interpretations of what the development of the cheap microprocessor might mean. One interpretation saw their application in mainframes, and IBM developed themselves into the number one microprocessor company. Another interpretation, which did not get the attention it deserved at the top of the company, was the use of these devices in small PCs, and the subsequent demand for this line of distributed computing. Thinking through scenarios of massive growth in this area might have suggested the importance of setting standards, something IBM "gave away" to companies such as Intel and Microsoft.

Answering the question of what would really make a difference allows the identification of a number of key uncertainties in the business environment. Scenarios are constructed on the basis of these and the predetermined elements (Figure 14). In this way we consider multiple futures, depending on different possible conclusions we reach on the underlying structure of cause and effect, depending on the key uncertainties.

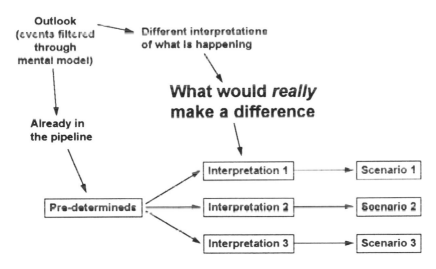

Figure 14. *Scenario building framework.*

More uncertainty means fewer variables to focus on

Scenario planning operates in the area where uncertainty is a major factor compared to the predetermineds in the situation. The discovery of predetermined elements in an uncertain situation creates the significant "aha" experience. The inherent uncertainty means that the analysis does not need to go into great detail; strategic management is the art of the broad brush, and of focusing on what is really important. There may be many sources of uncertainty but if these are considered orthogonally (independent from each other) then only those factors with the largest impact need to be taken into account. A handful of factors will normally overwhelm all the others (quadratic addition of standard deviations). And the larger the uncertainty the smaller the number becomes. Without this principle, scenario work in highly complex situations would be impossible. In this respect uncertainty helps the scenario planner, in that it allows focusing on a smaller number of key uncertainties.

SHARED THEORIES OF STRUCTURE

As we saw scenario planning provides structure for new data; it frames uncertainty and it balances the known with the new. In "Forms of uncertainty" (page 83) we discussed the difference between risk, structural uncertainty and unknowables. Scenario analysis is useful for analysing structural uncertainty, where possible future events are unique, lacking any basis for a probability assessment, but where the possibility of the event presents itself through a cause/effect line of reasoning. We will now turn to the question of how these structures can be understood and developed.

Prediction and uncertainty

As we discussed, the concept of strategy is based on the assumption that aspects of the contextual environment are to some extent predictable. The purpose of analysis is to reveal the underlying meaning in the business environment. Perception starts with observation. Events are the raw material we work with to build up our understanding of what is happening. We consider the events, and start to see trends and patterns. The human mind is particularly good at pattern recognition. (Patterns are an order we perceive in events over time or in place.) Once we perceive a pattern, we wonder where this order comes from. We start thinking in terms of causality. In this way we imply an underlying structure *behind* the events we are observing. We build a "mental map" of reality.

Once we have discovered the fundamental driving forces and levels of uncertainty we are in a better position to consider our responses to the challenges presented by the contextual environment. In this way environmental analysis makes it possible to test strategic visions, business ideas, strategies and plans.

Assumption of stable structure

The power of the scenario methodology lies in its ability to logically (causally) organise a large range of relevant but seemingly disparate data and information. This is done by the recognition of both pre-determined elements as well as uncertainty in the future.

The phenomenon of pre-determinism is based on the assumption of a deep stable structure pertaining over the planning time frame. We recognise stable physical structures (climate, geography) as well as social structures (belief systems, cultures). On the other hand elements of the future are seen as uncertain if we can explain events in different ways, see more than one possible structure driving events, and if there is no way to decide which structure will dominate in the future. Depending on which structure is considered different futures will be projected.

We will first consider the elements of the future where we feel we can imply a deep stable structure on the basis of which we are prepared to plan. Later we will discuss the other elements of the future, where different interpretations are possible, and uncertainty enters the picture.

Cues for causality

Scenario planners train themselves to find structure in a range of events. One useful way of thinking about data is through the categorisation known as the "iceberg" (Figure 15), which breaks down knowledge into three categories: events, pattern and structure (See Senge 1990). At the top of the iceberg "above the surface" are visible events, for example developments in the market or customers doing one thing or another, governments enacting legislation, and so on. Events can be observed. One sees the world through the events that present themselves and that we perceive. It is the visible part of the iceberg. Initially we describe the world in those terms.

But as soon as important events present themselves we try to discover underlying patterns and structure, in order to "understand" the situation. Consider for example the development of the interpretation of the 1995 Oklahoma bombing event. Initially no reason was obvious. A desperate search for some pattern made people consider a link with the earlier attack on the World Trade Center at New York. This led to a suspicion of a Middle East trigger, on the basis of which one false arrest was made. Through systematic causal

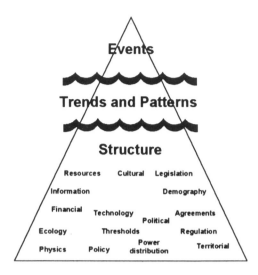

Figure 15. *The "Iceberg".*

analysis (and a degree of luck) a new pattern started to emerge later, leading to the arrest of the perpetrator. The new systemic interpretation introduced right-wing groups into the equation. Op-eds started to appear discussing "urban warfare" scenarios as a credible future. Eventually the FBI acquired new powers as a result of these deliberations.

The process is encapsulated in the saying: "CNN provides the events, Henry Kissinger the underlying structure".

Scenario planners start from the premise that there is much more to be said than just reporting events. They assume structure underneath events, driving these in one direction or another. The assumption is that events do not just happen at random, but they are related to each other through a structure where causes drive effects and one event leads to another. We can look at the world at three levels: events, patterns and structure. The thought of relatedness occurs to us as we start to see trends over time in the events. Events do not seem totally random. Some events may be entirely unexpected, but many seem to display some sort of organised behaviour in the way that we perceive them. Something may be going up with some consistency, or a growth path may be checked and starts turning down. Some variable may be cycling up and down with some regularity.

In order to get at the underlying structure we look for interrelatedness between multiple trends. Looking at trends ideas for structure present themselves. If variable *a* is going up and variable *b* is going up simultaneously we wonder whether they are in some way related. Our perception of causality is based on patterns we think we recognise in the events around us. Structure is based on our perception of causality. We use such patterns as cues for causality (Einhorn & Hogarth 1982). These can take the form of:

- Temporal order, events organised on a time line, for example trends over time in events.
- Co-variance, where we see different variables follow similar patterns over time.
- Spatial/temporal closeness, if one thing always follows another, we assume a link.
- Similarity in form or pattern

The discovery of cues for causality provides us with our second level of world knowledge.

Finally by discovering multiple cues for causality we infer elements of the underlying overall structure which we assume ultimately drives the visible events. In this way we compose our mental model of the world. The assumed structure we construct underlying all causality we have come to infer between trends is the third level of understanding of the world.

The "Iceberg" analysis

The causal structure we assume to exist we use to link history with the future. The total process in principle involves the following steps:

- Specify important events, things we can see happening.
- Discover trends, time behaviour we observe in events, leading to the conceptualisation of variables.
- Infer patterns, based on cues for causality applied to variable behaviour.
- Develop the structure(s), which connects the system together through causal links (multiple structures may result from different possible interpretations of causal patterns).
- Use the structure(s) to project future behaviour (with multiple structures leading to multiple scenarios).

Out of this we discover that some developments have already been set in motion, and are bound to come out at the other end. The inertia of the system will help us to understand predictable outcomes, on the basis of which we can plan our activities.

Following a process of this type we develop an understanding on predetermined elements, as the basis for future planning.

Structural uncertainty

But there is also a lot in the future that is fundamentally uncertain. As we saw above (page 83) uncertainty can be in the form of risk, structural uncertainty or unknowables. Scenarios operate in the area of structural uncertainty. This arises in most cases where developments in the environment can be explained in various different ways. We become aware of different cause-and-effect structures which could be alternative explanations of what is going on. This means that the future looks different depending on which structure we adopt for our scenario design. As it is not possible to assign probabilities to the different structures on any statistically sound basis the decision maker will need to confront multiple futures, which are all equally plausible.

An example of a structural uncertainty is the following: The economic outlook is often of considerable importance for a business. We therefore may often be interested in the economic performance of a particular industrial country. We read in the newspapers how commentators try to look into the future. Some may tell us that we are in a recession, and report the first signs of recovery. What is happening is that people are trying to fit observations into a pattern that they know from the past and extrapolate into the future. The implication of "our economic performance of the moment is determined by the economic cycle" is that we can predict that we will be coming out of recession and that growth rates will recover. Eventually unemployment will drop, people will go back to work. And the explanation implies that in five to ten years' time there will be another recession. Using the model of the economic cycle makes you predict the future in a particular way.

However, other commentators may come up with a different explanation. They may believe that a large contributory factor to the recent economic difficulties of Western economies is due to new overseas competition. They report that this is caused by the progressive opening up of new skilled low-cost labour markets, one after another, in the newly developing countries, causing the Western manufacturing sector gradually to disappear to these areas of lower cost. They point towards the run down of traditional industrial activities which has been going on for some time. Here we are confronted with a different interpretation of what is going on. If we accept this model, then the manufacturing sector is not going to recover in a few years' time. Based on this different interpretation of what is happening we see a different less attractive future on the horizon. Depending on the interpretation we find different ways in which the future will unfold.

An interesting example of alternative interpretations of an underlying structure was presented by the scenarios of drilling activity in the US oil industry in the 1970s and 1980s by a major oilfield equipment group. While the activity was increasing until 1981, the underlying model in general use related it to demand for oil and oil price. On the basis of this the forecast was for further increases. In retrospect we now know that the fiscal law was in fact a much more important driving force, making investments in drilling rigs a no-loss proposition, either one found oil, or the IR essentially paid for the investment. As soon as this anomaly was rectified the activity fell away. Following the oil price collapse in 1985 the activity fell to an all-time low.

Another example of different structures leading to different outlooks might be seeing the market for PCs driven by type of user (business products, consumer products), or by type of information processed (accounting, games).

There is never only one structural interpretation of a pattern of events, there are always multiple interpretations. Different interpretations of what is happening in the environment give rise to different scenarios of the future. These may contain the same pre-determined developments, but will differ in terms of these alternative interpretations. Figure 14 shows the scenario construction process schematically. The job is basically about finding structure in the events in the environment. Some of these will be considered predetermined and will be reflected in all scenarios. But the scenarios will differ in aspects which can be explained by different alternative structures. In this way the decision maker will take account of what is considered a reasonable planning basis, as well as test the robustness of his decisions across the range of uncertainty.

Referring back to the learning loop (page 37), the "reflection on

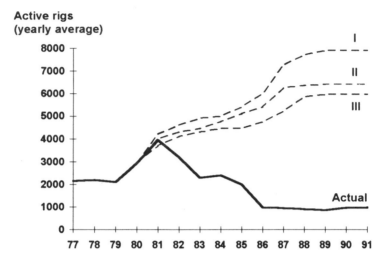

Figure 16. *Drilling scenarios USA 1980–1990.*

experience" stage in the learning loop, resulting in the awareness of new and unexpected patterns, is followed by building a theory (or mental models) of why things happen as we perceive them. This theory then becomes the basis for planning our next moves. In scenario planning understanding structure is the "building of theory" part of the learning loop. Structure plays a crucial role in all scenario design. This is often expressed as the need for internal consistency in scenarios. Internally consistent scenarios contain all the theory we can develop from our observations, and therefore become the institutional basis for the next step in the loop, the planning of new actions.

FORECASTING vs SCENARIOS

Leaving uncertainty on the agenda

Having discussed the principles of scenario planning let us now compare this with forecasting. Forecasting assumes that it is possible and useful to predict the future. It is the closely related to the rationalist assumption that there is one right answer and the art of strategy is to get as close as possible to it. The task of forecasting must therefore be given to the people with the best capacity in terms of intelligence and computer power as this will ensure that the answer will be as close as possible. Scenario planning has a fundamentally different, more processual oriented, starting point, based on the assumption that there is no one best answer, and there is a point beyond which accuracy cannot be improved. This means that it is important that irreducible risk is faced up to by the people who carry the accountability and responsibility for taking the strategic decisions. Scenario planning assumes that the future cannot be predicted and therefore irreducible uncertainty must not be swept under the carpet. Making a prediction where there is fundamental uncertainty is seen as a basically dangerous notion as it takes away from the decision maker the insights needed to come to a responsible conclusion.

Forecasting is done by experts, away from where the decisions are being made. That means that the decision maker who receives the result of the forecasting activity does not know the underlying thinking process and the uncertainties that have been taken into account to produce the prediction. The danger to the decision maker derives from this disconnection. If (s)he decides to use the forecast he does not know what risk assumptions enter his decision process. He is no longer in a position to see the different possibilities as they could unfold. He has shifted his responsibility on to the expert, who is not accountable. Uncertainty falls between two stools, the linear process runs out to an algorithmically inevitable outcome and thinking tends to stop. The decision process lacks basic information and therefore is essentially a chance event.

Forecasters box in the future, scenarios open up area of thinking

Forecasts are a statistical summary of expert opinion. A forecaster does not necessarily give just one number. He may give a range. He may put probabilistic information around his forecast. But this is always a reflection of expert opinion based on probability assessment. A scenario is much more a conceptual description of a future, based on cause and effect.

There is another fundamental difference. Forecasting requires that we first decide what we want to forecast. If you are in the automobile industry, you decide to forecast the demand for automobiles. Statisticians and experts go to work and, via GNP, spending patterns, etc. they come up with a prediction about the demand for automobiles in the various categories. The fact that the forecaster always decides in advance what he is going to forecast is crucial. Unexpected influences that may come at the business sideways are no longer part of the analysis; the unforeseen variables that do not feature in the expert's model of the business and its environment are not on the agenda. As soon as we are in forecasting mode we have boxed in our mental models and the unexpected has been shut out. Each organisation needs to be aware of the perceptual limitations caused by this sort of analysis.

Imagine a 1980 strategy meeting at IBM called to decide on the PC strategy. The meeting is told that the market forecast for 1990 is 275 000. The conclusion is clear, this is a side-show, we may as well outsource the DOS and microprocessor. Now imagine that some one walks in saying: "Yes, but imagine that the market is 60 million, think about what you would be giving away to Microsoft and Intel". He would have been thrown out.

Something else is required that will make the organisation look outside the framework of business-as-usual. What is needed is a processual approach that mobilises knowledgeable individuals throughout the organisation as well as outsiders. Next, the organisation as a whole needs to acquire the perceptual skill of seeing and acting on signals of change in the business environment across a wide front. This is where the scenarios come in. The scenario planner is not in the forecasting strait jacket. (S)he does not start from the notion of the product (e.g. automobiles), but takes a wider canvas. The starting point is "the main uncertainties facing this business". Perceptions of areas of concern in the management team are the agenda setting questions for the scenario planner. Demand levels for the product may be included in this, but questions will quickly move beyond that into driving forces. For example in the automobile industry the question of the future of transportation in general may come up. The scenario planner takes a broader view about the business environment than the forecaster does. The range of vision of the planning activity has been widened.

A forecaster's sources of uncertainty are generally not made specific. The forecaster will specify that demand for automobiles will be within a range of 80 to 100. There may be a high line and a low line with a probability attached. This is the information management will be getting. They will learn that the most likely outcome is 90 but it could be 100 and it could be 80, as the best forecast the experts can come up with. The sources of uncertainty have become obscured in the analysis. Compare that with scenarios. In scenarios we specifically address key uncertainties through chains of cause and effect. Because they differ on these key logics scenarios put these on the management agenda. Scenarios let the decision maker look not just at outcomes, but also at the driving forces which could move the business one way or the other.

Forecasts, efficient and impoverished

A forecast is a very efficient way of describing the future. But it is also, because of that, impoverished. It is a summary. Its efficiency derives from simple decision making algorithms. For example the size of the factory to be built is easily derived. Forecasting is efficient in reducing rich information into a simple form in which it can be passed on easily for operational purposes. Scenarios have much more information, they are richer because they give the whole cause and effect story, culminating in an understanding of why things happen. But for this reason they are also inefficient as input to yes/no type decision making. It is less straightforward to make a decision on the basis of a set of scenarios than a forecast. Later we will see that the reasoning from scenarios to strategy or decision-making is a significant thinking process in its own right. Scenarios require further judgements. A yes/no decision does not fall out from a scenario. For example in the case of the automobile forecaster we met earlier it may not be so clear, whether the new factory has to be built at all, let alone what its capacity should be. Scenarios do not normally produce conclusions in a mechanistic way. More work, thinking and analysis will be required before an action conclusion emerges.

Testing forecasts and scenarios

Forecasts can be tested after the event. You can compare what has come out with what was predicted. As we saw in a few examples earlier, sometimes it works and sometimes it doesn't. And unfortunately, it works least where it is needed most, in periods of rapid change. Scenarios, of course, cannot be proven or disproved. First of all there is no claim that they will materialise as such, and they are not supposed to be used on that basis. In fact, as one point on a continuum, the probability that one particular scenario will unfold in all its details is near to zero. But as a set they represent our current understanding of the range of uncertainty. If we draw the range of scenarios wide enough the chance that reality (less unknowables) will emerge somewhere in between them can be made high. Therefore they are not meant to be tested against what will happen. That information is simply not available when they are needed and therefore can have no bearing on conclusions drawn from them. The test is whether they represent our current best knowledge of the situation and outlook, and thereby lead to better strategies.

Different purposes

Summarising, forecasting and scenario planning have very different purposes. The strategic question has its origin in uncertainty, both in the environment and within the organisation. Uncertainty increases the further out we look. Forecasting is useful in the short term, where things are reasonably predictable and uncertainty is relatively small compared to our ability to predict. In this range rationalistic "predict and control" planning makes sense and is necessary. In the very long term where very little is predictable planning is not a useful activity. It is in the intermediate future where uncertainty and predictability are both significant that scenario planning makes its contribution. This is also the area of strategy. Therefore strategic management and scenario planning are closely linked.

Chapter Five

Scenarios and the Business Idea

The prime question to be addressed is whether the organisation is well-equipped for the futures we can see coming. The way this is achieved is by considering the Business Idea, the characterisation of the organisation, against the scenarios, the characterisation of the future business environment, to establish the degree of fit. This is what we compared earlier to the windtunnel where a model is subjected to tests to assess its strengths and weaknesses. The purpose is not just to accept or reject but to engage in an iterative process of adjustment and improvement, until a model has been developed which is sufficiently robust to deal with the whole range of environments that might develop. This leads to the fundamental rule of scenario planning: Once we have decided on the set of scenarios of the future which are considered relevant to our situation, each scenario is treated as equally plausible. This thinking process is described in this chapter.

CONSIDERING STRATEGIC FIT

The analytical task is to "walk" the Business Idea mentally through the various scenarios, to study how it would stand up if any of these futures were to materialise. As we have seen the Business Idea contains a limited number of key factors and Distinctive Competencies which are or will be brought together to meet a societal need and create value in a customer system. The business needs to apply its system of competencies to the provision of goods and services which the customer values. This ability to produce value for the customer is what we call an "overlap". This overlap will produce a surplus if the value is greater than the cost incurred in producing the transaction. In this case the supplier will seek to appropriate a portion of the value thus created (see page 61). While going through the scenarios one after the other the analysis addresses the following questions:

- Will the customer value system overlap sufficiently with the competence system envisaged to create significant new and surplus value?
- Will the organisation be able to appropriate enough of the surplus for its own development. Will its competence system be capable of being defended against competitive emulation?

While going through the scenarios events unfold, and with each of these the same questions are addressed, over and over again: how would this influence (1) the customer value creation effect and (2) the defensibility of the competence system (see Figure 17)?

Having gone through all scenarios in this thinking mode, a judgement has to be made on whether the answers are positive enough to instil confidence in the future strength of the formula. The answer may come out positive or negative. Depending on this outcome strategic attention moves in a different direction.

If the fit is strong the organisation will want to continue and expand

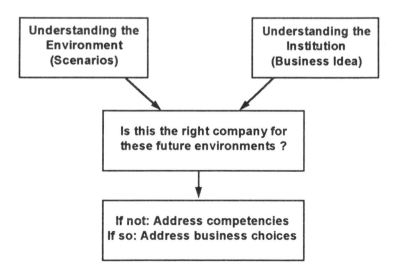

Figure 17. *Fit between the environment and the Business Idea.*

exploiting the Business Idea. In this case the strategic questions concentrate on finding new areas where the competence system can be exploited. This can take two forms:

- The offering, which constitutes the interface with the customer, stands and the organisation looks for new markets or market segments where potential customer requirements make it possible for this to be exploited.
- The organisation looks for new areas where the competence system can be made to create customer value.

In both cases the competence system stands as the basis of the strategy. Thinking then concentrates on options in the portfolio of businesses. Strategy development revolves around portfolio options.

However, if the confrontation of the Business Idea with the scenarios leads to less satisfactory results the strategic attention moves to the question of how to change and improve the competence system. In this case strategic thinking focuses on the development of new capability options.

In the process of testing a Business Idea in a set of scenarios strategists often develop a value judgement for the scenarios in the set. This is mostly related to the degree of change that a scenario requires in the Business Idea. If little change is required the scenario is considered a "good future", in which growth is possible on the basis of exploitation of existing strengths. If the existing formula does not do so well, the particular scenario is seen as less friendly. The narrower the business definition the more likely it is that certain futures are seen as uncomfortable. Companies who tend to define themselves in terms of a specific product often suffer from this. A wide definition of the "organisational self" will make the scenarios appear more neutral. Companies defining themselves in terms of general purpose competencies will have fewer difficulties. Underlying these value judgements are a resistance to change. If change is not judged negatively, but rather seen as the raw material of business success, then there are no good or bad futures. As we saw earlier, the world of business success is a relative world, in which every successful idea will be copied by competitors. It is a dynamic situation, a race, in which everyone who slows down will be overtaken. The winners are those who develop new business concepts, new Business Ideas. Companies who see themselves in the business of change will not find any scenarios good or bad, but will distinguish them by the different challenges they offer. In Part Three we will discuss how the scenario planner can help the company to avoid the good/bad syndrome in futures reconnaissance.

BUILDING FOR THE FUTURE

The Business Idea generally needs to evolve with changes in the business environment. Management needs to develop a view on what new Distinctive Competencies will be called for in the future, and they need to work towards getting these in place. This is best achieved by developing a coherent view of a future Business Idea that will be robust against the various futures the scenarios indicate (this is sometimes called a Strategic Vision, i.e. an as yet unrealised Business Idea concept one aims for). The challenge is to decide how to develop the Business Idea for the future.

Uniqueness as such cannot be bought, it needs to be invented and built. In principle there are two ways in which a Business Idea can be moved forward:

- By entrepreneurial invention. This means that new customer value potential is discovered and/or a new and more efficient way of creating already established customer value is invented.
- By building on the existing Distinctive Competencies, using old competencies to build new ones, which are better adapted to the new business circumstances envisaged (leveraging).

A plan to build new Distinctive Competencies for the future needs to be based on leveraging of the Distinctive Competencies the company has at the present time. The task of building the Business Idea for the future has the following characteristics:

- It needs to respond to future customer values.
- It needs to be a new unique combination of competencies, which can be exploited in a positive feedback loop.
- It needs to be created on the basis of the current Business Idea, leveraging existing Distinctive Competencies.

The ability to invent a new combination within these constraints constitutes the entrepreneurial task facing any management team interested in creating long-term profit potential for the company. **Building for the future means leveraging distinctive**

competencies which are present today. Most managers find this intuitive. However, what is often overlooked is that it can go terribly wrong if not considered in the context of a total Business Idea. For example building up the competencies for the future may involve acquiring another firm with complementary competencies. In almost all acquisition cases there is some expectation of synergy resulting from the new combination. However, the list of unsuccessful diversifications is very long. For example, oil companies expected to use their exploration skills in the metal mining business, EDS expected to leverage technology and people's entrepreneurialism by going into management consulting and digital video information systems (Lorenz 1993).

So why does acquisition go wrong so often? The oil companies discovered too late that exploration was not the "primary game" in metals mining. EDS discovered that distinctiveness in management consulting requires more than technology and entrepreneurialism. The argument here is that leveraging just one Distinctive Competency is not enough. A successful company needs a strong overall Business Idea. Success can only be expected from diversification if the Business Ideas of the existing business and the new business activity are fully understood and merged. Companies who intend to diversify need to be skilful in articulating and understanding Business Ideas.

ORGANISATIONAL ASPECTS

Developing the Business Idea for the future (the "Strategic Vision") in the scenario "windtunnel" is a prime managerial responsibility. But it is not the whole story. The Strategic Vision also needs to be shared by all parties with the power (formal or informal) to act (De Geus 1988). In the merger example discussed, the existence of a clear and detailed implementation plan to which all subscribe could be a manifestation of such shared understanding. The windtunnelling process must include all actors. The thinking process must be institutional.

Chapter Six

Scenario Planning in Organisations

How does scenario planning lead to strategic management in an organisational sense? This can be understood using the model of organisational learning discussed in Part One. This approach will allow us to create space for rationalistic as well as processual considerations, while maintaining uncertainty and unpredictability on the agenda all through.

As we saw in Part One, the way organisations cope with uncertainty is through learning. This is defined here as the institutional representation of the learning loop, where the organisation takes action, experiences deviations from plan, reflects on differences and synthesises these into a new mental model of the world, which is subsequently used for renewed action. In this chapter we will discuss how scenario planners intervene in this process, and how they help the organisation become more skilful in it. The most important aspects of this are twofold:

- Scenario planning affects and broadens perception, thereby providing the requisite variety in mental models necessary to see and perceive the outside world beyond the traditional business models.
- It provides a language through which the resulting issues can be discussed in the organisation, new theories of action can be jointly developed and shared, and alignment of mental models can be achieved, necessary for institutional action.

It assists in both the differentiation and integration aspects of the learning organisation. We will discuss the principles involved by reference to the three main components of the learning loop:

- Perception
- Institutionalisation
- Action.

ORGANISATIONS AS COGNITIVE SYSTEMS

Organisations are cognitive systems. They have ways of seeing and interpreting the world around them, and they have values that they pursue. The knowledge on which this is based is embedded in the people in the organisation, but also in its systems and in its artefacts. Institutions select recruits in their own image. Once living together individual members affect each other's views through more or less intensive interaction. They come to interpret developments similarly. Through a process of selection and mutual influence the organisational culture is created.

CORPORATE KNOWLEDGE

Corporate knowledge, defined here as that pool of knowledge on the basis of which the organisation can act, is not simply the sum of the knowledge of its members. Even in the most authoritarian environment very few corporate actions are the result of the views of one individual only. These views will have been influenced and formed by the interaction with others in the organisation. When we are looking at corporate behaviour we are not dealing with one individual, but with the "corporate opinion". When the world changes, managers must share some common view of the new world if a suitable and effective response is to be created. Individual members of the organisation may see and understand developments in ways different from the group, but the organisation as a whole cannot act on this knowledge if the individuals cannot make themselves heard. Organisational knowledge is less than the totality of the knowledge embedded in its members. Successful organisations in particular are prone to simplify the institutional mental model through the way they interpret the world, "it is difficult to argue with success" (Miller 1993).

SEEING THINGS IN DIFFERENT PERSPECTIVES

Managers have got where they are through their "good judgement" and they will not readily suspend that. When things remain stable it will serve them well. However, from time to time organisations experience turbulence in their environment. Explaining what is happening in alternative ways becomes a key corporate skill. The crux of this skill is a willingness to open up mental models, face conceptual uncertainty and arrive at a shared view of its meaning, i.e. become a learning organisation.

INDUSTRIAL EXAMPLES OF POOR PERCEPTION

There are many well-known examples of companies misjudging their environment. Above we saw how the refining industry and the oil tanker industry misjudged the 1973 oil crisis. A similar situation arises periodically in the petro-chemical industry, when the industry as a whole rushes into over-expansion without being able to do anything about it. Another example is the problem experienced by the American automobile industry interpreting pressures from the public concerning the environment, "Detroit would play ball if there were really consistent signals" (see page 48). The trouble is that there never are consistent signals, until interpretation creates consistency as an essential part of organisational perception.

Other examples include the misjudgement by the established computer industry of the personal computer phenomenon in the early 1980s. Even in the late 1980s, after personal computers were in existence and had been growing exponentially for ten years or more, I found that a major player in the mainframe computer industry was still largely disconnecting from the fact that computing power was increasingly being distributed away from mainframes. When I was asked to comment on their "scenarios", I found an example of what we have called the probability approach to scenario planning (see page 28). The scenarios showed a number of futures of demand for computing power, expressed in terms of MIPS (millions of instructions per second). The planners had not considered it opportune to work out in detail the form in which the market might require these. It was a prime example of how forecasting focuses on specific predetermined variables and closes the mind to wider exploration of the environment (see page 103). A lot of effort had gone into analysing possible future demand for computing power, but the resulting scenarios were created from the tacit assumption that computing capacity required would continue to be needed in the traditional form. Other developments, such as the growth of distributed personal computers were not seen as connected to the main forecasting question, their future development was simply not on the agenda. The fact that new players were redefining the game was probably seen by some individuals but these could not make themselves heard against the conventional view. New developments in the market simply were not an issue at the organisational level.

MEMORIES OF THE FUTURE

Perception is in the first place an individual activity, but having discussed how individuals perceive we need also to talk about how these perceptions are internalised by the group through interaction and discussion. Specifically we will discuss scenarios as perception devices.

What individuals see in the outside world is determined by the schemas and the concepts they use. If you want to be more observant you have to expand these. The expression "one track mind" encapsulates the idea that if someone can see only one future, thinking will focus on that, and perception will increasingly ignore outlying unrelated areas. Organisations, particularly the successful ones, often suffer from a corporate "one-track mind". To overcome this the organisation has to do the same thing as an individual does, namely rehearsing alternative pathways into the future as a way to expanding the area of vision.

The individual does this by considering future implications of what is observed, in this way providing a contextual framework in which these observations can be organised. The device used is a story line, in which events unfold over time through a progression of cause and effect. There is strong evidence that the human mind retains most of its concepts by relating these to elements of temporally organised schemas (Ingvar 1985, Rumelhart 1980). These are stored in memory as, what Ingvar calls, "memories of the future". Going through life, people spin stories about the future in their mind. For instance if a difficult interview is anticipated, thoughts continue to spring up in the mind: "If she says this I could react in this way". This mental preparation builds up a set of temporally organised concepts and schemas through which events are subsequently interpreted. This allows perception of developments which would otherwise pass by unnoticed. Even if the specific rehearsed scenario never plays out in reality, the mind has nevertheless built up a readily available set of concepts that allows perception and judgement of what is going on, causing more skilful observation and interaction in real time. In this way we are all "natural scenario planners".

Stories are efficient vehicles for organising things in our mind, relating data across a wide range of subjects. Making sense involves relating events causally, with one thing leading to another. Once we have decided what led to the occurrence of an event it has become more predictable, and therefore manageable. The human mind naturally arranges past events in this way. The causal framework provides natural "slots" for a multitude of events which no longer require our attention in isolation. Also stories about the future are in a way historical accounts but seen from a future perspective. They explain how the world has ended up in a future end-state, by a causal train of events, linking back to the well-known present. Scenarios make sense of future events in the same way as historical accounts make sense of the past. They provide the business planner with a flexible means to connect disparate data together into holistic pictures of the future, providing the context and meaning of possible developments. If they are carefully constructed, causal accounts of future events operationalise the insights gained, so that they can be used for drawing inferences and conclusions. (The historian may not have the same degree of flexibility as the scenario writer, although here also there is considerable scope for selective choice of events and of pattern inference).

In dealing with groups of people one has the additional problem of having to develop some commonality in individual schemas and language in order for the group as a whole to become skilful observers of the business environment. It is not enough for one person to see "it", more likely than not (s)he will be overruled by the conventional wisdom. The skill of observing the environment must become a group skill, such that the organisation is able to act on it. This requires that the knowledge is shared by a critical mass of people, who together are able to create action on the basis of their "consensus" view. The experience of not being able to make one's view heard in an organisation is common to most of us at one time or another. When things have gone wrong it is almost always possible afterwards to find someone who saw weak negative signals at the time the decision was made but who could not make his/her view register. The unheard view has no value for the organisation, what counts in terms of institutional decision making is the institutional knowledge embedded in its consensus view. If the Detroit executive complained of inconsistent signals, he in fact indicated that their shared mental model did not allow them to link these signals in a coherent account. As a consequence the company could not decide that the market was moving away from them. He indicated the lack of an adequate shared mental model in the organisation which would have allowed them to create consistency in what was observed. As a consequence they did not act. How can an organisation "complicate themselves" (Weick) so that they can develop a sufficiently varied account of the outside world, that can be shared among the members?

If properly developed a set of scenarios can be the institutional "memories of the future" to help organisations perceive their environment together. In this way it becomes an efficient vehicle for making sense out of a large amount of data and information. Scenarios structure data about the future in multiple stories. The concept of using multiple story lines to encapsulate learning is powerful for the following reasons:

- It reflects the uncertainty inherent in the future.
- It allows a multi-disciplinary approach to developing and discussing theories about the world.
- It presents findings in a tangible real-world context, illustrating theory rather than espousing it.
- It uses a causal mode of thinking, which is intuitively comfortable.

The language of scenarios is about the future, but they should make a difference in what is happening now. If it is successful in embedding different models of the business environment in the consciousness of the organisation, it will make the organisation more aware of environmental change. Through early conceptualisation and effective internal communication scenario planning can make the organisation a more skilful observer of its business environment. By seeing change earlier the organisation has the potential to become more responsive. Its decisions will also become more robust, there will be less "I should have known that". Generally the result should be an organisation more flexible and capable of adapting.

HOOKS INTO MENTAL MODELS

What sort of stories are effective in an organisational setting to achieve this perceptual goal? Like any other story teller the scenario planner needs to balance carefully the known and the novel:

- Effective scenarios should have enough hooks into the current organisational mental models to make them plausible to a "critical mass" in the organisation.
- But they should also contain an element of novelty and surprise in directions where the vision of the organisation needs to be stretched.

Experience has shown that scenarios that do not link in to current and ongoing concerns and anxieties in the minds of the decision makers are ineffective. They will be interpreted as irrelevant to the operational reality and be rejected. A scenario writer may find a story interesting, but a decision maker who has no mental connection to it will experience it as either boring or "science fiction" and it will end up on the book shelf without creating much effect. If on the other hand you set out to write a story that addresses the immediate concerns of the audience, their worries, the thoughts that keep them awake, then the product will be experienced as interesting. I observed this in Shell and other companies. Top management will listen very carefully to a scenario planner who produces a significant scenario exercise giving a new perspective on events or trends with which they are grappling. Over time it has become very clear that if the scenario planner sets his own agenda which does not relate to the concerns of the client hardly any attention will be paid to it. The biggest mistake that scenario planners can make is to fail to take enough account of the needs of their clients. The number one rule of scenario planning is "know your client". For this reason scenario planning is a customised activity, generic scenarios are less relevant to organisational behaviour.

Another essential condition for success is plausibility of the scenarios. Only plausible scenarios can be a platform from which to develop further the organisation's knowledge and understanding of the situation they may be facing. On the other hand, just feeding back to the managers the views they already share is not a useful thing to do, a new perspective needs to be added. The aim is to create a context within which the issue is seen afresh by the organisation. Creating such a new perspective is difficult for people who have been grappling with the issue, possibly for a long time. It requires new knowledge and insights that often only an outside source can provide. But it is easy to go overboard here, developing knowledge that is unrelated to the consensus view is not useful, as the message will not be heard. The project has to start from where the people in the organisation are now, but it needs to move on from there. Scenarios become a bridge between the existing understanding and new alternative views or frameworks that can be used to interpret what is happening in the outside world (Figure 18). That basically constitutes the most significant challenge of any scenario exercise.

Producing an effective set of scenarios is often compared with an art form. A writer who wants to get through to his audience starts from where they are now and then adds something new. The crux of the matter is finding the right balance between the known and the new. Erring on the side of the known doesn't make an impact through lack of interest. Erring on the side of the new makes the project lacking in meaning. Somewhere between the two the right answer has to be found.

The process is described by Vygotsky (1986). In his language, the scenarios "scaffold" the thought processes of the client. These need to be erected around the existing knowledge structure to allow the client to relate new experiences to existing knowledge. Vygotsky refers to the "zone of proximal development", which is the place where the client's newly acquired, but as yet disorganised concepts "meet" the logic of experienced reasoning. The learning

Scenarios need to connect

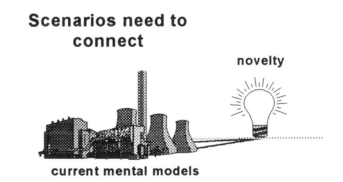

Figure 18. *Scenarios provide a new perspective.*

capacity of the client is limited to this zone of proximal development.

INTRODUCING NOVELTY

The "scaffolding" idea illustrates how scenarios need to move the thinking on. They need to throw a novel light on the existing thinking about the future of the business. Where do we find this novel insight? As we saw above, organisational knowledge is less than the totality of the knowledge embedded in its members. Therefore resources are available in house in the range of insights among the individual members of the organisation. The alternative views required are often available from individuals who, without scenario planning, find it difficult to make their views legitimate. This resource must be tapped in the first place. This requires a process through which people can make themselves heard. The process must trigger participants to:

- develop their knowledge through communication with the outside world,
- articulate their knowledge, and
- contribute this to the common pool of knowledge from which the shared view emerges.

Through conversation the process must enable structuring of elements of thought or observation, and of resulting perceptions of opportunities and threats. The process must be capable of taking in a wide range of initially unstructured thoughts and views, and create out of this coherent, internally consistent interpretations of the world in which the majority of the individual insights can find a logical place.

However, in most cases, external views must be brought in to enrich the new perspective. One of the most important objectives of scenario planning is to make the organisation a better observer of the environment. Its mental model needs to be stretched. This can often only be done from outside. Therefore scenario planners need to go further than just tapping internal views and incorporate a wide range of outside opinions in the scenarios. A set of scenario stories is an effective means of capturing and organising a wide range of ideas. The views of a number of outside experts can be canvassed. With this preparation the quality of the scenario process may be significantly enhanced.

LINKING THE OLD WITH THE NEW

Consequently the scenario analysis follows the following principles:

- Start from the platform of the existing "consensus view" in the organisation.
- Recognise the uncertainty and complexity in the business situation.
- Stretch by the introduction of new knowledge from inside and outside the organisation.
- Provide structure to seemingly unrelated environmental insights.

In this way scenario planning adds new "memories of the future", enlarging the area of vision in which the organisation will recognise weak signals of change. Less will pass the organisation by. It has become a more skilful observer, more flexible and more capable of adapting.

OVERCOMING PERCEPTION PROBLEMS

The following example illustrates how a company can overcome embedded perceptual limitations. In 1990, I conducted a scenario exercise for a company making machines used in microchips manufacturing. We spent a great deal of time analysing the main uncertainties. Some time into the project one senior manager suggested that he was worried about a possible recession. At this time, the recession was just starting, and the conventional wisdom was that it would be short, shallow, and lenient to high technology. This manager said, "That seems our assumption, but what if it turns out not to be true? What if we're entering a deep, 1981-style recession? What would happen to microprocessors and then to our machines?"

Discussion turned to how these assumptions were reflected in the plans in the first place – who decided what and how did this get worked into the cash projections. Initially no one in the management team could throw any light on this. The finance man looked at the sales man, they both looked at the marketing manager, no answer, they just did not know how it was done. The finance manager volunteered to find out.

A few days later he reported back. "Well," he said, "the way we do this projection really makes good sense. As a small company, we cannot afford to invest a lot of money in environmental analysis, so we buy projections from DataQuest, the top-rated high-tech market and economic research company. We don't think we can ever hope to improve on their research capability." "What's their assumption about the recession?" asked the manager who had raised the question. It appeared that DataQuest were assuming a shallow, short recession.

Now the room erupted in discussion. What if it wasn't to be shallow and short? The scenario exercise had shown them the value of questioning all such "inevitabilities". The CEO suggested that the finance manager ask their planners to produce a new set of projections. But this time, they would substitute a deeper, longer recession for the DataQuest prediction.

At the next meeting, the finance manager came back with some slides of spreadsheet numbers. "We have never done this before," he said, "but we made a few assumptions, and here's what it looks like." The results were dramatic. If there were a deep recession, the company would be in serious trouble. They were about to commit themselves to major research investments, and they could easily fall into insolvency if they were to lose the cash influx they had assumed would come. The conclusion was inevitable, management was betting the company on DataQuest's prediction coming true. As a result, over the next few weeks, they drastically cut back their research investment commitments. Today (in 1995), they are not doing as well as they had hoped several years ago, but they have weathered the recession. They know that if they had committed those funds in 1990, they would now be out of business.

They were fortunate to make the jump from an individual mental model to an institutional one. It is not a leap that can be taken for granted. The planner making his projections down in the finance department, from his perspective, did the sensible thing to rely on DataQuest's numbers. They were the best numbers available; it did not make sense to try to double-guess them. But nobody else in the organisation seemed to be aware of the underlying assumptions driving the cash projection. A question such as "I wonder about the recession" did not find an institutional response, nobody would know what to do with such a remark, there was no channel to deal with it.

All organisations are full of compartmentalisation problems. It is a fundamental part of the efficiency/adaptation dilemma. And a minor lapse in communication can cause a major dislocation. Compartmentalisation means that people down the line may make quite sensible individual decisions, which in aggregate can drive the company as a whole into serious problems. The strategic learning process needs to hit at the appropriate points in the organisational system where an impact can be created. This "node of effective intervention" may well be outside the management team, somewhere deep in the organisation. Finding these points requires processes which are part of the corporate culture, penetrating throughout the organisation.

INSTITUTIONALISATION

Above we defined institutional knowledge as that pool of knowledge on the basis of which the organisation can act. The scenario planning project needs to engage the organisation in a process through which the scenarios become part of this institutional knowledge. They should be discussed enough to become 'memories of the future' for a sufficient number of members so that they lead to common perceptions. The test of this is whether the scenarios become part of the institutional language. If people start using the names of the scenarios as a short-cut to conveying to each other the underlying world picture it is likely that institutionalisation has been achieved.

The process of institutionalisation requires infiltration of the strategic conversation. Scenario planners need to study carefully how strategic decisions are made, and become part of the high leverage points in that process. Not only formal decision processes need to be considered, the informal conversations are often at least as, if not more important.

STRATEGIC IMPLICATIONS

The example drives home the fact that full use of scenarios requires an institutional process through which they become embedded in the organisation and become part of the general consensus. This requires the discussion of strategic implications. This discussion starts within the scenario team and the commissioning client team. In principle this involves the team revisiting each scenario and looking for vulnerabilities and bottlenecks. As in the example above this may lead to ideas on strategies intended to strengthen capabilities and/or remove bottlenecks. The team should be on the look-out specifically for areas in which basic assumptions may become questionable. It is often helpful to try to articulate and question fundamental planning "axioms" and strategic recipes in use in the industry for each scenario. In a case of impending "paradigm shift" it may be possible to reframe the industry activities, for example by a redefinition of its business or customer interface. This may lead to the consideration of a reconfiguration of the players in the industry, through which new groupings may be determining competitive success (Normann & Ramirez 1994). It is at this level that the main payout of the scenario project has to be found. Using the newly developed scenarios the team mentally makes new combinations of scenario elements, leading to the invention of new and original strategy. The strategic repercussions discussion often starts already during the fleshing out of the story lines of the individual scenarios. The team needs to be aware of the volatility of ideas at this stage, and ensure that ideas are recorded as they flash over the table. One of the members should have the specific responsibility to ensure that no potentially useful contributions evaporate, but are recorded for later consideration.

The process is fundamentally creative, and cannot be too highly structured. For example setting time limits will in most cases kill it stone dead. The idea of "generating new strategy by five o'clock this evening" is a contradiction in terms. Teams approaching the task in this state of mind are invariably disappointed with the result.

In many cases it is preferable to avoid "option generation" as a specific objective of the project. The scenario project can alternatively be seen as a group learning exercise, which if kept alive will after a suitable gestation period produce new thinking and ideas in the organisation. This requires a somewhat mature attitude on the part of the client team, which will normally be found only in organisations that have developed a scenario culture. Managers of the "energetic problem-solver" type normally are less than satisfied unless a project has produced a recognisable result. The most productive results of scenario projects tend to surface later at unexpected times and places, and are often not even recognised as related to the scenario project. If the client team are looking for significant breakthroughs it needs a degree of patience and perseverance.

When client teams become aware of strategic options open to them, scenarios can be used to consider relative values and priorities. Option selection is powerfully assisted by the scenario process through the concept of "windtunnelling" described earlier. The one thing the client team needs to avoid is the selection of one scenario as a basis for "designing the future". If this is done the value of the scenario approach is lost, as from then onwards uncertainty is removed and robustness of options is not any longer considered.

SCENARIOS AND THE POWER TO ACT

The effectiveness of scenario planning can be measured only afterwards, in terms of:

- What actions have resulted that proved competitively important?
- What did they leave out that subsequently proved important?

Only scenarios that make a difference are worthwhile doing. In the institutional context, scenario planning is not only about developing the most effective set of futures, but also about transferring these effectively into the organisation, such that actions are affected through the new insights gained. The institutional context is important in deciding the ultimate quality and value of a scenario project: The test of whether the team has found a good structure for the scenario set and story lines is the degree to which these prove helpful to the client in conceptualising a previously unstructured area of concern, leading to new action that ultimately proves beneficial.

SHELL'S EXPERIENCE

This is best illustrated by means of an example. The following example should be considered against the industry background, discussed earlier (page 17). We saw how Shell became aware of the possibility of an oil crisis through the use of the scenario methodology. But the criterion for success of such scenario planning activity is not the discovery itself but whether this was internalised sufficiently in the organisation through an appropriate scenario process, such that it led to action in response to the new perception. Shell's managers saw, very quickly,

quickly, the results of two different responses to the scenario process.

. . . awareness . . .

One was due mainly to Jan Choufoer, the co-ordinator of Shell's manufacturing activity. A man with a strong research background, he was used to questioning practices that others took for granted. Even before becoming co-ordinator he had questioned one of the basic tenets of the oil business: that the purpose of the organisation is to meet all customer demand for oil and related products.

To understand what Choufoer was suggesting, it is important to realise that crude oil, as it is pumped out of the ground, is a mixture of many products, from light fuels (propane, butane) to medium (gasoline, kerosene, gas oil) to heavy (fuel oil, bitumen). The lighter products have more unique value; there is no easy substitute for light gasoline in engines. But under-boiler fuel oil can be substituted, e.g. by coal. Therefore fuel oil must be sold at a competitive price, while gasoline can command a premium. There is, however, a limit to this differential. Refiners can make light products out of heavy ones through secondary processes called "cracking". This is an expensive business, but if the differential is big enough, refiners can equip themselves accordingly. Normal practice was to build crackers whenever the markets showed an imbalance between demand for light versus heavy products. So in the US market, where demand for gasoline was always relatively strong, cracking was done a lot more than in Europe, which had a stronger fuel oil demand. Choufoer suggested that it might be more profitable to build additional cracking capacity, reduce fuel oil sales and make the same light product yield with less crude oil intake. This became known as the "upgrading policy". It implied advising the Shell marketers that they would not be supplied their full fuel oil requirement, handing potential customers over to the competition, a shocking idea that struck at the very foundations of the supply function.

In the early 1970s, calculations of projected oil prices showed, not surprisingly, that building additional upgrading capacity, while offering some opportunities for payout, would be mostly a break-even proposition. Although some Shell managers were intrigued by the prospect of questioning old established practice, and engineers liked the idea of building more upgrading capacity to get the best out of the barrel, the institution as a whole rejected Choufoer's proposal; it was at variance with the established mental model of serving market demand,

and no convincing economic case could be made. But then Pierre Wack in Group Planning emerged with scenarios showing the possibility of a crisis in crude oil supply, and a resulting explosion in oil prices. From our perspective today, it is difficult to understand the revolutionary nature of Wack's suggestion. The oil price had remained one of the most stable features of the global economic scene for as long as anybody could remember. An earlier Delphi forecasting exercise in Shell, involving the real experts, had come up with no price higher than $2 per barrel. People might be persuaded to consider that oil price might vary between $2 and $3 per barrel, but here was Wack suggesting a jump to $12!

Credibility was stretched to the limit, except with Choufer, who suddenly saw support for his idea. When crude oil prices jump, there is an even greater jump in differential between the price of heavy components (which cannot rise too much, because they compete with coal or other alternatives) and that of light components, for which there is no easy substitute. Motor gasoline, in particular, would become disproportionately more expensive. The scenarios implied that upgrading the heavy end of the barrel into light products, hitherto a break-even proposition, would (in the event of a price jump) become extremely profitable. Considering that without a price jump it would anyway break even, implementing the upgrading policy seemed a no-lose proposition. As Jan Choufer moved to head manufacturing, he continued to promote this policy. As a result, when the oil price crisis did actually occur, Shell manufacturing was prepared to act.

. . . and lack of awareness . . .

By contrast, Shell veterans could look at the example of Marine, the division responsible for transporting oil overseas. This organisation paid very little attention to an oil crisis scenario, it did not seem relevant to them. According to the conventional wisdom, a price jump would not really affect demand, not when people still needed energy and heat. People would pay the price, and Marine would still have to move the oil.

Then came the actual crisis of 1973. The Marine people (not only in Shell, but, as we saw, across the shipping industry) were shocked, but did not consider changing their policies. Investments in shipping capacity continued. When demand started to level off during 1974 and 1975 this was interpreted as a temporary aberration. Demand increased again in 1976, prompting Marine to assume the crisis was over. When demand fell away again, the following year, that was interpreted as the consequence of the economic recession, another temporary blip which would work itself out. Only near 1978 or 1979 did it start to dawn on oil shippers that, possibly, demand might be elastic after all. By then, they had built up such a massive over-capacity in the world's fleet, that profitability was destroyed for many years.

ACTION TRIGGERED BY INSTITUTIONAL PERCEPTION

Whilst in Marine, people continuously looked for signs (and found them) of reversion to the old pre crisis situation, people in Manufacturing saw the trend break as a fundamental change, as explained in the well-rehearsed and shared crisis scenario. They acted accordingly. While it took Marine years to realise what had happened to them, Manufacturing had a shared mental model of the changed situation to hand. Consequently they were ready to move. Shell refineries adopted the upgrading policy with remarkable speed. In the industry, while primary refining capacity ran into a disastrous surplus situation (like the tanker capacity), upgrading capacity became extremely scarce. Shell's early implementation of the upgrading policy provided the Group with a major competitive advantage which lasted well into the mid-1980s. This proved one of the major factors in Shell's climb up the rank order of major international oil companies, known as the seven sisters, from a position near the bottom to the top of the league.

BECOMING AWARE OF EARLY SIGNALS

The learning loop model shows us how scenario planning is intrinsically interwoven with action. Only through action does the organisation have joint experiences which will enable it to develop its mental model of the environment, and in this way become a more skilful actor, and only through more skilful action can the organisation benefit from its investment in scenario planning.

For this reason the scenario planner has to focus his thinking on the people with the power to act. They are the ultimate clients of the exercise, and they need to set the agenda. There is more required than just an intellectual thinking process. People need to get involved throughout the organisation, and mental models need to be aligned. What is needed is not just another technique, but a complete approach to strategic development and strategic management which scenario planning offers.

Once scenarios have become part of the institutional mental model they powerfully affect what is seen in the business environment. Scenario planners often comment after a scenario project on how they find themselves reading articles in newspapers which before the project they would have skimmed over, possibly even not have seen. The same applies to the organisation. This feature of scenario planning can be used to advantage through the institutionalisation of the concept of "early warning". If the scenarios have been done properly the team should have articulated a clear model of underlying structure to which the events in the scenarios are related. The same structure can be used to identify developments in the environment which could be the early signals of the world moving into the direction indicated by one of the scenarios. After the scenario project the team can identify such key variables and make these the subject of conscious periodic monitoring. The best monitoring variables play a central position in the underlying structure. By identifying such variables in the influence diagrams underpinning the scenarios the institutional attention can be directed in directions where manifestations of structural differences become evident first.

Part Three

The Practice of Scenario Planning

OVERVIEW

In Part Two we discussed the principles of scenario planning and suggested its philosophical base in learning theory. This has allowed us to integrate the three traditional paradigms of strategic management into one holistic approach. We have seen how scenario planning is the natural implementation of organisational learning, and we have discussed the benefits. We saw how scenarios are used to evaluate the characteristics of the organisation, expressed in its Business Idea, and how this leads to strategic conclusions, including the need for change.

Clearly scenario planning is more than inventing stories about the future. Its importance spreads across a wide area of organisational cognition, including:

1. In the pre-decision making situation:
   - Creating new concepts and language in the organisation.
   - Enhancing the quality of the strategic conversation.
   - Managing the focus of attention of the organisation.
   - Making the organisation more perceptive of its environment and therefore more adaptive.
   - Motivating action and change.
   - Making people think.
2. In the decision making situation:
   - Considering the strength of the organisation and its characteristics in its Business Idea.
   - Developing capability and portfolio options.

- Developing strategy.
- Making a judgement on a proposal.
- Making a decision.

Success in scenario planning depends on striking a good balance between the known and the novel.

We have presented scenario planning as a complete approach to institutional strategic management, based on an integrated philosophy of management around organisational learning.

Having discussed the principles of scenario planning, and how it relates to making organisations more resilient and adaptable, we now turn to translating theory into practice. In Part Three we discuss how a manager, or more likely a management team, can go about introducing scenario planning into its strategic considerations.

We argue that the preferred approach is essentially incremental. Some organisations may be able to make larger steps than others, but all start with an existing understanding of their business. The scenario planner or strategist starts by articulating the organisation's understanding of its business in the form of the Business Idea. Then the scenarist helps the organisation articulate the driving forces in its business environment. This information is a launching platform from which multiple scenarios of the future business environment are developed.

Options for improvement are generated by testing the Business Idea against the scenarios.

This part of the book takes as a model a management team wishing to broaden its views and think more strategically about the future of the organisation. Various exercises and workshops are discussed which will help the team get underway.

Chapter Seven

The Practitioner's Art

Scenario planning is a practitioner's art. Its origins are in the real world of management, it is therefore more a craft than a science. Over the years a number of general principles have emerged but most of the rules of implementation evolve from day-to-day practice. It has in common with any other craft that there is not just one way of practising it. Students of scenario planning learn their craft from other practitioners. Every practitioner has to learn from their own mistakes. This means that whilst new practitioners need enough input from their predecessors to make a start, each practitioner must still develop his own unique way of producing results.

Scenario planning always aims for the invention of strategy and the testing of related organisational characteristics against multiple representations of the future business environment. Even if scenario development is undertaken as an exercise in trying to understand ambiguous developments in the outside world there will always be a point where we will want to consider the repercussions of our thinking for the organisation. Scenarios are always a testbed for something. It is important to keep this in mind, because it means that scenarios must always be focused on a strategically relevant area if they are to be productive. Therefore logically we can distinguish a number of basic components in any scenario project:

- There will be a component characterising an internal issue or area of policy, where the project needs to provide new illumination.
- A number of scenarios will describe the multiple possible futures of the external business environment around this issue.
- Scenarios become productive in their interaction with the

internal characterisation. They are the testbed in which the area of policy is considered and judged.

Scenario planning can be used in a focused way, as a testbed for specific strategies, plans or projects. Setting the agenda in focused scenario projects is relatively straightforward However, in most scenario projects there is not a specific strategic issue on the agenda. Most scenario exercises are inspired by a general desire to do a more skilful job of monitoring and understanding what is happening out there in the business environment. They originate in the wish of management to improve the institutional learning skills of the organisation, in the sense expressed in the Kolb learning loop. Most scenarios are introduced as an organisational discussion device, to enhance thinking and perception of the changing environment, without any preconceived idea of any specific policy issues that may be at issue. This is the most difficult part of any strategy development, addressing the question whether the organisation as a whole is capable of seeing and perceiving in time any crucial trend-breaking developments in the business environment, outside the blinkers that every organisation develops over time. Managers generally feel quite capable of dealing with the strategic issues as they arise and mostly do not feel the need for another analytical approach to help them in that area. On the other hand many managers feel they could do with additional help in becoming a little better at observing the environment, understanding what goes on out there and in that way anticipating a little better. In those applications of scenario planning the intention is to let the policy repercussions of the exercise emerge naturally from the new insights developed. However, even in this case the scenario process in principle brings together a view of the environment and a view of the characteristics of the organisation, and tries to come to a considered view of what needs to be done internally in the light of the possible developments facing the organisation.

We will argue that it is important to try to articulate the "object to be tested" early on. It is of course possible to leave it embedded in the intuitive organisational knowledge of the participants in the process, letting conclusions on organisational repercussions naturally emerge as a result of the thinking process and conversation. This is a legitimate approach, preferred by many experienced scenario planners and managers. It requires that all involved are insiders with excellent knowledge of the organisation. However, there is a potential danger lurking here that needs to be recognised. The main purpose of the exercise is to surface possible trend-breaking developments in the business environment. One has to face up to the question whether the organisation itself has the requisite variety in its mental model to pick up the weak signals that may indicate a possible major trend break in the future. As we saw in Part Two, what we see is determined to a large extent by what is already in our mental model, and this filtering is even stronger for organisations than for individuals. In particular the well-run successful organisations almost inevitably develop blinkers, and suffer from institutional myopia. There is only one way of overcoming a narrow myopic organisational mental model and to create more differentiation, and this is by bringing in fresh outside signals. Most successful scenario projects involve both internal and external people who together interact on the issues involved. A device is needed to articulate the organisational characteristics that matter, serving as an agenda for the strategic conversation the organisation needs to have with new outside conversation partners. This device should not be an already conceived strategy, as this would introduce new blinkers in the strategic conversation. In Part Two we have introduced the concept of the Business Idea to play this role. In the most general scenario planning project the scenarios describe the external business environment in which the Business Idea of the organisation will have to live, survive and flourish.

Although, if possible, scenario planners should try to articulate a Business Idea whenever they undertake a scenario project, the more intuitive approach is also feasible. In both cases the essence of the scenario project is the interplay between the two sides of the strategic-fit analysis. The scenarios must constitute a suitable testbed for the characteristics of the organisation, the conditions in the windtunnel must fit the model to be tested. Therefore, even in the intuitive approach towards scenario planning, there needs to be some prior understanding of the sort of issues to be considered before the scenarios can be conceptualised. The world is very large, and much of it is of secondary importance to the organisation.

We are in a dilemma here. On the one hand we wish to concentrate on issues that are relevant and important for the client. On the other hand too much pre-specification of the issues facing the organisation creates the danger of focusing down to the known and traditional, thereby missing important new/weak signals. If the intuitive approach is preferred, and the Business Idea is not articulated in advance, a scenario agenda needs to be drawn up early on. This should be general enough to include study of adjacent territory which could be of unanticipated importance to the organisation.

ROLES AND ACTIVITIES

We will discuss the various issues involved from the perspectives of two actors in the project, the scenario planner and the client. The scenario planner is the person (or the group of people) involved in promoting and facilitating the learning process. This could be anyone in the organisation, a dedicated staff person, a member of the management team or the CEO him(her)self. Or it could be an outside consultant brought in for the occasion. When we consider the issues from the perspective of "the scenario planner" we primarily consider the process issues involved.

The other actor we call the client. This is the individual or group of people struggling with the strategy question itself and who will benefit from the thinking as it develops. Typically it could be a management team who are interested in understanding better the developments in the outside world, with the aim of reviewing the general strategic thrust of the organisation. Or it could be a team trying to develop a specific project of strategic importance. Another possibility might be a management drawing up a strategic plan for discussion with other stakeholders, such as shareholders and finance providers. In this way we identify the separate roles of conducting the organisational process, and determining the content agenda of the thinking process.

The scenario planner and the client need to work together to get the show on the road by setting the scenario agenda. This can be done on the basis of the intuitive knowledge of the client, brought to the surface by the scenario planner through the application of elicitation techniques. This approach may well be adequate for groups with considerable experience with scenario planning. However, the Business Idea will help the scenario planner to structure the data collected in the elicitation process, in interaction with the client. The aim is to create a joint conversational device which will help to organise the creation of relevant scenarios, suitable for the discussion of strategic implications for the organisation.

We will first discuss practical ways of eliciting strategic insights and intuitions from the client. We will then move on to the use of the Business Idea concept for structuring understanding of the fundamental success drivers of the organisation. We will see how this can be generated by a management team in a programmed way, and used as focusing device in their strategic discussion. We will then move on to the development of the scenarios themselves. We will consider the issues involved and practical ways of moving forward on each of these. We will then discuss how the scenarios can be used in conjunction with the Business Idea to come to useful strategic conclusions, and we will consider how these can be expressed in terms of strategic options open to the organisation.

In Part Four we will discuss how all this can be incorporated in an institutional process that involves all those with the power-to-act to make the scenario process part of the institutional learning experience of the organisation as a whole.

SETTING THE AGENDA

The business environment is very large. How to select where to look? This is the first crucial decision the scenario planner has to address. The most important stipulation here is the imperative that the work remains relevant to the client. Under no condition must the scenario planner "lose" the client on the way. This means that a very clear picture must be obtained of what is strategically important to the client, as the starting point of the project. Any new idea must address these basic needs of the decision makers, if they are to make any impact.

The next problem the scenarist faces is: how to surface and articulate the strategic agenda? The assumption here is that each organisation manifests a basic driving force for success, akin to what we have called a "Business Idea". Sometimes managers may be able to articulate this in some degree of detail, more often it remains tacit in the background while people go about their daily activities, confident in the experience that what they are doing seems to "work". Even in situations where the Business Idea remains in the background managers use it intuitively to prioritise actions. Their thoughts, worries and anxieties are manifestations of a discrepancy between such a tacit Business Idea and perceived reality. By discussing these concerns for the future elements of the manager's Business Idea will emerge. Therefore an agenda for the scenario planning exercise can be developed by asking business leaders to express concerns and anxieties about the future. Through a process of discussion an agenda may be developed of issues that managers intuitively feel to be important to the future success of the organisation, on which the scenarios are to throw new light.

As suggested earlier, it is advisable for scenario planners to develop an explicit representation of the underlying Business Idea of the organisation, based on the views expressed by the managers. If the process of scenario planning is to lead towards reasoned, rather than intuitive conclusions concerning the future health of the organisation this step becomes essential.

ELICITATION OF VIEWS AND INSIGHTS

The scenario planner needs to start from the client's insights, intuitive or otherwise, of what drives (or should drive) the success of their organisation. (S)he needs to get access to these insights by engaging the business leaders in a process of elicitation. This can be done through either group brainstorming or individual interview and feedback. The interview process is more elaborate, but more productive in terms of detail generated. However, the time and resources are not always available for the complete job, in which case the group brainstorming approach must suffice.

We will discuss two models of team elicitation. The most basic approach, in which a management team discusses its strategic insights, is called the SWOT (strengths, weaknesses, opportunities, threats) analysis. An exercise of this type can be conducted in half a day, and provides the scenario planner with a useful insight into the strategic agenda of the management team. The more in-depth approach uses individual interviews, followed by team feedback. Either of these approaches can serve to trigger the managers into articulating what seems important for the future.

After this first step in the elicitation process further work with the team of client-managers is required to structure the insights obtained, until a workable agenda of issues results, which is suitable to set the scene for a scenario planning exercise.

The elicitation process in itself can be an important contributor towards enhanced understanding of the business situation. By providing a sounding board the scenario process facilitator at this stage helps managers to express and structure their thoughts. The process of articulating tacit understanding in itself often makes the situation seem more manageable.

The process needs to elicit from the mind of the client what they believe is important in the strategic situation. Not all aspects of the business situation draw the attention of the client to the same extent. Some elements are further away for the client, some are close in. The task is to build an understanding of this and map out a representation of this thinking.

Figure 19 shows an outline of the elicitation cycle. We get into the cycle by asking trigger questions in a SWOT workshop or individual interviews. The most effective triggering takes place in an open atmosphere, conducive to creating a free-flowing discussion. This generates responses which need to be carefully recorded in a response database.

Following a series of individual interviews, for example covering a management team, the response database is analysed. The result of this is fed back to the client team in a joint session, showing how their insights, as the analyst has heard these, have been mapped out. The presentation highlights clusters, and how these are inter-connected. The client normally recognises much of what is fed back, but the new element introduced at this stage is the ordering of the various views in a coherent framework. Interestingly, there are also surprises. Individual managers often have different perspectives on the business, depending on their area of responsibility. Therefore participants are confronted with views on the business that are different in some places from their

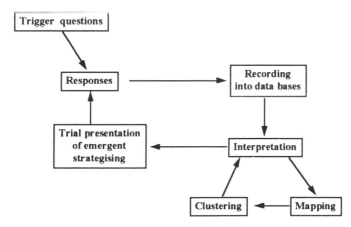

Figure 19. *The elicitation cycle.*

own perception of the situation. Managers often do not realise the diversity of thinking in their own management teams. They are often surprised at what their colleagues have to say on strategy and the long term. It seems that most management teams concentrate on discussing operational day-to-day questions and problems, and issues of a longer term strategic nature are not often on the agenda. Through individual interviews differences can be surfaced and presented back to the team in one or more feedback meetings.

Being presented during a feedback session with a representation of affairs that does not coincide with his own understanding of the situation will cause the manager to articulate his own views. In this way further responses are generated. This new data can then be included in the response database to make it more complete. A further feedback session can be held, in an iterative process, until no further progress is made. The complete cycle of individual interviews and joint feedback is generally experienced as a highly positive experience in most management teams. Reasons for this include:

- Managers are forced to articulate their assumptions and opinions about strategy, helping them in their thinking through verbalisation.
- The ordered database provides an overview of the main strategic issues in a framework which makes the situation cognitively more manageable.
- Managers become aware of the diversity of thinking available in the team.
- Successful interviews create a feeling of a "common experience" among the group of interviewees, helping to improve the dynamics of their strategic conversation.

Following a SWOT workshop it is advisable to feed the results back to the client-team to allow them to validate and modify. The SWOT process is designed to make one cycle through the elicitation loop only.

THE SWOT WORKSHOP

A SWOT analysis is a way of recording important features of the business situation. It provides a database for a scenario exercise and further discussion on strategy. The four letters SWOT stand for

Strengths, Weaknesses, Opportunities and Threats.

The SWOT is developed in a client workshop, facilitated by the scenario planner. It consists of:

- an opening in which the purpose of the exercise is explained,
- a brainstorming session, during which contributions are invited from all participants, without critique,
- an analysis of the recorded results of the brainstorming.

After the opening and introduction the participants are invited to write down individually any aspect of the company or its business environment that seems to them either good or bad. The facilitator should not try to be too specific at this stage, people should follow their intuition in deciding what good or bad means. These lists do not need to be exhaustive, they only serve to get the ball rolling in the group. While participants think about this the facilitator prepares four flip charts, which he identifies with a S,W O or T.

After (say) 10 minutes the facilitator invites participants one by one, going around the table, to call out one of the points they have written down. Before recording this he invites the team to identify the item as S,W,O or T. Only questions of clarification are allowed. When everyone understands what is meant by the point raised the facilitator writes the indicated point in a few words on the appropriate flip chart. The facilitator ensures that everyone agrees with the choice of words. The convention for deciding where particular features need to be noted down is as follows:

- A favourable feature of the company is noted under Strengths.
- An unfavourable feature of the company is noted under Weaknesses.
- A favourable feature of the business environment is noted under Opportunities.
- An unfavourable feature of the business environment is noted under Threats.

It is important to be somewhat relaxed with where items end up. Many views of the business cannot be neatly put into one of the categories. If this problem arises it is often useful to discuss the various aspects, and enter separate points in more than one flipchart.

This ideally should become a true brainstorming session in which ideas trigger new ideas. When this happens the facilitator should make room for the discussion of these new ideas and they should be incorporated on the flip charts in the same way. When ideas dry up the facilitator continues with the next person going around the table, and so on until no further new ideas come forward.

As a next step, participants are invited to overview the whole table as assembled on the flip charts, and to ask themselves the question whether this characterises the company in all its important aspects. A holistic overview of this type often triggers further ideas on aspects that have been overlooked so far.

To finish the generation of the SWOT table, participants are now invited to critique the result so far. Participants particularly need to discuss the features that feel uncomfortable. This may lead to a reformulation of what is written down, or the challenged point may have to be annotated, or even removed, as the case may be.

ANALYSIS OF THE SWOT

The four categories of data collected are now analysed further.

Step 1

It is important to identify which Strengths can be considered distinctive, distinguishing the company from its competitors. If a strength is annotated as distinctive the meeting should be capable of providing a suitable answer to the Devil's Advocate question: "Why would others be unable to emulate it" (refer to Part Two, page 62).

Step 2

Weaknesses should be broken down into three categories:

- Symptoms
- Hygiene weaknesses
- Structural weaknesses.

Some features on the list of weaknesses will be symptoms of weaknesses in the company. They cannot be repaired directly, but will come right when the underlying causes of weakness are tackled. Examples might be high debt, poor profits and low share value.

A second category of weakness are known as "hygiene factors". These are conditions that are generally agreed to be the essential basics for running any business enterprise. They represent current codified knowledge in society about sound management. No professional manager can be ignorant of this knowledge. It can be picked up by studying the practice of well-managed companies as codified in textbooks on management. Examples are adequate accounting systems, personnel policies, a minimum level of information systems and internal communications, succession plans, cash planning, inventory and working capital management, etc. Looking after hygiene factors puts the company on the starting line. It doesn't as such give a company any competitive advantage, but their absence will make surviving very difficult indeed.

The third category of weakness concerns structural weaknesses, and indicates areas in which the company would like to have, but lacks, a Distinctive Competency, at least for the time being. Examples would include such things as low market share, relative size vis-à-vis main competitors, lack of brand awareness, etc. When specifying the Business Idea the management team needs to keep these in mind, and test whether the Business Idea they come up with can stand up in the light of these weaknesses.

Structural weaknesses often indicate the direction in which the Business Idea for the future (the Strategic Vision) needs to be developed. Most of the structural weaknesses can be interpreted as a lack of a strength which the management intuitively feels the company should have. It is therefore likely that these indicate areas of desirable development.

Step 3

The team identifies opportunity areas. It is likely that so far opportunities will be expressed as options for the company and the facilitator now asks the group to rephrase these in terms of "opportunity areas open to us". Opportunity areas can be of two types:

- Portfolio areas
- Capability areas.

Portfolio opportunities are areas of potential business where the distinctive nature of the company's Business Idea might be capable of developing profitable business. In general a portfolio opportunity involves exploiting one (or more) of the company's distinctive strengths. Capability opportunities are areas where the company might develop new capabilities which are felt relevant to future success. Capability options indicate potential development territory towards the Business Idea of the future (the Strategic Vision).

Step 4

Threats are features in the business environment which could undermine the strength of the company. They should be carefully scrutinised by management for signs that the current Business Idea is becoming obsolete and in need of major overhaul.

Step 5

The SWOT data can be used as a quick way of coming to a scenario agenda. Overviewing the complete SWOT analysis the team addresses the question of what this indicates for the areas in the business environment that need to be looked at. A new flip chart is used by the facilitator to write down ideas that are highlighted. This can often add up to a considerable list of items of very different levels of potential importance. Therefore this step is completed by clustering the items recorded, in terms of their potential impact on the organisation. The facilitator needs to end up with a list of not more than (say) five broad areas of concern to the client management team about the business environment, as the basis to be used by the scenario design team.

The SWOT data have wider use. They can be of importance in subsequent steps of the strategy thinking process. Apart from the scenario agenda they give important indications about the current Business Idea, and where this needs to be developed. In conjunction with an explicit Business Idea SWOT data can also be used to trigger a discussion on options open to the company. Generally the SWOT analysis provides a database which can be used by the team during various stages of the strategy discussions.

INDIVIDUAL INTERVIEWS

Normally one works under a time constraint, and the number of iterations through the elicitation cycle will be strictly limited. It is therefore important that the best possible starting point is obtained. The most effective way of developing this is by means of a series of individual interviews. There are a few general rules that should be followed by the interviewer to create a successful interview.

Interviews are as much as possible of an open-ended nature. This means that the interviewer does not arrive with a ready set of specific questions concerning the business. Instead questions are general, and intended to trigger a free-flowing conversation, in which the interviewee sets the agenda.

Each interview is opened by explaining the purpose of the exercise. It is important that the interviewer explains what will happen to the data collected. It should be clear to the interviewee that any data will be stored anonymously. Data items will be sorted by subject, such that for each topic an overview is obtained of the range of views in the client team. In this way total anonymity is assured. This understanding will help the interviewee to talk more freely.

The challenge for the interviewer is to establish him(her)self as a genuine listener. Genuine listening involves paying attention to what arises in the mind of the listener during the conversation (active listening), and feeding this back to the interviewee. In this way the listener signals that (s)he "cares". Some degree of interaction of this type is required to establish a trust relationship between the parties in the conversation, a pre-condition for a successful interview. On the other hand, if it is overdone the interviewer risks dominating the content of what is said in the interview, reducing its elicitation value. A careful balance has to be found. This will be different in each case, depending on the characters of the individuals involved and their relationship.

The start of the interview sets the tone for the rest. Some personal trust needs to be established as quickly as possible. This is important to enable the interviewee to express what (s)he cares about, in his/her relation to the business theme of the interview. A useful way in is to ask the interviewee to briefly relate how (s)he came to be in their present position where the interview issue has become of importance. This introductory question allows the interviewee to express a personal viewpoint relating to the subject under discussion, and helps to involve him/her in the exercise. This question immediately follows the preamble, explaining the purpose of the exercise.

After this introduction the interview proper starts. The interviewer must refrain as much as possible from setting the agenda of the discussion. This means that questions must be designed so that they trigger a conversation, but influence the agenda as little as possible. These are known as trigger questions. One example of a set of trigger questions that have been found to be effective is known as the "seven questions". The core of these originates from the work of the Institute of the Future (Amara & Lipinsky 1983), but further questions were added later in Shell by the scenario planners.

The first three questions form a set, the purpose of which is to elicit a list of the main uncertainties in the business and its environment. It is an intuitive point to start, as uncertainties and concerns overlap. The interviewees could be asked straight out to list their concerns and uncertainties, and for some clients that may be the best approach. For most interviewees it is productive to impose constraints. This can be done by suggesting a situation in which the client could pose only three questions to a clairvoyant, somebody who could actually foretell the future. How would the interviewee use these three opportunities? In this way one introduces the issue of priorities and relative impact. There is much uncertain in the business environment and the client is encouraged to reflect on what is really going to make a difference.

There is a distinctive advantage in posing the first question in a "lighter" way. It takes the weight off the interview and makes the atmosphere more comfortable. It signals "feel free to explore various unusual avenues". Asking trigger questions in a somewhat playful mode is helpful in opening up the interviewee.

When the conversation starts to slow down the next question is introduced. The situation is turned around, and it is suggested that the interviewee might take the role of clairvoyant, answering his/her own questions. However, as we are dealing with an uncertain world, which could turn out in various different ways, the interviewee is asked to concentrate on a future that turns out favourable. "Imagine that the future is a good one, rolling out as you would like it to be, how would you, as the clairvoyant, answer your own three questions?" In response the interviewee produces a "good" scenario, revisiting all uncertainties, and working out how they develop out in a scenario that is considered "good". This question is followed by a similar one in which the world develops in an undesirable direction, representing the interviewee's worst fears.

Earlier (page 109) I argued strongly that the idea of "good" and "bad" futures in the scenario design stage lead to poor quality scenarios. In most circumstances the scenario planner does best to stay away from good and bad worlds, instead focusing on what is plausible and internally consistent. However, in the elicitation interview the discussion of good and bad worlds tends to be powerful in triggering ideas of what could be important factors to look at, leading to the discovery of underlying driving forces.

These tend to be productive questions. It often happens that one does not get much further than these three questions, and that time runs out before the interviewee runs out of steam. People find it easy to spin stories in this way, particularly after the uncertainties have already been articulated. The good or bad scenario questions must follow the clairvoyant question if they are to work well. The major uncertainties must already be on the table. The questions do not only surface the interviewee's ideas of how things hang together in the world, but what is considered good and bad will also emerge, and in this way value systems start surfacing. The interviewer does not specify good or bad, the interviewee fills this in.

The contribution of the interviewers during the conversation needs careful consideration. The objective of the interviewer is to engage in a conversation with the client without directing what the client says. This is not a simple matter. In principle, by participating in the conversation the interviewer affects what is being said. On the other hand one cannot expect the client to engage in a monologue of two hours or more. The interviewer must participate, preferably only in a reactive mode. This is done by means of questions of clarification or feeding back what has just been heard. The art of this type of interviewing is to do that in the least obtrusive way possible, such that the effect on the client's line is minimised. Interviewers must be aware of what they are doing while they are engaged in this conversation. They need to continuously try to judge to what extent they are capable of keeping the conversation natural and normal without steering. The challenge is to participate in the conversation while standing apart from it at the same time.

This requires that the interviewer has more open-ended questions up his/her sleeve. A useful technique is to alternate questions about the past with questions about the future. Ideas about the future are anchored in the past. Therefore questions about the past make the interviewee realise where some of the ideas come from.

Follow-up questions that have proven useful include:

- *Inheritances from the past:* "What pivotal events can you identify in the past of this organisation, good or bad, that should remain in our memories as important lessons for the future?" This question acknowledges that mental models are representations of patterns we have seen in past events. These can be powerful elicitation entry points, leading into territory that has not yet been explored. The interviewer should listen carefully for organisational "myths", stories known to all members of the organisation. Groups of people tend to use myths to codify and remember some of the most basic assumptions underpinning their culture. Surfacing these can be particularly productive in mapping the organisational mental model.

- *Important decisions ahead:* "What major decisions with long term implications is the organisation facing at the moment, decisions that need to be tackled in the next few months?" The time period indicated may vary and should be appropriate for the major decisions that will have to be faced. This question aims to get at the sort of issue that are currently exercising the client's mind, and where help from a scenario project could be particularly welcome.

- *Constraints in the system:* "What major constraints are you experiencing inside or outside of your organisation that limit you in what you can achieve in your business situation?" Many constraints are strongly felt and prove a powerful trigger for elicitation. Internal constraints often are the subject of political battles, and some interviewees may require some encouragement to bring these out. The interviewer may want to follow up with: "Please do not forget to include cultural constraints in your own organisation".

- *The epitaph question:* "Please consider the situation in the future when you will have moved on from your current position, to the next job or retirement, what do you hope to leave behind that people will associate with your period in office. What do you want to be remembered for?" This question is aimed directly at the interviewee's value system. Following an initial response, and to help the interviewee to get as close as possible to personal values the interviewer may want to follow up with the suggestion that the interviewee should try in his/her mind to remove all constraints; imagine (s)he is in total control, and only personal values will shape the response.

CONDUCTING THE INTERVIEW

During the interview two activities need to be carried out at the same time; the conversation has to be kept going in a natural but non-directive way and what is being said needs to be recorded. Maintaining a natural conversation without influencing the agenda requires significant mental effort. The interviewer needs to think carefully about what (s)he is going to say so that (s)he does not steer the conversation too much. On the other hand the conversation needs to be natural and relaxed, to keep the interviewee at ease. It cannot be combined well with note taking.

Should interviewers record the interviews on tape? A lot depends on the culture in the organisation. The most important objective of the interview is that it feels to the interviewee like an informal natural conversation, encouraging airing of personal opinions, rather than espoused theory or the "party line". The interviewee must be convinced of complete confidentiality if this is to be achieved. Most business managers are not used to their conversation being recorded and have "Watergate"-type visions when confronted with such a device. They start wondering what might happen with the tapes and cannot help being put on their guard. Pragmatically it must be assumed that in most cases tape-recording is counter-productive. It is preferable to miss a few observations in hand-written notes, if the rest gains in substantive significance. In most interviews notes need to be taken, requiring a second person in the team.

A team of two people often works well, particularly if they can switch roles during the interview. This requires some practice in the team, but after a few interviews the style and approach of one's partner become clear. Switching roles during the interview gives it a feel of a natural and comfortable conversation. Experienced interviewers learn to switch roles frequently during the interview.

Adding more people to the team tends to reduce the quality of the interview very quickly. There is a risk that a team of three (or more) interviewers entering the interviewee's office is perceived as an event, requiring a "performance". More than three progressively reduces the value of the interview further, due to the increased stress created.

Interviews can be conducted by people belonging to the organisation or by outsiders. Internal people have the advantage that they know the language and much of the background of what is being said. On the other hand this may sometimes turn into a disadvantage. The external person is not expected to know much of what is going on. This may lead the interviewee away from the usual formulation of business issues, into aspects of the world taken for granted which are normally not verbalised. This often proves particularly productive in surfacing theories about the world which the person actually uses to guide his/her actions, rather than theories through which people traditionally articulate the situation to each other (espoused theory). The other advantage of the external interviewer is the absence of prior history of interaction with the interviewee, which often inhibits free expression. On balance the external person has the advantage, provided that (s)he has acquired some of the language of the organisation in advance.

Interviews of this type seldom take less than an hour and a half or more than two hours and a half. Realistically one can do three, or at most four, interviews in a day, more would be difficult to handle. This is a quite consistent finding, allowing reliable planning of an interview project over time.

WHOM TO INTERVIEW

In a normal organisational situation focused on a management team it seldom proves necessary to interview more than fifteen or so people. Early interviews generally add a lot of additional information. But number ten produces clearly less, by that time a lot has already surfaced. A typical management team works together in the organisation, communicates on a daily basis, meets regularly in corridors or in business meetings. For this reason, the fifteenth interview does not surface much new. (The interviewer can use the later interviews to test emerging theses, moving beyond the agenda setting framework. But only after having tested the trigger questions first.) The fact that in most cases the number of interviews can be limited to between ten and fifteen is another important data point enabling the planning of the scope of the exercise. (Some strategy projects require many more interviews, for reasons other than data collection, for example to create ownership across the organisation by allowing a wider cross section to be heard.)

NOTE TAKING

Good listening and note-taking is absolutely crucial, it is *the* big challenge of this project. Fortunately it is also something one can learn to do better. Gaining experience helps people in being able to push back their own preconceived idea filters and to give increasing space to the ideas of the interviewee. Comments need to be captured as completely as possible. Judgement on what is important and what will prove interesting needs to be developed.

It is useful for the two interviewers to compare notes immediately after the interview. Invariably one finds that overlap between the two is not total: one just does not hear all that is being said. While memory is still fresh a lot can still be recovered. At this stage it is useful to identify and agree on the important ideas.

Having completed the notes the next step is to identify the important insights. This is a judgemental process, where again the two-person team has the advantage over the single interviewer. The interviewers go through their notes and consider the important observations to be processed further. The test for inclusion is whether the view expressed is relevant and significant in the context of the organisation's position and behaviour in its business environment. This includes internal issues if these are relevant to the way the organisation will react to the outside world. Any views on where the environment might be going are obviously important.

Typically one interview may produce between 40 and 60 important insights that need to be taken forward. The interviewers will write these down as short bullet-style statements, each expressing one significant thought.

INTERVIEW ANALYSIS

Any strategy project ultimately is about considering the fit between the organisation and its environment. For this reason these two domains need to be separated as early as possible in the project.

Interviewees will not have made this distinction, and the interview notes will be a mixture of external and internal points. The first step in the analysis is to separate statements into these two categories. The analysts need to create two data files, one including the statements about the external business environment, and one containing all other points relating to internal characteristics and phenomena in the organisation. The allocation criterion is whether the company has control over the issue.

One must be aware of language traps that lure here. Very often a statement ostensibly about an internal policy issue is really about the environment. For example the statement: "we may soon have to double our capacity if we want to remain a key player" includes a statement about the rate of growth in demand. Similarly "we should adopt a more customised approach in our product design" may imply the insight that the market may be moving towards giving higher value to customisation. These implied business environment assumptions should be included as separate statements in the business environment file. Before the separation is made all statements seemingly addressing internal issues should be tested for any embedded content on the contextual environment.

Once the statements have been divided between these two files, the data in each file need to be sorted and clustered. Initially the statements are unconnected, like a set of random thoughts. The subsequent analysis of these statements involves a process of clustering and linking. It is important that no clustering rules are laid down in advance. It is preferable to let cluster categories emerge naturally out of the material collected. Intuitive clustering will force the analyst to pay attention to conceptual meaning, for example through cause and effect reasoning. As a result clusters will start emerging which combine statements together in context. By overviewing the total set of insights produced the analyst will start to see patterns, similarities and natural couplings. The material now needs to be arranged into these emerging categories. At this stage the purpose of the analysis is to cluster ideas and arrive at a smaller number of higher level concepts, which can be related to each other. Total overview is required in the early stages until the first level categories have emerged.

Technically there are various ways of doing the clustering, dependent on the number of statements to be considered. Visual methods tend to be more comfortable in view of the large amount of material the analyst has to overview. Statements can be written on slips of paper, Post-its or magnetic hexagons, moved around on a display surface or wall-mounted area. If the team has been disciplined in note taking this should be a relatively simple step. The human mind is particularly strong in seeing or inferring patterns. As the purpose of the exercise is to acquire an overview, it is important that text on each Post-it is limited to not more than a few (say, eight) words. These should be written in large heavy characters, so that they can be read from a distance. By scanning the whole display ideas for clustering present themselves.

For small projects this approach suffices. However, if one is dealing with a ten-interview project some 500 Post-its may be generated, which stretches the visual approach to the limit. In this case it is preferable to use a computerised database in the analysis. Sorting and clustering then becomes an exercise in hierarchical outlining. However, creating overall overview, required for the first level of clustering, is difficult in a computer database. The analyst will therefore still want to use a parallel visual approach using only main statement categories. Once the first level categories are established in this way, sub-categories can be developed on the computer itself.

Initially there will be statements that do not seem to link up naturally. These may be put aside temporarily while progress is being made on the rest. Following completion of this stage further iterations are needed to try to integrate the odd statements that have been left out so far. The first clustering will be somewhat random, depending on what caught the eye first, but it may not be the most effective way of incorporating as many of the insights as possible. If there are unconnected ideas left, the analysts need to try to find a home for these by reclustering. They should consider whether any other higher level criteria can be found, on the basis of which the data can be re-clustered, which accommodates the so-far-unconnected ideas. It is worthwhile iterating a couple of times, until there is no further progress.

The exercise is basically iterative. The decision whether clustering has been satisfactorily completed depends on whether clustering principles have become clear, and whether clusters are reasonably independent, with each idea falling naturally in one cluster only. The analyst should try to get as close as possible to this state of affairs. One way of testing this is through naming of the clusters. A cluster name should be a short and unambiguous indication of the principle that keeps the ideas within the cluster together, while distinguishing them clearly from any of the other clusters identified.

From then onwards the analysis moves into each of the main clusters to develop a second level of categorisation. The process of moving and clustering the Post-its on a display area is now the same as moving data in a computer outliner, using principles of hierarchical outlining. The detail required in the categorisation depends on the quantity of the material collected. If the number of statements runs into many hundreds, a three- or four-level outline may suggest itself. The ultimate aim is to arrive at a level of hierarchical categorisation where each of the lowest sub-categories contains not more than (say) 15 statements. On the other hand the number of statements in a category may be as low as one or two, if statements are self-standing and cannot be grouped with any others. The final step in the process is to move the statements within each sub-category in an order which suggests a logical progression from one statement to the next.

Finally within each of the clusters the analyst identifies common and divergent views and assumptions. These need to be highlighted as powerful triggers for the feedback meeting. In this way the analyst gradually creates a picture of the management team's mental models, including overlap and divergence within the team.

With the initial material divided into internal and external points, the analysis results in two sets of cluster hierarchies. Two products will emerge from the data structuring stage, the scenario agenda and the internal agenda.

INTERNAL AND CONTEXTUAL DATA

The interviewees will have talked widely, dealing with external and internal issues, during the interviews. Many of them will have been concerned with areas where the client firm has a great deal of control, but where the interviewee is unsure about how to exercise this. These are strategic option issues, including internal client policies, their business policies, actions by other players that can be influenced, and "games" that are being played in the market place or with other stakeholders. Outside the areas where the client has a degree of control, known as the transactional environment is the contextual environment where the control of the client organisation is insignificant (see Figure 20).

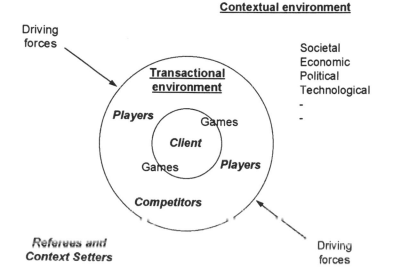

Figure 20. *The business in its environment.*

As discussed scenarios address driving forces in the contextual environment. Any useful and productive conclusions in scenario planning will derive from the exploration of strategic options in possible future worlds expressed in the scenarios. For this to work it is essential that external issues are expressed and developed in scenarios separately from internal issues that are processed into strategic options.

There are various taxonomies of external contextual factors. The most well known is called the "September formula" which categorises the environment into:

- Societal development
- Economic developments
- Political developments
- Technological developments.

(The next E in September is sometimes used to indicate ecological developments.) It is useful to address each of these four (or five) areas consciously.

However, detailed strategy cannot be developed with reference only to such generic categories. It also requires a detailed analysis of the structure of the industry and market the organisation operates in.

Industry structure is the result of power structures among the generic categories of competitive forces, which all try to appropriate as much of the overall profit potential as possible. At the contextual scenario level these competing forces include (Porter 1980):

- Generic competitive forces among the existing competitors in the industry.
- Relative power of suppliers.
- Relative power of buyers.
- Relative power of potential new entrants.
- Potential influence of substitute products.

It is useful for the interviewer to make a check that each of these categories has been consciously addressed.

At the level of the contextual scenario we are not considering the behaviour of the individual players in the game whose power and stake depend on the strategies adopted by the client organisation. Testbed conditions must be independent of the strategies and plans to be tested. As we saw, it is important that clients do not play a role in their own scenarios.

THE SCENARIO AGENDA

The first product of the elicitation exercise is known as a scenario agenda. A scenario agenda is a list of typically up to four or five broad themes or areas of interest in the business environment where it has become clear that the project has the potential of helping the client. These are areas of major uncertainty that the client is significantly concerned about. Following the clustering exercise a larger number of agenda issues will tend to emerge. However, a scenario project should not attempt to, and mostly does not need not to address more than five themes in its agenda. A good in-depth scenario exercise cannot really handle more than five broad themes simultaneously. More than that would make the outcome cognitively difficult to handle. Very few customised scenario exercises need to go beyond that if the agenda themes have been chosen reasonably orthogonally (mutually independent). In this respect uncertainty actually helps the scenario planner, in that more uncertainty tends to reduce the number of key uncertainties.

By clustering and re-clustering the analyst tries to make the categories as independent as possible, such that uncertainty in one affects uncertainty in the others as little as possible. It often happens that this will reduce the number of clusters to manageable proportions. If this does not prove possible the analyst will have to take the final result back to the client and suggest a ranking exercise to decide the top five themes. The ranking should be conducted using the level of concern and anxiety in the client team on specific possible items as the criteria. This means that themes that score lower this time may be ranked higher on another occasion in the future. The analyst needs to clarify that the current ranking does not mean that the lower ranking themes are not important. These areas may have their turn of being included in a scenario project on another future occasion.

In many cases it may be tempting for the analyst to define, with the client, an "organising question" at the conclusion of the elicitation exercise. This needs to be carefully considered, as there are advantages and disadvantages to this. An organising question helps in giving a strong focus to the project, and ensures that any outcome has strong relevance to the client. It may be particularly helpful to those client teams who lack common understanding of the business environment, and who find it difficult to move forward due to this confusion. On the other hand, strongly cohesive teams, who have little problem moving forward on the basis of their one-track view of the future need to consider alternative interpretations of the world which are not currently part of their shared mental model. In such a case, where the main purpose is to stretch existing understanding, an organising question may introduce constraints limiting exploration trips into the future into those areas where these novel insights need to be developed.

THE INTERNAL AGENDA

The second product of the elicitation exercise is a first cut at mapping the fundamentals of the organisation itself, the organisational "self". Scenarios play out in the contextual environment. But the client has not only been talking about the contextual business environment during the interviews. A lot has been said about the organisation itself, in terms of problems and concerns, what is wrong and what is good, problems with other people, why the culture is not right and so on. Typically, more than half of the interview material contains data not about the contextual business environment, but about the organisation itself. This part of the data is important as a starting point for mapping the strategic fundamentals of the organisation, ultimately to be expressed as its Business Idea.

THE HORIZON YEAR

One of the first decisions by the team is how far the scenarios will look forward. Each scenario exercise needs to be based on what is known as a "horizon year", determining how far into the future the exercise will be taken. This decision will be made by reference to the issues on the identified scenario agenda and the nature of the Business Idea. The horizon year needs to be selected on the basis of the future impacts of today's decisions and strategies. Major capital investments require consideration of a period up to 20 years. Decisions relating to developing the Business Idea, often of a cultural nature, may also have long term implications. On the other hand organisations with a robust Business Idea may be involved with business portfolio strategy with shorter term repercussions. Similarly companies in survival mode may not be able to afford the luxury of looking too long-term. The horizon year decision to some extent prejudges the outcome of the scenario planning exercise. The guess made may prove to be inappropriate in which case the team needs to decide whether another iteration needs to be made.

Chapter Eight

Articulation of the Business Idea

Using the concept of the Business Idea requires explicit recognition and exploitation of a system of Distinctive Competencies in a positive feedback growth loop. A simple form of graphical representation is suggested as the basis for in-depth discussion in the management team of the current and future Business Ideas.

SURFACING A BUSINESS IDEA IN A MANAGEMENT TEAM

All managers carry the elements of a Business Idea in their head. The process described here is intended to articulate these views, for subsequent discussion, adjustment and agreement in a management team. The process described is an iterative one, in which a prototype representation is quickly developed. The managers then react to this model, expressing their understanding of what drives success. Through a number of iterations the prototype representation is gradually brought into line with the views of the managers. By employing this process in the management team the managers debate their differences of view while they go along, such that when a stage is reached where not much more progress can be made, the result represents a shared view of the business owned by the team as a whole.

The process needs to be facilitated. The facilitator's role is to remind the management team of the concepts involved, to introduce and lead the process, to take the team through the various steps and to record the views expressed. Choice of the facilitator is important, and will normally be limited to team members or well-trusted outsiders.

In this chapter we describe a process of articulating and discussing the Business Idea in a management team. The process is presented as a series of three management workshops, separated by days or minutes as preferred. If necessary the process can be completed in one full-day session.

ELEMENTS OF THE BUSINESS IDEA

As discussed in Part Two the essential elements of a Business Idea describe the following drivers of business success:

- The customer value created.
- The nature of the Competitive Advantage exploited.
- The Distinctive Competencies which create the competitive advantage, in their mutually reinforcing interaction.
- All this configured in a positive feedback loop, in which resources generated drive growth.

The recording medium is the cause-and-effect influence diagram, (see Figure 23 below). A word representation cannot bring out adequately the systemic features of the Business Idea. The concept is a description of mutually reinforcing Distinctive Competencies working in a positive feedback loop. Bringing this out requires the medium of the influence diagram.

INITIAL DATA REQUIREMENT

If companies are dominated by one or a few major business sectors, customer value, Competitive Advantage and Distinctive Competencies may be easier to define at business unit level. It may be useful for the top management team to prepare the ground for their corporate Business Idea review by arranging one or more sessions with the business sector managers, in order to develop joint understanding of the basics of these businesses in the team. A possible way of approaching this is by means of one or more Strategic Evaluation Sessions, in which top management discusses the strategic aspects of the business in a "for information only" exchange with the business manager. A possible model is discussed in Part Four, page 285.

The discussion of the Business Idea in the management team requires a shared database which ideally should be generated through an interview/feedback round, to be undertaken by the facilitator as discussed. Alternatively the facilitator develops with the client a SWOT analysis on flip charts. This is done preferably in a separate team session, such that the results can be suitably worked up and presented, but if necessary the management team may start the Business Idea workshop with a one-hour SWOT analysis.

The most difficult part of the process of developing a joint Business Idea is getting to the first prototype diagram. The facilitator needs to do some preparatory work in order to be able to help the team along if they have difficulty negotiating this first step. From preparatory work the facilitator needs to develop some initial understanding of the key elements that may end up in the Business Idea diagram, and to prepare these as a checklist of triggers, to be used during the meeting if required.

THE PROCESS

Step 1. Deciding on the company's Competitive Advantage

The SWOT analysis, developed from individual interviews or as a team exercise, are displayed on the walls of the meeting room

The process of drawing up the first prototype diagram starts with addressing the question of Competitive Advantage. To get the process going, the facilitator poses the following question: What is the basis of the company's Competitive Advantage?

A useful way to think about this is to articulate how one would explain to potential customers why they should prefer this organisation as supplier/business partner over any other competitor. It raises the question who the customers are in the first place and what their cares and worries are. The facilitator may introduce this by suggesting to the client-team that they formulate a sales-pitch that clearly differentiates the offering in terms that motivate the customer to buy from this organisation rather than another one.

The follow-up question – "What does this organisation have to do well in order to deliver on this promise?" – turns the focus on competencies. It is surprising how much time many teams need to answer these seemingly obvious questions. As we saw earlier many teams take the basic strengths of the organisation for granted, and do not think a lot about the underlying driving forces while they carry on with the day-to-day tasks.

The purpose of the competitive advantage question is to come to an understanding of the way the organisation is or will be successful. Success can be based on doing better things than others or on doing the same things but at a lower cost. The final answer to the competitive advantage question should be one, or a combination, of the following two:

- Product/service differentiation
- Cost leadership

A company produces a differentiated product if the nature of the market allows a price premium on product differentiation, and if it has a system of Distinctive Competencies allowing it to put a product/service on the market with enough unique features, in design, quality, support, availability and so on to make the customers want to pay the premium price.

A company is a cost leader if it has a system of Distinctive Competencies which allows it to make a product/ service available at a cost consistently below any competitor (cost leadership should not be confused with cost management as part of any "good housekeeping").

When agreement has been reached the facilitator records the answer to this question on a flip chart.

Step 2. Addressing the Devil's Advocate question

Having done this the facilitator poses the Devil's Advocate question: "What are the unique factors that allow this company to exploit this competitive advantage, and why are others unable to emulate it?" The purpose of discussing this question is to force the managers to burrow deeper into their mental model to search for evidence of the underlying system, not stopping at superficial symptoms at the event level. A company can be a differentiator in the market only if it has competencies that nobody else has. Why would this be? Why would other competitors not simply copy what this organisation is doing when they see the success of the formula? The same applies to a consistent cost performance. Competitors have always tried to copy each other's successes. The name of the game today is benchmarking, in which companies study each other's way of doing things carefully. Companies need something that is distinctive and difficult to emulate.

Initial ideas on elements of uniqueness are recorded on a flip chart as well, as preparation for the following stages of the process.

Step 3. Developing a cause and effect picture

The facilitator now starts the development of the first prototype Business Idea diagram. As this is an iterative approach, the most flexible recording medium available should be used (see below).

The facilitator begins the development of the influence diagram by recording the agreed Competitive Advantage. He then draws an arrow to an element he puts up, called "profitability", and from there another arrow goes to an element called "investment".

● An arrow from A to B means: A is a (part) cause of B!

The team has started to discuss the sources of the agreed Competitive Advantage by addressing the Devil's Advocate question. The facilitator now formalises this part by inviting the group to specify succinctly the characteristics of the company causing the Competitive Advantage These are recorded, and arrows are drawn from the sources to the competitive advantage recorded.

The attention now moves to the sources identified. The facilitator raises the question: "What causes these sources to exist and how are

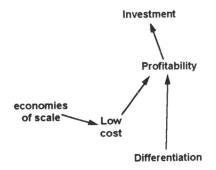

Figure 21. *Start of the Business Idea diagram.*

they being sustained?" In this way new elements enter the picture, connected up with what is already there through cause/effect arrows. This line of questioning is continued until no further progress can be made.

Step 4. Completion of the diagram

When the diminishing returns stage is reached the diagram will contain a number of loose ends, elements for which no sources are shown. This may be due for a number of reasons:

- The element may be sustained by investments, either in capital expenditure or operating expenditure. For example, an R&D capability may be maintained by expenditure, personnel loyalty may require generous rewards, or customer loyalty may be bought by a "low everyday price" policy. In such cases the facilitator will complete the diagram by drawing an arrow from the "investment" box already entered to the element under consideration. All expenditure made to buy a hard or soft asset creating long term value is considered an investment.
- The element may be due to investments, sunk or otherwise, made in the past, the fruits of which are enjoyed by the current organisation. In relation to these elements no further entries on the diagram are required, as the explanation resides in the past only.
- In some cases the organisational success may be related to the leadership by an individual. If the organisation is strongly identified with this individual, e.g. in the case of an owner/manager then similarly no further explanatory entries are required.

In all other cases questioning should continue until all elements in the diagram are explained, i.e. are supported by explanatory arrows.

Step 5. Identifying the Distinctive Competencies

When loose ends have been tied up, the facilitator needs to complete one more task in this team session. This is to identify the Distinctive Competencies in the diagram. Referring to the Devil's Advocate

question again the facilitator asks the managers to identify the elements
in the diagram which are:

- Unique to the company, and in which it distinguishes itself from
  its competitors.
- Impossible or difficult to emulate by existing or new
  competitors.

As explained in Part Two, five categories of Distinctive Competencies
can be distinguished, and the facilitator needs to take the team
through this list, making sure that suggestions by the team fit in one of
these:

- Based on sunk costs:
    Activity specific assets
    Legal protection
    Reputation and trust
- Based on uncodified knowledge:
    Embedded processes
    Networked team knowledge.

Elements on the diagram that are agreed on this basis to be distinctive
are suitably annotated.

Recording media

Drawing up an influence diagram "on the fly" during a workshop is
greatly facilitated by the most flexible recording medium available. A
number of possible approaches is listed here in order of reducing ease
of manipulation:

- For facilitators with a developed computer aptitude the ideal
  medium is the computerised systems diagram, using auto-
  connecting flow diagram software, and made visible to the team
  by means of an LCD projection device.
- The systems diagram can be built up using movable adhesive or
  magnetic stickers on a white board, each showing one element
  in the diagram. These are interconnected through arrows drawn
  on the board, to be wiped out and re-drawn whenever a change
  is made.

- Instead of using moveable devices the elements can be written on the board itself. This makes the process of making changes rather more difficult.
- The use of flip charts must be discouraged. The resulting "spaghetti" makes the process unwieldy and unattractive.

The choice must be left to the individual doing the facilitation as the first requirement is that (s)he feels totally comfortable with it.

Step 6. Cleaning up

The first part of the team session is now completed. The flip charts with the SWOT analysis will be displayed again during the next session. The Business Idea diagram will be in need of cleaning up, and needs to be re-drawn in an orderly way, with minimal cross-overs etc. The facilitator undertakes this as preparation for the next part of the meeting. The result at this stage may look typically as shown in Figure 22, which gives an example of a first-stage Business Idea diagram. This diagram shows the usual convention with boxed items indicating Distinctive Competencies.

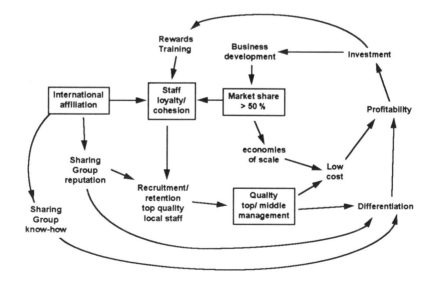

Figure 22. *First stage Business Idea diagram.*

Step 7. Review of the Business Idea

After reconvening the management team needs to consider the results obtained so far. To allow members of the management team to prepare for this part of the discussion the facilitator may want to circulate the cleaned-up version of the Business Idea diagram in advance of the meeting. Normally the re-arranged picture indicates areas for reconsideration, and the facilitator should be prepared to make numerous changes as requested by the team. During the meeting these are discussed and incorporated.

Having made the necessary changes the management team needs to test the results obtained. The first test is against the strengths and weaknesses developed in the SWOT analysis. This gives rise to the following questions:

- Have all strengths been reflected in the diagram?
- Can the Business Idea overcome any structural weaknesses identified?

A useful trigger question to open the next part of the discussion is the following: "If we, as a management team, swapped places with that of our best competitor, what would we do to eliminate the competitive advantage of the company we now belong to?"

In the final analysis it is the distinctiveness that determines the quality of the Business Idea. We already discussed the "Devil's Advocate" question. A more comprehensive final test – called the 3E test (Marsh 1993) – is now made:

- *Emulation:* How easily could the competition emulate our Distinctive Competencies? Not only must a company have more than one Distinctive Competency, it should have competencies in more than one category of distinctiveness. If this is not the case the Business Idea is weak and easily subject to competitive onslaught.
- *Emigration:* Will customers move on elsewhere and seek new satisfaction from other products having properties our offerings do not possess in adequate measure? What do our scenarios teach us on the possible evolution of societal developments in the future and the consequences for customer behaviour?
- *Erosion:* Can our Distinctive Competencies be eroded by neglect, by the passage of time, by the normal course of business?

Step 8. Drawing out the essentials

This completes the second team session. The facilitator has another task before the Business Idea articulation exercise is completed. In most cases the resulting Business Idea at this stage is too complex. The systemic nature of the concept is fundamental and it is crucial that the Business Idea is understood as one whole, rather than a combination of many interconnected elements. The human mind cannot simultaneously retain more than some seven concepts (Miller 1956), and the number of elements in a workable Business Idea diagram should, if at all possible, be reduced to this order of magnitude. There are ways of reducing the number of elements. Very often a rather more complex idea can be reduced by combining elements, or replacing them with other concepts which look at the situation from a higher perspective.

It tends to prove rather difficult to do this in a plenary session, and it is recommended that the facilitator drafts a proposal in advance for subsequent scrutiny and approval by the management team. For example the above diagram might be simplified without losing anything essential as shown in Figure 23.

In the example quoted, the essence of the strategic thrust has now been condensed to three elements:

● Investment in people to retain status of most attractive employer and to achieve "best in class" management.

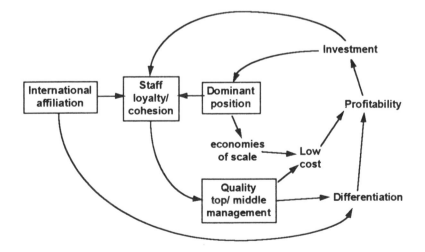

Figure 23. *Reducing the Business Idea to its essentials.*

- Maintaining a dominant market position by continuous investment, to retain a cost leadership position and to support status as most attractive employer.
- Using international affiliation as a source of differentiation in the market and to support status as most attractive employer.

Step 9. Strategic repercussions

Having reached this stage the facilitator brings the result back to the management team in their next strategy meeting for discussion and final agreement. The analysis so far looked at the Business Idea against the situation in the past up till the present. Can the result serve as a powerful leading principle for the future as well?

In order to consider this the management team confronts the Business Idea developed so far with the opportunities and threats identified in the SWOT analysis.

- Does it constitute a strong basis from which to exploit the opportunities?
- What would happen if the threats identified were to become reality?

Ideally, this part of the discussion requires the scenarios as testbed. If the Business Idea exercise is undertaken as an isolated project, without further scenario planning, the question has to be dealt with intuitively. Even so, the principle of scenario thinking, i.e. multiple equally plausible futures, should be the basis of the discussion. What do multiple scenarios teach us about possible evolution of societal values and consequent customer values and behaviour? Will the distinctiveness portrayed in our Business Idea be relevant and functional under these possible future circumstances?

The outcome of this deliberation may be to indicate that the Business Idea stands firm as the basis for future business, allowing the discussion to move on to the question of how it can be exploited to best advantage.

Alternatively a Business Idea, even one which has proved to be successful in the past, may not stand up to these questions, and the management team may decide that it needs to be developed to create a better fit with the future business environment. This may be because structural weaknesses or threats stand in its way, or because there are

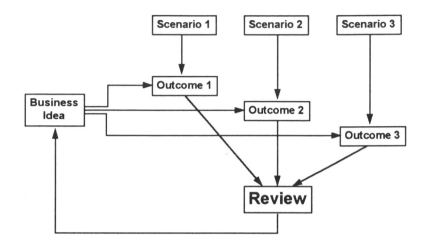

Figure 24. *The Business Idea considered against scenarios.*

not enough opportunity areas to exploit it. (In the example above, market dominance may be threatened by possible new and well-funded competitors. Or the company may have reached a relative size where further development is no longer possible, etc.)

If the fit is less than ideal the management team need to address the question of how the Business Idea can develop in a direction to make it more robust. A CEO who at this point comes to the conclusion that there is a significant misfit will want to repeat the foregoing steps. But this time rather than looking at the past (s)he will want to look at the desired Distinctive Competencies and Competitive Advantages to create a better fit. For example has a long-standing Distinctive Competency inadvertently been allowed to decline and must it be re-invigorated? Or can fit be improved by careful nurturing of a dormant Distinctive Competency whose time has now come?

During this part of the discussion the facilitator needs to remind the management team frequently that the only building blocks the company has are its existing Distinctive Competencies. The following important point from Part Two needs to be projected frequently in the management team: "Future corporate success is based on future strengths, but these can only develop from existing Distinctiveness. Strengthening and development of Distinctive Competencies comes from internal renewal, nothing else. Specifically it cannot be bought". In our example there are a number of important Distinctive

Competencies which can be leveraged, namely Group affiliation, staff loyalty, quality of management and dominant position in the market place. Exploiting these what new Distinctive Competencies can be developed that are more robust in the future? For example, can the affiliation and staff resources be used to branch out in a new direction? Or can the size-based economies of scale be used to create synergy in a possible merger or takeover deal? And so on.

When a conclusion has been reached it is useful to express the results of the discussion in terms of qualitative strategic objectives. These can take two forms:

- If the existing Business Idea is seen as a good basis for future business development, objectives will be formulated in terms of existing business areas to be further developed or new business areas to be entered where the Business Idea can be exploited. The direction will be towards doing more with what the company has got.
- If the existing Business Idea needs development, objectives will be formulated in terms of the development of new unique capabilities and competencies, to be created in the company by the leveraging of existing Distinctive Competencies.

Or the result may be a combination of the two.

The facilitator will ensure that the conclusions are recorded on a flip chart and that the wording is agreed all round.

With agreement in the management team the current strategic thrust has become clear. It has been comprehensively discussed and documented, and can serve as a source of coherent management action.

SUMMARY OF BUSINESS IDEA SURFACING PROCESS

Following preparation of a database, by means of a round of interviews or a SWOT analysis, the process of articulating and analysing a Business Idea in a management team consists of the following steps:

1. Identification of Competitive Advantage.
2. Addressing the Devil's Advocate question.
3. Mapping of causes of Competitive Advantage.
4. Closing the circle of the prototype Business Idea.

5. Identifying the Distinctive Competencies.
6. Finalising the prototype diagram.
7. Vulnerability analysis, testing and reworking of the Business Idea (3E test, SWOT).
8. Drawing out the essentials.
9. Considering strategic implications.

This process is the sort of entrepreneurial thinking which every team can only do for itself. What has been achieved at the end of it is that the team's current success formula has become clarified, and can now be challenged against scenarios of the future business environment. The model to be tested has been articulated, the next job is to design the test conditions.

Once the Business Idea has been tested and found robust against a range of possible futures it articulates what is really important, forming the basis of the strategic direction which will be taken. The rest of the strategic management process can now be focused. Priorities have become clear. Strategy is the art of making choices. There is no better tool for this than the robust Business Idea. It is holistic, shared and focused on the essentials.

Chapter Nine

Competitive Positioning

A STRUCTURED DISCUSSION IN THE MANAGEMENT TEAM

Having developed its Business Idea, management needs to consider its distinctiveness against competitors in more detail. Here we move on to the "playing field" (the transactional environment) where the organisation can influence what is going to happen. It is a true "game" situation with all players having interest in and power over the outcome. All are trying to figure out what competitors are going to do, in the full knowledge that competitors are doing the same in the opposite direction!

In Competitive Positioning, as in most other things in management, knowing what is strategic is the key question. The focus must remain on the fundamental driving forces of success as expressed in the Business Idea.

Top management will normally want to approach the competitive positioning question at a generic level, approaching it from a top-down perspective in the following six areas:

- Identifying the customers we are competing for.
- Testing business definitions.
- Identifying the competitors.
- Competitive cost driver analysis.
- Competitor response profiles.
- Summarising the most important competitors.

One member of the team needs to take responsibility for organising the discussion. In many cases a facilitator can be useful. The most senior report to the marketing manager is one possible choice. Data and some analysis will be required, mostly from Marketing, but also from other areas of activities. The following paragraphs are designed to be helpful in this preparatory task. In each of these areas the main conclusions should be summarised in a few OHP slides. These are the basis of the discussion in the management team. It is preferable that findings are presented by the facilitator, or even by the analysts who can provide back-up information.

The issues worth exploring must not be interpreted as a series of logical steps which, following one after the other, will automatically lead to specific results. Achieving a favourable competitive position cannot be the result of a mechanistic methodology. It requires creative insights, generated during discussion of important aspects of the competitive situation. The six issue areas indicated should be seen as six perspectives on the competitive situation, the discussion of each being capable of triggering new and innovative ideas. Once again note taking during such discussions is one aspect that needs careful attention, to ensure that ideas do not evaporate as quickly as they come.

The availability of data is a perennial issue. Data may be a particular problem where a Management Team are analysing a new entry. However, even in such a case a format such as suggested here will help to meaningfully structure a discussion in the important area of competitive positioning.

Issue 1. Identifying the customers we are competing for

Every competitive positioning exercise starts with identifying customers who are the subject of the competition being analysed. Their views and values must be articulated before it is possible to make a judgement on the relative position of those competing for their favour. This issue has been addressed conceptually in terms of the competitive advantage driving the company's Business Idea. This now needs to be analysed a bit further.

Identification of customers is mostly relatively straightforward, by considering who are "the people who pay our invoices, and make the buying decisions". In a top-down review it is normally not possible to review every individual customer. Therefore customers need to be categorised in groups which bring together those who respond in similar ways, and who require similar attention and treatment from the company. Appropriate segmentation of the business is a critical first step. This involves grouping customers on the basis of who they are and how they are served.

This is a perennial issue as many business units have grown incrementally to exploit potential synergies between existing businesses and new activities. In this interlinked structure segmentation may be justified on the basis of the geographical area of operation, features of the customer groups served, types of (augmented) products, or the technology used to produce products. Criteria for segmenting business activities into independent areas of operations should be guided by the question: Does the segment clearly represent specific customer choice, which drives profit potential and competitive focus?

Normally, management has a good intuitive grasp of the commercial situation. Therefore the job is best tackled using a common-sense approach.

Issue 2. Testing business definitions

When the company operates in a commodity market where it is difficult to differentiate the offering, taking the buying decision as the primary driving force can focus attention away from the most important stakeholders involved in the transaction. In a commodity market the ability to provide a particular service may depend more on concessions and the powers of concession/franchise holders than on the favours of the buyers of the products.

A helpful notion is the "competitive moment of truth" when the die is cast concerning the allocation of future business, margins, profitability and competitive success. Normally this occurs when the consumer of the product decides to buy from the company rather than from someone else. In that case competition is for the favours of the consumer. However, sometimes the buying decision is effectively made for the consumer. This happens if a supplier has obtained certain exclusive rights of access. In that case competition is for the favours of the concession giver, who becomes the prime customer.

The management team need to identify the customers being served in these broad categories. This needs to follow the exploration of the "moment of truth" question, in order to identify those categories of customers which are less than immediately obvious, though crucial for an appropriate business definition.

All along, a powerful instrument for choice is the current Business Idea. This identifies the most important elements of uniqueness on the basis of which the company intends to compete. Segmentation needs to be done such that real or potential competition in the areas of Distinctive Competencies is clearly identified.

Issue 3. Identifying the competitors

Having identified the main groups of customers, many managers will consider identifying the competitors a straightforward question. They will argue that if you are not aware of your competitors they are not really competing. However, the question can be cast a bit wider than those competitors who are out there in the market trying to take customers away from the company. First of all the management team need to think about potential competitors, who can come from two directions:

- New entrants into the existing market.
- Substitute products, existing or new.

Most companies know how to deal skilfully with existing competitors. But potential competitors are not so visible, their competition may not yet be felt, and it is easier to overlook them. This is why they are doubly dangerous, and require awareness and preparedness on the part of the company. The first need is for their identification, and this should be attempted here.

Having included potential competition the management has not yet identified the complete playing field. Its margin may be competed for by other players, which would normally not be classified as competitors, but who have potentially the power to affect the outcome of the competitive game. These include the following categories:

- Suppliers of goods and services.
- Buyers of goods and services.

Few companies do everything themselves; all companies buy some part of their requirements. It is interesting to consider the position of the company vis-à-vis their suppliers. Sometimes these are not very powerful, and if the company is unhappy with the service it gets it may switch over to another supplier. On other occasions there is only one supplier and the company has to deal with it. In that case it will be much more difficult to strike an attractive deal and a larger part of the potential margin of the company ends up with the supplier. It shows that suppliers compete with the company for the overall margin obtainable, and it depends on the relative power of each player where the balance will fall.

The same situation applies between the company and its buyers – its customers. If there are many buyers, and not too many suppliers, the company is in a strong negotiating position, and buyers will have to accept the deal on offer. If the company depends on a very small number of buyers, the latter are in a much better position to get a better deal. Therefore, as with suppliers, buyers and the company compete for the overall margin and the outcome of this "game" will depend on the relative power of both players.

From the above it follows that there are five categories of competitive forces, known as "Porter's five forces" (after the originator of the concept, Figure 25). In summary they are:

- Rivalry among existing competitors.
- Potential inroads from new entrants.
- Potential competition from substitute products.
- Relative power of suppliers
- Relative power of buyers.

It is useful to assess the relative importance of each of these forces. This will result in the identification of a few to focus on. Once again,

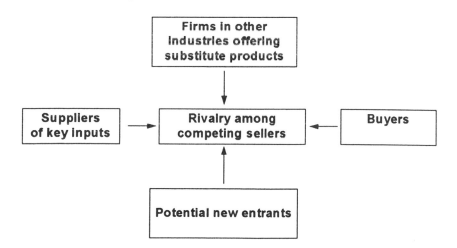

Figure 25. *The five-forces model of competition.*

the discussion needs to be framed by the Business Idea which should already have been defined. The question to be discussed relates to the way customer value creation and Distinctive Competencies could be threatened or otherwise affected by competitors, new entrants, substitute products, suppliers and buyers.

The discussion in the management team focuses on the ideas generated. But while discussing the five forces the participants will consider specific examples of players in each category. These examples should be carefully recorded on a flipchart as they come up. At the end of this exercise the team should end up with a list of important players and have a good feel for the relative importance of each competitor.

They should now divide these into two categories, "immediately important" and "to be dealt with later". For practical reasons not too many should end up in the first category. A degree of prioritisation is required here, and everyone in the team needs to understand that not everything can be resolved in one fell swoop. After some negotiation a short-list should be prepared which is the basis for the further analysis.

Issue 4. Cost driver analysis

Relative costs vis-à-vis those of competitors is always a major issue in competitive analysis. Cost analysis is particularly important in the more mature stages of a business when products are perceived in the market as commodities. In such markets price competition often dominates and lower-cost companies have the upper-hand. In a commodity business the Business Idea is likely to be based primarily on cost-related issues.

Relative costs cannot be discussed usefully in the management team until some analysis provides the basis for such a discussion. In the following paragraphs we discuss a few of the most important analytical approaches which should be commissioned by management to provide the necessary input to the management review.

Some cost categories are more important than others and a good way to develop a picture of relative levels is by developing a company cost chain (sometimes called a value-chain, see e.g. Porter 1985). The purpose of this is to identify the main cost elements to focus on in the discussion. The principle is that costs are allocated only if they can be argued to be directly incurred by the activity. No arbitrary allocation should take place. If costs are incurred to benefit more than one activity it should become an overhead item. However the task is approached, a compromise needs to be struck between interesting, but paralysing detail, and undue simplification which renders the analysis uninformative.

The next step is to compare one's cost position with that of the main competitors identified. An estimate is made (and presented in the same format) of the cost chain of important competitors and any significant deviations from one's own position is worthy of consideration.

Focusing on the main cost items, cost drivers need to be defined and analysed. Improving the relative cost position is based on finding an advantageous position for the cost drivers. Examples of some of the most important drivers worthy of consideration include:

- Price paid for raw materials.
- Differences in age and efficiency of plant and equipment.
- Economies of scale.
- Economies of scope (shared activities, cost synergies).
- Learning effects (e.g. the "experience curve").
- Differential wage levels.
- Logistics differences, geography, productivity, working capital.
- Differences in marketing costs.
- Mark-up differences.

Cost analysis is often too extensive a task to discuss exhaustively during one management team meeting. In that case the discussions serve the purpose of highlighting areas of importance, and the task of completing the analysis will have to be commissioned for presentation during the next management meeting.

Issue 5. Competitor response profiles

The next part of the competitive positioning discussion relates to behavioural characteristics in the competitive market. Such competitor profiles are closely related to their organisational culture, and these are worth studying carefully. This can often be mapped simply by listing the main behavioural features, e.g. as follows:

	Company A	Company B
Nature of competitive thrust	Based on few major investment decisions	Based on day-to-day control of investment mix
Decision making process	Slow Committee Analysis	Frequent individual decisions based on intuition
Organisational structure	Complex	Simple
	Matrix	Functional
	Consensus	Authoritarian
Personnel	Long-term career	Short-term career
	Generalists	Profit orientated
	Risk aversion	Entrepreneurial
	High quality	Specific experience

The analysis is driven by considering the following questions:

1. *Offensive*
   - Do they take the initiative for strategic change?
   - What are their probable moves?
   - How serious are their intentions?
   - What are they likely to gain?

2. *Defensive*
   - How vulnerable are they to offensive moves, or to environmental change in general?
   - What offensive moves would induce retaliation?
   - How effective would retaliation be?

3. *The battle ground*
   What are the market segments or strategic dimensions where competitors are:
   - Ill-prepared (in skills and competencies)?
   - Least enthusiastic (in goals, in emotional attachment)?
   - Frozen out, by committed position?

Issue 6. Summarising the most important competitors

The essence of successful strategy is in being different from others. Unique features of a company are expressed in its Business Idea.

Therefore, the final step relates the findings so far directly to the Business Idea. Having specified the behavioural profiles the following questions are addressed for each main competitor, and/or the market in general:

- Who are our competitors now?
- How are they competing with us?
- What does this tell us about our Business Idea?
- How can we change this to be more effective?
- If we change who will be our new competitors?
- How can we be effective in relation to these new competitors?
- Where will our competition be coming from in 5 years' time, 10 years, 20 years?
- What does this tell us about our Business Idea?
- What new Distinctive Competencies will we need to develop?
- What transitions will we have to make?

After having analysed each of the important competitors in the context of the Business Idea the discussion may be summarised by creating a table with competitors listed vertically and Distinctive Competencies laid out horizontally. Each of the boxes should be considered and where it is felt that a real threat exists this should be annotated, e.g. with a "W" for weak; a "SS" for strong, short-term; "SL" for strong, long-term. In this way the company team analyses the really crucial competitive questions around their basic formula for success at a holistic level, and can debate:

- Are our Distinctive Competencies really unique?
- Do competitors pursue the same or different ones?
- Could our Distinctive Competencies be under threat from existing or new competitors?
- If so, what do we do about that?

Viewing the competition in such broad terms encourages rethinking of the nature of one's business and the strategies being pursued.

SUMMARY OF MAIN POINTS OF COMPETITIVE POSITIONING

At the end of the Competitive Positioning discussion the management team will have considered some or all of the following:

- Identification of main customers, and reframing of the business definition based on the "competitive moment of truth" question.

- Identification of main competitors, not only existing but also potential competitors and others competing for the overall margin and profit potential.
- Analysis of the main cost drivers and the position of the main competitors along this dimension.
- Competitor response profiles.
- Competitive overview indicating the main areas of threat to the Company's Business Idea.
- Learning from best practice, both in and outside the industry.

The result of this analysis should give a much better insight in the strength of the company's Business Idea. This is based on a system of Distinctive Competencies, and the question of distinctiveness can only be tested vis-à-vis the existing and potential competition. It is likely that following this analysis, the management team may want to revisit the Business Idea to incorporate the lessons learned from the competitive analysis.

Chapter Ten

Scenario Development

In this chapter we assume that the scenario planner has developed the scenario agenda — areas in the outside world that need to be looked at in the scenario project — preferably based on a series of in-depth open-ended interviews and anchored in an articulated and carefully tested Business Idea representing the organisation's success formula. The attention now turns to the outside world in which this Business Idea will have to perform.

We have argued that a productive scenario planning project must under all circumstances remain relevant to the client. The specific scenario agenda will ensure that this is the case. On the other hand not much is gained if the client's thinking is not changed by the process. This means that the client needs to find in the scenarios an element of novel thinking in areas where they are concerned and anxious. Having set the scenario agenda the next task facing the scenario planners is to develop new insights in the indicated areas. While sticking to the agenda new thinking needs to be developed on the agenda themes. This is known as the "knowledge development stage".

SCENARIO TEAM

Developing new knowledge on the basis of the identified scenario agenda is an activity for a scenario team. The selection of the team members is important. Scenarios are multi-disciplinary, and this should ideally be reflected in the composition of the scenario team.

Team members need to be able to suspend disbelief, think the unthinkable, and let intuition and premonitions flow freely. Therefore a necessary skill in team members is tolerance for ambiguity. The collection and development of outside knowledge needs to be approached open-mindedly. During the "opening-up period" team members must be open for any surprise. This means that they must learn to take what they observe at face value, refraining as much as possible from putting a structure and judgement around observations they make.

The team's task is to look for rich data about the external environment, that might illuminate the agenda. A successful team will develop novelty in their thinking. The most important challenge in this work facing the scenario planners is to find the optimal balance between:

- Relevance to the client.
- Novelty.

INTRODUCING NOVELTY

The client interviewees will be the first to provide a lot of ideas and insights. Obviously the client will have thought a lot about the business situation and therefore there will be a lot of rich information to get. However, as we saw scenario builders use the client's agenda as a starting platform only, from which they need to take things further to produce a product which is successful as reframer, idea generator and testing device. The scenario planner needs to try to find new ways of conceptualising the agenda area. Although the "maverick" view in the client team is helpful here, normally the search for innovative thinking needs to take place outside the organisation.

How does a scenario team go about creating novelty in their scenarios in areas relevant to the client? Where does one start? In principle there are many ways of going about attempting to discover new insights, including reading and carrying out original research. But experience is that the practical way of doing this is through interaction with people who combine expertise with innovative insights, i.e.:

- who have studied areas specified in the scenario agenda, but
- who are not normally part of the organisation's network and therefore can contribute original insights.

The challenge is to identify such centres of knowledge in the indicated agenda areas. Literature research may be a way to start. The team is looking for those experts who are not in regular contact with the client organisation, such that an original contribution may be expected. These are known as "remarkable people", experts who can produce an insightful "aha" reaction for the client. A typical remarkable person is a professional observer of an area identified in the scenario agenda. They could be academics, commercial researchers, writers, artists, consultants, or perceptive business people. An organisation that has institutionalised its scenario planning will maintain a dynamic list of potentially useful "remarkable people". Whenever a scenario project is undertaken and the client's scenario agenda is identified, the list is consulted for possible candidates for the remarkable person role.

At this stage the scenario team splits up in sub-groups, each dealing with one or two scenario agenda themes. The job to be done entails:

- Finding the remarkable person.
- Introducing him/her to the issue.
- Eliciting a first contribution, possibly in the form of a written paper of what the expert believes can be contributed.
- Followed by a workshop in which the expert is confronted with members of the scenario team and the client organisation.

Participants to these workshops should prepare themselves by studying the issue area, doing their own reading and should internalise the report by the expert. On the basis of this a discussion is held in which the new and unexpected views of the remarkable person are elicited, challenged and developed. Capturing of the conversation is once again crucial to retain views as they emerge (and otherwise quickly evaporate) in the give and take of the discussion.

Typical questions for discussion includes:

- What is happening that matters/could matter?
- What is the relevant system to study?
- What is the appropriate level of "granularity" (detail) of observation?
- What are other ways of looking at this?

Through such contacts it is not difficult to source the new ideas required.

The scenario planner needs to refrain from structuring the information obtained while this search is going on, to avoid closing the mind to further new and unexpected promising lines of thought that might present themselves. This is not an easy thing to do as it often leads to a feeling of information overload. However, scenario planners need to remember that creativity at the time of scenario development requires a degree of overload. They need to develop a tolerance for this. It is helpful if scenario planners set themselves in advance a clear date on the calendar when search stops and structuring of findings will start. Before that date the discipline should be maintained that everything will be considered as potentially worthwhile.

All this makes it all the more important that members of the scenario team train themselves to record any findings, however seemingly small and insignificant. All members should carry a field note book with them, in which observations are noted down. It has proven useful for scenario planners to regularly take time off to annotate what has been written down to ensure that the crux of the observation is understandable later on.

Practice has taught that instilling a note taking discipline in a scenario team is one of the most difficult things to manage. Scenario planners, beware!

DEVELOPING THE SCENARIOS

Overview of the scenario building process

The scenario team should set themselves a clear date on the calendar when searching for new knowledge stops and structuring starts. This date needs to be set in relation to the delivery date of the scenarios as promised to the client.

So far the scenario team has developed a considerable amount of data pertaining to the future. They have surfaced the perspective of the client interviewees, and explored novel ways of looking at it, through the eyes of the remarkable people consulted. They may now feel a degree of overload, with many ideas concerning the scenario agenda requiring attention, without any significant structure so far.

The next challenge is to find a suitable structure in which all this seemingly unrelated data can be expressed, contextualised and thereby made operationally useful to the user, for the purpose of idea generation and testing of policy ideas and strategy. This is akin to an artistic task. McLuhan once suggested that "for the artist, information overload becomes pattern recognition. What the average person sees as increasingly unmanageable complexity, the artist sees as a new figure/ground relationship, and tries to get that into a form the average person can cope with." This task description is not far from what the scenario planner needs to achieve at this stage. Ted Newland, one of the people working with Pierre Wack, sees it as follows: "If you want to get answers frustrate very intelligent people and they will find them. In scenario planning, if you frustrate people for a few days the subconscious takes over and you awake to find the scenario is there. The subconscious is more powerful than the conscious mind. However, it will not intervene until it has been frustrated". Tolerance for overload will help in dealing creatively with the task of scenario conceptualisation.

The main decision to be made is how to create the necessary structures around the data collected. This will determine which data will be put in which story, and how these data will be connected up. This means that we have to decide on how many stories we will tell, and what will be the organising principle of each story. It means that we have to cluster the data down to a point where no further category reductions can be made. At that point the irreducible categories become the organising principles of the scenarios.

How can this category clustering be done? There are a number of principles we can bring to bear on this process:

- At least two scenarios are needed to reflect uncertainty. More than four has proven organisationally impractical.
- Each of the scenarios must be plausible. That means that they must grow logically (in a cause/effect way) from the past and the present.
- They must be internally consistent. That means that events within a scenario must be related through cause/effect lines of argument which cannot be flawed.
- They must be relevant to the issues of concern to the client. They must provide useful, comprehensive and challenging idea generators and test conditions, against which the client can consider future business plans, strategies, and direction.
- The scenarios must produce a new and original perspective on the client's issues.

Except for these general rules the scenario planner has flexibility in deciding how the stories will be built, what ends up in what story, and what organising principles will be applied to cut up the territory into individual story-lines.

We will discuss various ways of processing a large collection of unrelated data and ideas into such scenarios. Some are more formal than others. But in any scenario project the tools are there to help, they should never stand in the way of intuitive leaps of imagination in the scenario team. Our process suggestions should be taken in that spirit, use them while they feel useful, but if you have an another idea feel free to follow that.

Scenario structuring mostly takes place in workshops, which ideally should take place away from the daily workplace. A typical workshop requires the scenario team to work together for a period of two to three days as a first step. This may be followed with further more focused workshops of shorter duration as required. At this stage no outsiders are involved, only permanent members of the scenario team. The team should also arrange for a more permanent central recording workroom, with plenty of display wall space where progress in thinking is recorded and displayed for all team members to inspect. This should be available to them until the end of the structuring phase.

FIRST DATA ANALYSIS

Initially collected ideas tend to be highly unstructured across a large spectrum of levels of conceptualisation, something often found in a typical brainstorming situation. The first task is to create some degree of overview of what initially seems chaotic.

For this it is necessary to perceive the connections between variables and data in the total system (surprises often arise from seeing a new interconnectedness in the system). This will lead to understanding of the driving forces in the system. Soft data will prove as, if not more, important than hard data.

Once again graphical techniques can be of considerable help here. A simple approach based on the use of Post-it displays has already been discussed in the interview analysis paragraph of the chapter headed "Setting the Agenda", page 137. At this stage the purpose of this technique is to cluster ideas and arrive at a smaller number of higher level concepts, which can be related to each other.

A good point to start is for the team members to write down, in bullet form, points of learning and discovery obtained during the knowledge development phase. If the team has been disciplined in note taking this should be a simple, albeit laborious step, which each of the team members undertakes individually, possibly even before arriving at the workshop. Once again text on each Post-it is limited to not more than (say) eight words, which should be legible from a distance.

During the workshop each of the team members puts up the Post-its they have developed, in no particular order, while explaining the short labels to the other members of the team. When all team members have done so the job is to try to find logical clusters by moving the Post-its in the display space. Once again there are no rules on what constitute suitable clustering criteria. Clustering may be based on patterns, cause and effect, association etc. However, at the end the team should have created a limited number of clusters, which logically contain the elements put into it, while being clearly distinguished from the other clusters. A good test whether a suitable result has been achieved is if the clusters can be given clear short names, indicating that the clustering criteria that have emerged can be articulated.

Each cluster in turn should now be studied in some depth. The purpose of this step is to identify driving forces. A driving force is a variable which has a relatively high level of explanatory power in relation to the data displayed in the cluster.

HISTORICAL STUDY

Part of the work at this stage should include analysis of the historical behaviour of important variables that the knowledge development stage has thrown up as potentially interesting. It is useful to look back as far as the scenarios will look forward, to ensure that these will constitute a seamless continuation of history and present trends.

This continuation depends on the interpretation put on historical developments. For this reason a set of different scenarios can be seen as a set of different interpretations of what is happening in the present (see also Figure 14. Scenario building framework). Earlier (page 100) we discussed the example of the interpretation of economic difficulties. If these are seen as an economic recession the scenarios will show a recovery in the not too distant future. On the other hand, if economic problems are attributed to decline of the indigenous manufacturing industry, due to low wage competition from newly developing countries, activity will stay at a low level in the medium term future.

Historical research needs to find such possible interpretations, which are the basis of the continuity in the scenarios. Therefore the analysis needs to be in some depth, and should consider such factors as typical rate of change, major driving forces, elements already "in the pipeline" and cause and effect relationships. Typical questions raised at this time include what are the key driving forces and causal relationships in the system, which forces can be predicted to be there in the future, and what are the important uncertainties about the future. From time to time the question needs to be raised: "What are other ways of looking at this?".

Activities the team might engage in during this stage:

- Listing the key patterns and trends.
- Mapping of causal relationships in influence diagrams.
- Listing of the underlying driving forces.
- Ranking of driving forces by unpredictability and by impact on the strategic agenda.
- Listing of the candidate branching questions.

As a result clear and deep understanding needs to be developed of how the system works and might work. This will include a list of predictabilities (predetermined elements) and key uncertainties (branching questions) in the system.

DRIVING FORCES

In Part Two we described the "Iceberg" analysis, a method for understanding the underlying structure of the situation by inferring patterns and trends in the events which are observed. By documenting such a discussion in the form of an influence diagram this underlying structure can be surfaced.

This starts with the articulation of a number of key variables, considered important for the situation being considered. The next step is the development of simple influence diagrams around these variables. Kemeny, Goodman and Karash (1994) suggest that this step can be facilitated by first drawing diagrams illustrating the nature of the variable's trend over time as observed. There should be no attempt a this stage to quantify, only the nature of the movement should be shown (up, down, stable, cycling etc.). While addressing the question why these movements might occur the influence diagram is drawn up. Initially this will bring in new variables into the discussion. This may trigger further ideas about what might be important. Therefore the list of key variables is revisited, and the process repeated.

As an example, assume that an issue has been raised around a place of instability somewhere in the world. The scenario team would become interested in discovering some underlying structure in what is actually going on there. The first task is to surface events and trends in events in what's happening. Then they need to look at the events, and try to establish a trend over time in some of the underlying variables. For example they might be looking at the development of violence. They may decide that they can see a trend which can be expressed in a graph of how violence is changing over time. Let us assume that it is increasing.

The next question would be "What other events do we see there that might in some way or other be related?" Ideas come to mind, media coverage may seem important, the economy plays a role and so on. What would be the relation with media coverage? Someone might argue "More cameras mean more violence". What would be the relation with the economy. How do we express economy? Someone might suggest "level of personal income". Other ideas for related variables might include government control, with government interference in the economy seen to be on the increase. These could also be expressed in simple graphs against time.

In this way trends emerge and while the team are discussing these they start identifying certain elements of structure. For example the idea that media coverage means more violence is an element of structure, a cause/effect relationship. They now could start drawing an influence diagram in which media coverage contributes to violence, indicated by an arrow from one to the other. Another variable identified was the economy. Someone might suggest that performance seems to deteriorate and the suggestion presents itself that this might be related to violence. Low incomes might increase violence. Another suggestion was government interference. This raises the question whether this is a cause or an effect. Someone might suggest that violence leads to polarisation in society, which leads to state repression. Meanwhile it might be suggested that foreign investments might suffer,

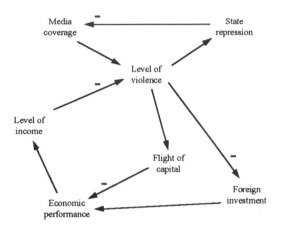

Figure 26. *Starting an influence diagram.*

which drags down the economic performance. If violence increases that may well lead to a flight of capital, causing further economic deterioration. What emerges here is known as a positive feedback loop, which underlies all growth phenomena. At this point an interesting influence diagram starts emerging (see Figure 26) representing an upshot of the discussion so far.

At this point someone might want to bring in history. For example the suggestion might be made that historically people resort to violence because groups become threatened by sudden change: But with change the problem may move over time from one group to another. "It's group A who are now creating the violence, whereas previously it was a different line of violence, triggered by opposition to the then status quo. There's a difficulty there with one straight line indicating violence, while we are looking at two violent groups following each other in time. They are not one phenomenon. You cannot explain all violence in terms of the causes presented so far, whether it is media coverage or economy. The earlier deaths occurred when there was less media coverage, they have to be explained by a different group being violent for different reasons. It is more complex that you have it so far".

And so the diagram grows and insights develop.

The example illustrates the three levels at which we can look at the world. At the event level we talk about the occurrence of violence. By plotting the number of deaths we defined a variable and we looked at a trend. Every trend implies a variable. While we were doing that we started to map out the underlying structure by seeing patterns. By looking for patterns we discovered that looking at violence just as one statistic was too simplistic, we needed to look at different groups at different times. While going down the iceberg the quality of the discussion improved significantly. This is what is meant by identification of driving forces. It involves moving from events through the trend and pattern stages into the structure, to identify the forces that fundamentally affect the situation.

Following the interviews with clients and remarkable people and the historical studies the scenario team have collected a data set which contains elements at all layers. At this stage the team needs to move down into the structure part of the iceberg and discover something of the more permanent structure of the situation. The task is basically to express events in terms of trends and patterns and to explain these in terms of structure in influence diagrams, leading to an understanding of ultimate driving forces.

The above example illustrates the use of an influence diagram, see Figure 26, in which variables are linked by arrows indicating the influence they exercise on each other. Variables that play a central role in such a system are likely to be driving forces. The example above shows how, in order to develop such an influence diagram from a cluster, the analyst distinguishes events from variables. Variables should be capable of going up and down over time, check whether you can put "the level of" or "the extent of" in front of it. The analyst tries to identify trends over time and expresses this as variable behaviour over time. An explanation is then sought for these trends. Why would variable X be going up, and Y going down? Such explanations provide insight in what is driving what. Once this has been established another link in the diagram has been uncovered. The activity is continued until everything in the cluster has been accounted for.

For example a scenario team was discussing whether demand was an appropriate underlying driving force. One of the members suggested that demand might be driven by technological development, which would therefore be a more basic driving force. In order to consider this suggestion the team came up with a simple influence diagram as shown in Figure 27. Having considered the structure of the influences identified the team decided that it needed to consider both

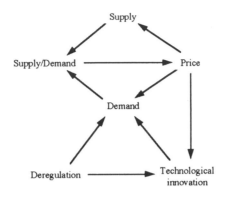

Figure 27. *Example of a driving force analysis.*

technological development and deregulation as independent driving forces in the analysis.

In summary, systemic analysis of the surrounding world looks at the situation in steps:

- Break down the database in events, trends, patterns and structure.
- Specify the important events, the things we can see.
- Discover trends, time behaviour we observe in the events, leading to the conceptualisation of variables.
- Infer patterns, based on cues for causality applied to variable behaviour.
- Develop the theories, which connect the system together through causal links (multiple structures will be required, resulting from different possible interpretations of causal patterns).
- Use the theories to project future behaviour (with multiple structures leading to multiple scenarios).

GRANULARITY OF THE ANALYSIS

A significant challenge in this work is hitting the right level of granularity in one's analysis. The team are looking for a general pattern which can be developed into an explanatory theory (or one out of a number of alternative possible theories) of driving forces explaining how things work in general. It is not very clear how the human mind recognises these patterns, it is largely based on intuition. Slowly, while working with the data collected an ad hoc model is taking shape of how driving forces might produce the data. This activity can be aimed at an inappropriate level of amalgamation. For example "overfitting" the pattern on specific data must be avoided. It's easy to fit the data perfectly, but that makes it difficult to generalise, and the key is to generalise. One must lean towards a fuzzy fit of a somewhat imprecise generalisation, with enough validity to be useful in understanding underlying structure. On the other hand, if events are amalgamated at too high a level the structural relationships between patterns of behaviour may prove too ephemeral.

For example a scenario team may conclude that explaining the pattern of world-wide demand for gold pitches the analysis at too high a level, providing little evidence of causal relationships with other variables. On the other hand explaining the demand for gold at the level of every individual gold buyer will not develop a theory general enough to use for scenario building. The analysis has to be pitched somewhere between these two extremes. For example the scenario analyst may decide to break down the world-wide demand into a few categories, including use for technical, adornment, investment and monetary purposes. At this level it may become possible to start seeing some fuzzy relations with other variables, which can be extrapolated.

The process is essentially one of trial and error, trying various levels until one finds relationships which seem to be sufficiently firm to indicate underlying driving forces. The hard part is keeping it simple. And as we have seen, the more complex the problem, the simpler the causal models that prove most useful.

SCENARIO STRUCTURING

So far the scenario team has collected the basic data from which the new scenarios will be constructed, and structure has been put into these by clustering and categorising and by a search for trends and underlying causal structure. The next step is to create a limited number of scenarios in which the insights gained can be reflected. As we discussed in Part Two, story lines are an efficient medium through which ideas across many disciplines can be linked in context. The process we have described so far has ensured that the totality of the data available at this stage are highly relevant to the client and also contain an appropriate level of novelty. The purpose of the next step is to develop a number of internally consistent story lines which project as much as possible of the learning obtained in the project so far. There are a number of ways in which this can be achieved, which we will subdivide into inductive, deductive and incremental methods.

In the inductive method the approach builds step by step on the data available and allows the structure of the scenarios to emerge by itself. The overall framework is not imposed, the story lines grow out of the step by step combining of the data. In the deductive method the analyst attempts to infer an overall framework to start with, after which pieces of data are fitted into the framework, wherever they fit most naturally. The difference between the inductive and deductive methods is between letting the framework emerge in the process of building stories from the data upwards, or deducing a framework from the data as a first step.

A third way of developing scenarios I call the incremental method. This approach aims lower and is useful if the client team still needs to be convinced that the scenario approach offers an opportunity to enhance the strategic conversation. In situations where scenario planning is not yet embedded in the thinking style of the organisation the client team may still be strongly attached to an "official future", a shared forecast that is implicitly the basis of all thinking about strategy. For such a client the first steps on a scenario planning road are easier if the official future is used as the starting point, from which the scenarios make excursions into surrounding territory.

The degree to which the three methods produce similar or different scenarios depends on the clarity with which the team has come to see the main uncertainty bifurcations in the future. If there are only a few major overwhelming uncertainties the three approaches tend to produce similar results. Pierre Wack put it like this: "Good scenarios just emerge from an intensely experienced polarity." If the team does not have this clear understanding of the main uncertainties facing the client it may be advisable to spend more time discussing the findings and the underlying structure to try to develop a better insight in the crucial driving forces in the future.

INDUCTIVE SCENARIO STRUCTURING

Inductive scenario structuring can be done at the level of events or at the level of structure. At the level of events the understanding and new insights gained by the scenario team are turned into illustrative events. Each of these are recorded on an event card, with annotations for possible timing and actors involved. Cards also show clearly whether the event is seen as predetermined or as one pole of an uncertainty (see Quinn & Mason 1994). Predetermined events need to end up in all scenarios, while uncertain events are included in only one. If events contain predetermined elements as well as uncertainties this is reflected by representing them in multiple event cards. For example if it is considered predetermined that OPEC will set a production ceiling, but it is uncertain at what level that will be, then more than one card is generated, for example one with the ceiling set at 30M barrels per day and one at 35M barrels per day. The team then needs to make sure that one of these cards is part of each scenario.

The next step is for the team to start building scenarios from the events generated by putting them in time order. Some cards are bound to form a natural cluster while others seem unconnected. In that case the team will start different scenarios, so that both can be accommodated. The jigsaw puzzle is finished only when all cards have found a natural place in one of three or four scenarios. The team invents new events and generates new event cards while it is allocating events to scenarios in order to create connections and overall logic. This is necessary to ensure that the final scenarios all meet the requirement of internal consistency, i.e. events should naturally follow from each other. This will be indicated by the team by drawing causal arrows between event cards on the display board. In this process the events come first, the logic follows from putting them in time order, and implying causal relationship. After a number of iterations this tends to produce satisfactory scenarios which reflect team learning during the earlier scenario process. When the team members are satisfied that no further progress can be made the scenarios are named and an overall logic is inferred from the story lines generated.

The inductive method can be applied at the level of logic. In this approach understanding gained during the preparatory phase is expressed in bits of logical relationship. The vehicle used is a short part of a story, connecting up a few events through a cause and effect relationship. These have become known as "snippets". They are often generated by interpreting influence diagrams developed by the team. So a typical snippet might indicate that the level of inflation affects the level of business confidence, which in turn affects the level of investments. Or a level of cash generation beyond absorptive requirements would lead oil producers to reduce production levels, which would increase the price. The activity of generating snippets usefully alternates with alternative expression of the situation in influence diagrams, in an iterative process. This type of approach requires sufficient time to be spent on the prior analysis of data, and the articulation of driving forces.

Once diminishing returns are reached in this the snippets developed are written on cards. The next step is for the scenario team to allocate these cards to three or four piles, on the basis of intuitive clustering. Once this has been achieved each of the piles are sorted and turned into an overall story logic. This is achieved in the same way as in the event method, by implying a time dimension and sorting the cards accordingly. In the process of doing so new events or snippets may be generated to make the story hang together better. For example inspired by the inflation snippet someone might suggest: "Let's assume that inflation goes up". Over time this then leads to lower investment and recession, according to the relevant snippet. Someone might suggest to link in the OPEC snippet. If demand goes down then production goes down, cash generation falls below requirements, and the pressure is on to produce. This has the interesting effect of lowering prices, reducing cash generation further. In the longer term lower energy cost will lead to reduced inflation, and recovery in the consuming countries. In this way snippets are chained together into story lines. The approach differs from the event driven process, in this case causal logic generates events, rather than the other way around.

While the inductive method is capable of producing powerful scenarios the team needs to be on guard for the in-built danger that the scenarios end up in a "good/bad mode". There seems to be a natural tendency for developments considered favourable for the client to end up in one scenario and unfavourable developments in another. This is highly undesirable and significantly reduces the value of the scenario exercise in the application stage. A basic tenet of the scenario planning methodology is that all scenarios are equally plausible. The best set of scenarios contains only futures which the client will find worth preparing for. If some scenarios are experienced as too unpalatable for the client to contemplate, or too rosy to be credible, the team needs to make another iteration with this requirement in mind. As a general rule the team should avoid thinking in terms of good or bad futures, see page 109. Only plausibility and internal consistency should be the yardstick.

Following is an example of inductive scenario construction. In it Adam Kahane describes a project with a group of political leaders in South Africa (Kahane 1992b).

Some South African political leaders have been struggling recently to find common languages with which they can talk about the future. In 1991, an economist at the University of the Western Cape named Pieter le Roux wondered if scenarios would help, and he invited me to facilitate a project. Scenarios were well-known in South Africa because during the 1980s a scenario exercise led by Clem Sunter, a senior executive at the Anglo-American Mining Corporation, with important help from Pierre Wack, had played an influential role in building public discussion about the future of the country.

This project would be different. The scenario team was to include 22 members from across the spectrum of South Africa's diverse constituencies. The multi-racial group included left-wing political activists, officials of the African National Congress, trade unionists, mainstream economists, and senior corporate executives. Our purpose was to investigate, and hopefully develop, common mental models about the future of the country. When we started, many people in the group were pessimistic; they expected to spend the meetings in endless dispute, unable to agree on anything.

Because of the charged political atmosphere, a "visioning" exercise might not have worked here. In fact, at the first meeting I said, "We're not going to discuss what you would like to happen. We're going to discuss what might happen." This turned out to be a liberating choice of words. If I had asked what future they wanted, each participant would have pulled out their party platform. In the end, the process did produce a scenario they all preferred, but they would never have got there if we had started by looking for it. Instead, we were looking for a common understanding.

We started with an exercise that made people realise that they couldn't predict what would happen. Dividing them into sub-groups, we asked them to come up with stories of what might happen to South Africa, seen from the vantage point of 20 years in the future. When we reconvened in plenary, we had 30 scenarios to consider. During the presentations, no one was allowed to say, "That's a stupid story," or, "You shouldn't be saying that." I allowed only two types of interruptions: "Why does that happen?" and "What happens next?" If the presenter couldn't answer those questions then they had to sit down; the story was no good.

It turns out that this is a great exercise. People came up with all kinds of wild stories, including stories inimical to their own interests. For example, one left-wing sub-group proposed a story called "Growth through repression," suggesting that South Africa might have a tough authoritarian left-wing government. Another story suggested that the Chinese government would provide arms and support for a Communist liberation movement, which would overthrow the government. I don't know whether it was originally proposed seriously, but when people asked, "Why does that happen?" there was no way to substantiate it. So it fell by the wayside, almost immediately.

The rest of the whole exercise was a narrowing process – pruning our scenarios from 30 down to three or four "useful" stories. To be useful, they had to be logically consistent and plausible, which are difficult criteria to meet. But the discussion of plausibility and consistency was very good for this politically charged, diverse group.

Then we asked, "Which of these stories are useful to tell to an audience?" In other words, what did participants believe our audience needed to think about? In our plenary group, after much discussion, we narrowed our selection down to four distinct stories, all focused on the nature of the political transition (perhaps the most important single uncertainty in the country), and all named after winged creatures. As I write this, in summer 1993, all four are still plausible.

The first was called "Ostrich". The De Klerk government "sticks its head in the sand". Some path other than a free election occurs. White segregationists gain in influence, as do extremist black groups; they stop communicating, and polarise the country. "Eventually, the various parties are probably forced back to the negotiation table," said the group's report, " but under worse social, political, and economic conditions than before." This doesn't work very well: it might lead, for instance, to civil war.

The second scenario, called "Lame Duck", envisaged a prolonged transition with a constitutionally weakened transitional government. Because the government "purports to respond to all, but satisfies none", investors hold back, and growth and development languish amidst the mood of long, slow uncertainty. This was an important scenario because many people expected a coalition government to form, and now they could see the potential dangers.

The third, called "Icarus," ended up being the most influential. Originally proposed by some of the black left-wing members of the team, it suggested that a black government would come to power on a wave of public support and try to satisfy all the promises it made during the campaign. It would embark on a huge, unsustainable public spending program, and consequently crash the economy. For government and business observers, the existence of the Icarus scenario was a reassuring phenomenon, but it also influenced the policy debate on the left. For the first time, a team which included prominent left-wing economists discussed the possibility of government trying to do too much. This was hopeful, because only by discussing a potential catastrophe can you prevent it.

"Flamingoes" was the most positive of the four. Like Lame Duck, it concerned a coalition government, but this was a good coalition. The name was chosen because flamingoes rise slowly, but fly together. In this scenario the economy gets no kick-start. There is a long, gradual, and – most importantly – participatory improvement, with all the diverse groups in the country "flying together". Because the scenario process keeps asking what would have to happen for each future to take place, the group emerged with a sense that this optimistic future, in which economic growth and political equality reinforced each other, was possible.

By the standards of Shell, these were not very deep scenarios; they had little research or quantification behind them. But their significance came from the fact that they were arrived at collaboratively by a very broad group. All members of the team endorsed all of them - not as desired futures, but as valid mental models for how the future might unfold. When they present the scenarios to other groups and forums, they all stick exactly to the basic points, even in cases where they disagree with the formulation. This has made the presentation of the scenarios enormously effective. When the scenarios are presented to an ANC audience, for instance (nearly always by presenters who include an ANC-affiliated member of the team), it provides a non threatening way to bring up the unpalatable message of "Icarus" – that a crash public-spending program might not work. The Lame Duck scenario gives the National Party audiences a way to confront the dangers in their inclination to encumber the transition process with safeguards, and the Ostrich has a similar message for the conservatives.

When the team came together, they had no common view on the difficulties of transition. By arguing over the distinctions between Lame Duck and Flamingoes, what distinguished Lame Duck from Flamingoes, they came to a common view, on a moderately detailed level, about some of the problems around limiting the power of the transitional government. I'm sure that very few of them, before the meeting, had considered the question of macro-economic constraints on a newly elected government. Now, through the Icarus scenario, they are deeply familiar with it.

You may wonder what keeps people, in these highly charged meetings, from walking out. Conservatives and radicals kept coming back because they felt they were learning a great deal – and enjoying themselves. The advantage of scenarios is that, unlike in a negotiation, people don't have to commit their constituents, but they can see a common language – a common way of understanding the world – emerging fairly early in the process. Once the scenario process is over, that common language should make subsequent negotiations easier to conclude successfully.

This exercise has made me hopeful about the use of scenarios as a foundation for collaborative action, especially among people who are enmeshed in conflict. As writer Betty Sue Flowers put it, "In a scenario team, you develop two or three different pairs of glasses to see the world through. You can put them on and off, and by doing that, it gets easier for you to see the fourth and fifth way."

DEDUCTIVE SCENARIO STRUCTURING

The deductive methods aim to first discover a structure in the data to be used as a framework for deciding the set of scenarios to be developed, rather than let the scenarios emerge from it as in the inductive methods. The resulting framework identifies the scenarios in the set by means of a few crucial descriptions, such as end-states (state-of-affairs in the horizon year, described in terms of the key dimensions). Having established the basic nature of each they are then filled in from the data available or even from new data as required. Trying to name the scenarios at this stage with one or a few words expressing the basic nature of the story line is an effective way to test that the team has reached consensus on what this basic structure is.

The framework is developed by study and manipulation of the data in a few stages:

- Grouping of data in a hierarchical structure.
- Identification of high level orthogonal (mutually independent) dimensions at event, trend or structural level.
- Ranking these on the basis of predictability and impact on the client.
- Selection of the most important as structuring dimensions.

The process starts with grouping the data hierarchically, in a similar way as the interview data are processed (see Interview analysis, page 151). Each insight gained during the research period is summarised in a few words on cards or Post-its. The next step is clustering of these notes. The process alternates intuitive clustering with testing of clusters on mutual independence and internal consistency in an iterative way, until every insight has found a natural place in the context of all other notes.

From this point onwards the structuring process can be conducted on the basis of events, trends or structure. Most scenario teams will want to try all three approaches to see which one produces the most insightful framework.

If the event approach is followed the team now needs to decide on a limited number of key events which will have overriding influence on the future. It is often helpful to express these in an event tree, if decisions logically follow from each other. An example are the Mont Fleur scenarios discussed above, where the group agreed that three events seemed to be of overriding importance:

- Will a power-sharing agreement be reached between the parties?
- Will the transition of power take place quickly or will the process of transition get bogged down?
- Will the new government follow sound economic policies, or will it be more populist?

As shown in Figure 28 the resulting four scenarios can be structured in an "event tree":

- If no agreement was reached the "Ostrich" scenario would unfold.

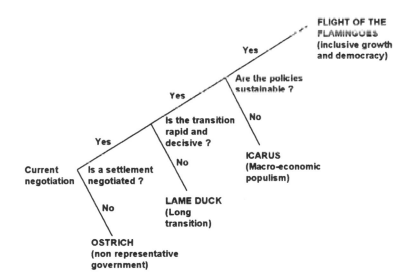

Figure 28. *The "Mont Fleur" scenario structure.*

- If the transition got bogged down the scenario was called "Lame Duck".
- If the policies were populist the "Icarus" scenario showed quick development followed by collapse.
- If all these hurdles could be taken the future would develop in the "Flight of the Flamingoes" scenario.

In this way a sensible scenario framework can be derived from key events, depending on how these play out one way or the other.

However, it may not always be possible to find a limited number of key events which have such overriding influence on the future. In that case the team may wish to look for key trends. If the structured data show a few key trends which may compete for dominance in the future the scenario framework may be based on these. An example of this approach is the 1989 Shell scenario set (Kahane 1992b). Having clustered the data as discussed above the team concluded that developments seemed to fall into two natural clusters, based on economy and ecology.

Popular opinion seemed to indicate that developments in both of these areas could reach serious constraints, which would have major repercussions on the way the future would play out. Parts of the new international economy were clearly developing outside the control of the traditional national control mechanisms; as a consequence overheating could develop out of control, and the world might end up in a depression, to recover from the consequent collapse. On the other

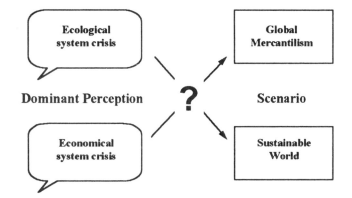

Figure 29. *The scenario matrix.*

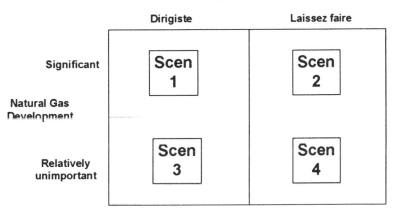

Figure 30. *Scenario structure, based on dominant trends.*

hand society was becoming more and more aware of ecological limits, and this might lead to priority being given to restructuring action, with the possible effect of diverting the economic crisis. The team concluded that if the ecological trend dominated, attention would move to restructuring of global governance systems, creating significant new investment levels, and leading to the economic confidence being maintained, or restored. But if the economic system hits its limits first, a serious recession would push ecological considerations to the background. As a consequence a framework results (see Figure 30) in which two scenarios are indicated, depending on which trend dominated perception in society. The dominant trend would create the scenario driving force, pushing the other into the background to become relatively insignificant.

The third deductive approach is based on identifying two or three key structural variables or driving forces, on the basis of which the scenarios will be distinguished from each other. Expressing each of these driving force variables in terms of two opposite ways in which they could play out in the future will then create a 2 × 2 (or 2 × 2 × 2 in the case of three driving forces) matrix, indicating four (or eight) scenario end-states as candidates for the scenario set. This approach is only practical if two or three overwhelming driving forces can be identified, as with any more the number of candidate scenarios multiplies exponentially. This means that the team needs to delve deeply into the structural "iceberg" of the data to define those elements that really matter for the future in terms of only two or three driving forces. An example of this approach is given by Wack (Wack 1985a) for the French energy business in 1965, when every future uncertainty seemed to be dominated by the two crucial variables:

- The future of the government regime vis-à-vis the industry ("dirigiste" or "laissez-faire")
- The possibility that nationally significant indigenous natural gas reserves would be found (subsequently answered in the negative).

The 2 × 2 matrix is shown in Figure 29.

The choice of the key driving forces takes account of their potential impact on the client, but should also take account of their relative level of uncertainty. If a dominant driving force is predetermined it does not distinguish the scenarios in the set. Because of the way that orthogonal uncertainties "add up", uncertainty in the future tends to be dominated by only a few key variables which we have called the driving forces. If everything else is equal it is those more uncertain dimensions that are most effective in distinguishing the scenarios from each other. Therefore the discussion on which variables should be used as distinguishing driving forces takes account of both impact and level of uncertainty, and we are looking for those which are most impactful and least predictable. A useful way to structure this part of the discussion is by using the impact/predictability chart, in which potential candidates are located depending on how the team ranks these on the two characteristics. As we are looking at relative notions here (everything is important, but some things have more impact than others, everything is unpredictable, but some things are more predictable than others) the axes are moved until roughly similar numbers end up in each of the quadrants. The dimensions we are looking for have to be found in the more impact/less predictable corner.

The next step is for the scenario team to fill in the detail in each scenario, and to create a story of how the end-state is reached from the current state of affairs, through a series of events, with one leading to another over time. A story line needs to be developed, based on a cause and effect logic. One way to achieve this is by translating research data into illustrative events, and to record these on event cards, as discussed above under the inductive method. In the deductive method the basic scenario structure has already been decided, and event cards are allocated to one of the different scenarios where they seem to fit most naturally. Following that the team arranges the cards in time order, to create the story line, filling in new detail wherever this is helpful to create a satisfactory story.

The more successful the team is in identifying truly orthogonal scenario dimensions the more successful they will be in developing a scenario framework which will allow them to encapsulate the findings from the scenario research process. This will allow the team to better explain their findings and show new ways in which history and present developments can be interpreted. This will help the client to get on top of the business environment through reframing of traditional mental models, and to test, and if necessary challenge, strategic plans for the future.

The way scenarios are developed deductively, through the selection of key scenario dimensions, helps in avoiding scenarios in the "good/bad mode", but it can still happen. Therefore the same test needs to be made as indicated for the inductive approach. If it is found that the scenarios call up very different value judgements (positive or negative) in the client group it is worthwhile to make another iteration with this criterion in mind. All scenarios should reflect worlds in which the client would want to live and be prepared for.

AN EXAMPLE; INDUCTIVE AND DEDUCTIVE METHODS COMPARED

How can we organise and govern ourselves successfully in a world of rapid change and increasing interconnection? In 1993 a group of senior Canadian public servants and private-sector executives got together to discuss this area of concern. They decided to adopt the scenario methodology to structure their conversation. After inviting a number of interesting people to discuss the theme with them, they met for a workshop for the purpose of structuring their findings in a few scenarios. They invited Adam Kahane to facilitate the activity. The following description is an excerpt from Steve Rosell's account (Rosell 1995)

> After an initial introduction an essentially inductive process was adopted to develop a set of scenarios for how the information society might shape the environment for governance over the coming decade. Prior to

the workshop, we had worked in smaller groups to identify some of the major certainties and uncertainties in how the environment for governance might evolve. Early in the workshop we reviewed the reports of the small groups and synthesised these.

Then, working individually, we were asked to write snippets, short causal sequences describing how various of those key elements might develop. An example of a snippet: education focuses on information technology skills $\rightarrow$ surge of young people entering information industries $\rightarrow$ Canada becomes key player in software. We were encouraged to write the snippets in telegram style.

The next step was to break into 3 small groups, which worked to combine the snippets that their members had produced into several longer story-lines. Those were given a name and presented to the plenary session.

We then worked together, in plenary, to organise these bits of story-lines into an initial set of scenarios. Each of the snippets was written on a yellow adhesive Post-it note. The story-lines were constructed by stringing together sequences of these notes. As the story-lines were presented in plenary and then developed into first-cut scenarios the walls of the meeting room soon became covered with large and lengthening streamers, snippets becoming story-lines, becoming scenarios.

In that plenary discussion a generally positive scenario began to be developed, build around such story ideas as a wired world, a new economy and the global teenager, along with a largely negative scenario based on unemployment, social unrest and disintegration. There was also a generally positive middle-range scenario that started to emerge around a combination of reconstruction of the social contract, shared transfer of wealth, life-long learning and world institutions for the environment and peacekeeping, while a more negative mid-range story started to emerge around increased polarisation, the lack of shared myths and identity and decreasing legitimacy of opinion leaders in all sectors. At a number of points in this discussion a participant suggested a possible structure to order the stories that were emerging, but none at this stage received general consent.

The process of combining and recombining the story-lines and arguing which made the most sense, and which structures to differentiate the scenarios might be most useful, was complex, fractious, generally good-humoured, frustrating, stimulating and often chaotic. The pivotal moment came when one member suddenly saw a new way in which we might structure the scenarios we had been developing: "It seems to me that the starting point of all these stories is that the information society changes the world. Then there are two dimensions that basically define the scenarios. The first is whether we have economic growth or not, and the second is whether we have structural change or not. So in the first scenario information technology changes the world, we do have economic growth, and we do make structural adjustments. The result is the scenario built on 'Wired World' and 'New Economy'. In the second scenario information technology changes the world, but we don't get economic growth and there is no structural change and the result is a 'Dark Age' scenario. In the third scenario information technology changes the world, we do get economic growth but we don't get structural change, and the result is a 'Social Fragmentation' scenario, disparity increases, the rich get richer and the poor get poorer. And in the fourth scenario information technology changes the world, but we do make structural changes and the result is a very Canadian form of muddling-through."

Amidst the general agreement that greeted this insight there was a sudden spark of recognition among some members. Some weeks earlier three of us had been reviewing the findings of our first several meetings and trying to determine, through essentially a deductive process, what scenarios it might be possible to derive from that complexity of information. That deductive process had begun by noting that in our discussion of the information economy two polar possibilities had been on the table for the development of the economy over the next decade, either:

- we learn how to use the new technologies to their potential, and embark on a new secular boom, or
- the structural changes in the economy produced by the information age produce persisting unemployment and low or no growth (as conventionally measured)

Similarly our discussion of the social and cultural dimensions had defined two polar possibilities, either:

- we manage to find a way to construct a new social consensus, appropriate to the information society, that rebuilds social cohesion and renews the social contract, or
- we face continuing and accelerating social fragmentation and disparities, as the realities of the information age undermine our ability to construct a shared perspective.

These two sets of possibilities, while necessarily over-simplified, had illustrated different ways in which the information society could shape the environment for governance over the next decade, through the changes it might produce in our society and economy. The next step in our deductive process was to try to interrelate these two dimensions. We constructed a matrix with society on one axis and economy on the other, to illustrate the possible environments for governance that might result from an interplay of such social and economic changes.

But once we had constructed this matrix we did not know what to do with it, and whether there were viable scenarios that could be devised to fill the various cells. So we had put the matrix aside and did not circulate it. Now, as one of the members presented this structure to the workshop, we all were struck by the degree to which the scenarios, which we had constructed through the inductive process of the last days seemed to fit within the matrix that had been developed deductively earlier. Somehow, the inductive and the deductive routes had led us essentially to the same destination. With this striking realisation, and with the basic structure for differentiating the scenarios now agreed, we broke into four syndicates to develop each scenario further.

THE INCREMENTAL METHOD

In situations where scenario planning is well established the deductive and inductive methods are the preferred approaches. They offer the best opportunities to bring the new thinking that the scenario team has developed to bear on the strategic conversation. However, not all client teams are always quite ready for this approach yet. For example, in a situation where scenario planing is just being introduced the client team may still have to be convinced that it offers an improvement over the traditional forecasting method, and that it is cost effective. Very often interest in the scenario approach will have been created by means of a "challenge scenario" (see page 217), but there may still be a strong attachment to the shared forecast of the business, the "official future". A lot of time will often have been invested in this and once it has been accepted as the agreed plan, people who want to open this up again are not always welcome. This is the world of management as described by Lindblom (page 33) where decision making is a negotiative business, and where people are expected to stick to an agreement. Mavericks are not welcome here.

The scenario planning team needs to tread very carefully here, if they want to avoid being rejected altogether. In such a case the incremental method may be indicated. This takes the official future as the starting point. The team will first of all try to identify flaws in the official future. This often does not prove too difficult, as forecasting methods do not force analysts into in-depth analysis of driving forces. The team will then develo alternatives which convincingly challenge the official future. Or the team will develop scenarios as excursions from this. Superficially what the scenario planners are doing may look to the clients as what they will know as "sensitivity testing". However, the scenario planners will make sure that there is a fundamental difference, namely that alternatives will not be conceived as variations in business variables, but as variations in underlying driving forces, and that each scenario will be conceived as an internally consistent story on that basis.

The first step in this approach is for the scenario team to analyse carefully the official future scenario. Specifically the team needs to establish the degree to which this can be considered as internally consistent. This requires two specific analytical jobs:

- Trend analysis. In this step the analyst tries to identify any trends in a direction that can undermine the structure on which the forecast is based, such as the existence of a breaking point or threshold in that trend. Such breaking points, where trends cross "fracture lines" can therefore be written up as branching points. They can be thought of by considering similar events in the past and/or by extrapolating trends implied in the official future further out into the future, until they clearly hit such fracture lines.
- Actor logic. In this step the most important stakeholders in the official future are identified, and the forecast is analysed from the perspective of each of these. The question here is whether the forecast is consistent with the logics of the actors in the game.

If the official future violates the requirement of internal consistency in either of these categories, the first alternative scenario will be an adjustment to the official future which addresses this problem.

The team then follows the deductive approach up to the point where the Predictability/Impact matrix has been completed. At that point a ranking will be made of the high impact, but unpredictable driving forces, using the need to project these in the organisation as a criterion. Alternative scenarios are designed, each of which incorporates an alternative way in which one of these key driving forces could play out.

SELECTING AN APPROPRIATE METHOD

How should a scenario planner choose between the three methods available? Which approach is appropriate in which situation? In addition to personal style of the facilitator, and time available for the project, diversity of thinking and tolerance for ambiguity in the client group seem to be important. The deductive method offers a more codified step-by-step approach than the other methods. If time is at a premium it has distinct advantages. Also if the client group thinks cohesively, and has difficulty in widening thinking its more regimented nature helps to force the thinking into new areas. Generally if it becomes necessary for the facilitator to force the pace it offers advantages.

If a cohesive group does not accept the more regimented approach of the deductive method, and wishes to take its own time to explore the situation step by step the incremental approach is indicated. Often a team has developed a shared understanding of the environment and feels an intuitive reluctance to open this up for scrutiny. In this situation the thinking process needs time to evolve. The pace cannot be forced using the incremental method. It does not do well if there is only a limited amount of time available for the scenario project.

A divergent client group, or a group with a high degree of tolerance for ambiguity often does well with the inductive approach. The method exploits the diversity in the group to the maximum, and enriches the scenarios by providing scope for a wide range of views to be incorporated. Groups that have difficulties compromising and coming to joint conclusions often do well with the inductive method. However, the method, if done well, cannot be forced, and suffers under time restraints.

In many cases facilitators use more than one approach. Often client teams started off on the incremental or inductive methods run into time constraints, and switch to the deductive method to finish the job. Or teams working through the incremental or deductive methods may halfway decide to take stock of the range of thinking in the team by doing an inductive scenario exercise. Switching of methodology during the project can enrich the process, and should be considered an option by the facilitator at all times.

DEVELOPING THE STORY LINES

With the general scheme of the scenarios now established the team needs to turn its attention to fleshing out the story lines. The ultimate product needs to be a set of scenarios that compellingly transfers to the user the important discoveries the scenario team has made. The stories need to be provocative, memorable, eliciting a rich imagery. The task before the scenario team is to find a way to develop the most interesting and enlightening stories. Scenario planners should feel free to engage their own creative talents to do this as they see fit. Interest and memorability derives from originality which should have free rein.

A story needs to have a beginning, a middle and an end. A number of points need to be kept in mind while this task is being carried out:

- The scenario is a story, a narrative that links historical and present events with hypothetical events taking place in the future. In order to establish plausibility each scenario should be clearly anchored in the past, with the future emerging from the past and the present in a seamless way.
- Each scenario must elicit a *gestalt*, an integrated structure that must be apprehended as a whole rather than as disconnected parts. The basic logic of each scenario should be capable of being expressed in a simple diagram. Similarly the fundamental differences between the scenarios should be equally transparent.
- Internal consistency implies that each story is based on an underlying structural (mostly qualitative) model. Creating this in the scenarios is facilitated greatly by the use of influence diagrams discussed earlier, to establish and develop the causal train of events in each scenario.
- Agreed predetermined elements need to be reflected in all scenarios.
- Key variables need to be quantified and leading indicators listed.

Within these limits there is significant room for artistic inspiration in the scenario team. It is often helpful to consult professional story writers. A clear influence diagram of the underlying principles involved can be extremely helpful in fleshing out the story line into an internally consistent result.

TESTING FIRST GENERATION SCENARIOS

One of the most demanding requirements of the scenario process is ensuring that story lines developed are internally consistent. As soon as scenarios are used for testing strategic projects any consistency weakness will quickly emerge as a major obstacle to their effective use. At this stage of the process this still needs to be tested, as internal consistency may be violated by an element of logic that has so far escaped the attention of the scenario team. For this reason the scenarios developed so far, either through the inductive, the deductive or the incremental method, are called first-generation scenarios, subject to further consistency testing.

The two most important internal consistency tests are the following:

- Quantification of the scenarios.
- "Actor-testing" of the scenarios.

Detailed quantification is often not required by the client, if the scenarios are intended for future exploration or if strategic plans are still qualitative, and if activities are difficult to capture in numbers. In other cases, in particular where scenarios are used to "windtunnel" strategies and project proposals, quantification is often required. But even where the client organisation does not require quantification the team may wish to do some on their own accord, as it is a worthwhile discipline to check for internal consistency. Quantification brings into play many causal models that may not have been on the agenda as yet. Through quantification the new scenario logics are tested against traditional quantification models, and discrepancies will almost always surface. It is important that the scenario team identifies these discrepancies and decides whether or not these are a deliberate part of the story line. Some of these may not have been foreseen and require thinking through. It is almost invariably the case that even the most logical narrative will require some adjustment if numbers are applied to the developments in the story line. If time and resources can be made available quantification proves useful in the majority of cases.

Actor analysis surfaces inconsistencies by confronting the internal logic of the scenarios with our intuitive human ability to guess at the logic of the various actors in the game.

Actors/stakeholders around a strategic issue can be sub-divided in a number of categories, as defined in Figure 31.

The contextual environment is populated by "referees", i.e. actors whose stake in the situation is such that they cannot be influenced by individual players, including the client organisation.

Subjects cannot influence the situation and could be ignored, unless this is objectionable for ethical reasons. Another reason to consider subjects is that they might create coalitions through which their power increases and they gradually move over to the category of players.

Players require our attention, as they are in a position to influence what will happen, and they have a stake in the outcome, and will therefore be active.

In the "actor test" the team first identifies the most important actors in the business environment considered. The next step is to classify them according to the categories of Figure 31. Following this the team are particularly interested in the category "referees". The task is to test the scenarios against the logic of each of them. The team puts itself in the shoes of each of these actors in turn and then, in this role, walks through each of the scenarios, checking whether the detail of the story line is consistent with the behaviour that might be expected from the actor considered. Almost invariably in this process a point will be reached where the team has to admit that a particular actor will find it very difficult to live in a scenario without taking some action which is not part of the scenario and therefore invalidates it. This is an important discovery, at this point the team learns something important about the future that would otherwise not have surfaced.

Further actor tests need to be made in the other three boxes, to ensure that no individual actor can logically invalidate the scenarios developed.

An example is reported by Pierre Wack in his article on the development of scenarios about the future oil price (Wack 1985a), in which testing of first generation oil demand scenarios against the

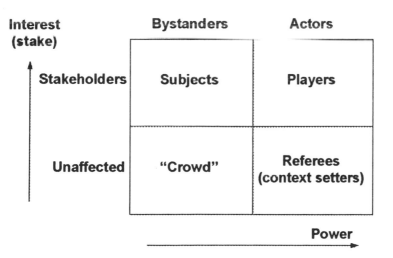

Figure 31. *The actor/stakeholder matrix.*

intuitively plausible logic of oil producing countries identified such a possible discontinuity. It was shown that a situation could arise where producers would start to question the wisdom of ever-increasing production levels as required, increasingly beyond local absorptive capacity of the funds generated. This discovery identified the need to test strategies against a possible supply crisis, where producers would no longer meet demand, which therefore would outstrip supply, resulting in oil prices shooting up. This seemed to indicate a strong reinforcement of the initial decision not to meet all demand. Having identified the possibility and the self-locking nature of such a crisis, the team then analysed its dynamics, and identified the conditions under which it might happen. As we saw, this discovery allowed Shell to prepare themselves for such an eventuality ahead of most of its competitors in the industry.

Actor-testing of scenarios is a crucial part of any scenario building process, and should never be left out.

SPECIAL TYPES OF SCENARIOS

The structured approach to scenario construction as discussed here aims at serving the general strategic needs of the organisation. However, from time to time the scenario team may have a number of more limited specific objectives. There is often a need to project a specific message in the organisation (or to management), and scenarios may be an effective way of doing so. Three examples of such specific use of scenarios are discussed here:

"Surprise-free" scenarios

From time to time a scenario team have to come up with scenarios which are considered by the client as challenging. This often happens when the client team are not well experienced in the use of scenarios, or where they do not have much experience with discussion of strategic issues in general. If a client is used to thinking in terms of a one line future the idea of challenging scenarios can be daunting. Particularly when members of the client team have their own strategic agenda and are used to dealing with each other in an "advocative" mode the introduction of new ideas in scenarios may be difficult.

In such cases it has proven useful to include in the set of scenarios one that represents the common traditional wisdom of the organisation, a scenario which will be recognised by everyone. This is the "surprise-free" scenario, based on a business-as-usual world which can anchor the set of scenarios in the belief system of the decision makers. This "link with the old world" serves as a basis of recognition of change and can be helpful as a platform from which to develop the more challenging futures.

"Challenge" scenarios

Working through a surprise-free scenario may look simpler than it often is. What scenario teams often find is that the "business as usual" outlook is the result of inertia and not of detailed analytical work. As a consequence serious analysis often reveals the inconsistencies in the set of beliefs which together make up the official future. People may be making assumptions in different parts of the business that, if put together, will be seen as incompatible. Or by carefully considering the underlying structure of the situation the team may develop an understanding of predetermined elements or structure which are ignored in the "official future". If the scenario team finds this situation to prevail it needs to make itself heard. A useful technique is to produce just one challenge scenario, which through its internal logic exposes the flaws in the conventional wisdom. The message the team puts across is the following: "The organisation is assuming both *A* and *B* at the same time. Did you realise that for both to happen the following conditions need to be in place?" The challenge scenario then describes a more consistent set of conditions, taking account of the structure and the predetermineds in the situation. It is up to the client team to decide whether this is a plausible development or state of affairs. If the scenario team are proven right and the client accepts that an alternative view of the environment is urgently required the discussion then needs to move on to the development of a full scenario set as a basis for an evaluation of strategies, policies and plans as currently pursued.

Challenge scenarios generally are useful if the scenario team have made a discovery which is important enough to pass on to the client team as quickly as possible.

"Phantom" scenarios

A phantom scenario is a further development of the challenge scenario. It is a useful device if the scenario team finds that the client team strongly project ideas which are simply infeasible. Rather than attacking these ideas straight on, or developing a challenge scenario in which the team tries to create a logical alternative framework, it is often more effective to develop the unlikely scenario in which these ideas would be valid. The aim of the exercise is to make the intellectual authors of these assumptions consider the logical consequences, in order to suggest that these may not be the ideal planning basis.

SCOPE OF THE SCENARIO PROJECT

Strategy projects

So far the discussion has focused on exploration and strategy design. These tend to be the biggest and the most visible scenario projects. Particularly if the project is aimed at reviewing the entire Business Idea and business plan of an organisation elapsed time can run into months. Scenarios developed in this mode have a "shelf-life" problem. A tremendous amount of work is done, a great deal is learned, but the value of the scenarios themselves often vanishes within months, as they are rarely used again after their initial life in the strategy project. For this reason most scenario projects are of a much more modest scale, and aim at thinking through a particular strategic question or concern. Or the project may be initiated to help in a particular strategic decision. Such projects can be conceived at any level of sophistication, from a three-month-long exercise down to a two-day workshop. A typical satisfactory focused scenario project would involve introductory discussions with the client, discussions with two or three carefully selected "remarkable people", a two-day scenario structuring workshop, and a short scenario write-up, and would take a couple of weeks to complete. This would be followed by a discussion with the client team in a workshop on scenario "windtunnelling" of possible options for the decision to be made.

Scenario projects are often identified with the very large global scenario research projects that large organisations engage in. This is not necessarily the most effective use of the methodology. The most successful scenario projects have been focused and as a consequence modest in effort and expense. The crux of the matter is to introduce multiple futures thinking in the strategy area where forecasting is counter-productive. The scale at which this is done is a secondary issue.

Project development

Many focused scenario projects are developed in the context of more or less precisely defined business projects. Many corporate decisions are made around projects; and global or overall strategy scenarios don't always address the issues involved. In the final analysis it is the client who decides the focus of the scenario exercise. If the client is responsible for a project then the scenarios developed should be project scenarios.

Scenario planners who listen carefully to their clients do not have a relevance problem. However, many scenario planners find it difficult to make the client's concerns the focus of the planning project, particularly if they are convinced that the client focus misjudges the situation. This is a potentially dangerous state of affairs. It has been shown time and again that a scenario planner who goes his own way, however right he may prove to be later, will produce a product which is received as irrelevant and therefore has no impact on organisational decision making. Relevance problems occur frequently but are unnecessary, if only the scenario planner can adopt a "client service" approach.

Short-term/tactical decision making

There is no time constraint on where scenarios are useful. The criterion whether scenarios can help in short-term decisions is related to the degree of uncertainty against predictability in the decision situation. In many organisations long-term strategic work may be inappropriate, particularly if short-term problems are faced which threaten the continued existence of the organisation. The message for this often comes from the financial markets. In such a situation a point may be reached where long-term implications have become irrelevant, and everything needs to be focused on survival in the short term. It is important for scenario planners to be able to recognise such a situation. This is not always the case. A typical complaint by scenario planners is the following: "We write scenarios about trade and values and politics, then the financial markets push into a company with their point of view and careful thinking is out the window". The answer to this problem is the same as for projects: The client is the referee. If (s)he thinks short term we need to make short-term scenarios. Scenarios are made to help the client, so the scenario planner needs to address his/her anxieties.

In every scenario project there is some scope for initiative from the scenario planner. As long as the client anxieties are taken as the starting point, the scenario planner can introduce novelty in the direction (s)he considers necessary or desirable. For example if the planner's conclusion is that the thinking is too short-term, and that there is some scope for longer-term considerations, then there is no reason why the scenarios should not be stretched in this direction. But to stay effective this needs to be seen as an extension of the client's needs, not as a separate starting point for the exercise.

A related problem may arise if there is a discrepancy between the time horizons of top management and operational management. In such a case it is often found that the scenarios developed for top management are considered of little use to the operators. In this case the need arises for reconciliation of the long term views with the operators' short term views. This need is not always recognised down the line. The culture may not yet be ready for integrated scenario thinking. The best the scenario planners can hope to do is to be as persuasive as possible in their presentations of the long-term scenarios. Meanwhile top management needs to consider the various aspects of the institutionalisation of the scenario thinking culture (see Part Four). The first thing to do is to let it be known that the organisation is moving towards a strategic management style, and to insist on discussing decisions in a strategic context. Consistent signals from the top in this connection are crucial for success (see page 244).

Having said this it would be unrealistic to expect that operational management will eventually be able to develop their strategy on the basis of the same scenarios as top management. The coal face and top management need their own focus in their scenario projects.

Crisis management

Many organisations have made arrangements to deal with unspecified emergencies as these may arise. These normally entail ensuring that the appropriate personnel is involved, that communications are established and that requisite information is passed around to the parties who need it. Such arrangements often involve physical facilities, e.g. for communications, as well as the people involved in crisis management. Once such systems have been put in place these need to be tested, and the people involved need to be trained, such that when the crisis arrives they have a readily available set of schemas according to which they will be able to act. These objectives are achieved by running simulations of real emergencies in which the system, including its human component is tested out. The testing of crisis systems by simulation involves scenario planning. This is a typical example of the "windtunnelling" principle, as explained on page 57.

The problem facing the crisis management scenario planner plays clearly in the S area of Figure 13, page 92. Therefore the design of the scenarios follows the same principles as any other scenario project. Ideas on what might happen need to be generated, the structural connections between the variables involved need to be established, and scenario dimensions need to be ranked on impact and predictability. On the basis of this a number of scenarios need to be designed which are reasonably representative of what might happen. Once again, plausibility and internal consistency are important.

Scenarios in crisis simulation should confront the participants in the simulation with what might happen, in order to develop desirable behaviour in the crisis context. Therefore the simulation must be as close as possible to plausible realities, and must "feel" realistic. For this reason the scenarios need to be worked out in a lot more realistic detail than is usual in strategy projects. Most of the scenario projects in crisis management involve creating a realistic interface between the imaginary outside world of the scenario story and the participants in the exercise. Crisis management scenario projects tend to be manpower and time consuming.

Exploration (consensus building) scenarios

At the other extreme some scenario projects are undertaken to make exploration trips into an unknown future. In these cases the focus is somewhat blurred, the client does not want to set too much of an agenda, but to explore widely in a broadly defined territory. There are no particular decisions on the agenda, no particular threats to react to, the client simply wants to explore possible futures.

Exploration scenarios are often used when individuals in a group of people look at a situation from different perspectives and come to different descriptions of the essentials of it. Particularly when the group is charged (or charges itself) with a degree of responsibility for the situation, it may find that lack of consensus stands in the way of joint action. This situation often arises outside the organisational context if groups of people without formal power (or who have suspended power for the purpose of the exercise) get together to attempt to pursue a common objective. An excellent example are the Mont Fleur scenarios as discussed on page 199.

In a situation where participation is voluntary by participants who are potential competitors the scenario planner needs to tread carefully to arrange the project in a way in which participants do not feel in any way threatened by the discussion. In politically difficult situations trying to develop a common policy may be counter-productive, exploration may be the only and most productive objective the group is able to pursue.

In any situation in which the project is threatened by political tension the danger is that scenarios are used to enhance personal power; or are defeated when someone's personal power is threatened. In those circumstances the scenario planner should ensure that any decision making is clearly not on the agenda, and that the rules of the game ensure that it cannot creep in. If decisions can be avoided the scenario approach becomes powerful, as it allows all participants to project their views in one of the futures discussed. The awareness that one's own view is clearly "on the table" enables people to pay more attention to other views being expressed in the group.

The approach adopted by Kahane for the Mont Fleur scenario project is a good example. He asked all participants to invent scenarios, which they subsequently were asked to explain to each other, but under the following rules:

- No evaluative comments allowed in any way.
- Only two questions allowed: "Why would this happen?" and "What happens next?"

The underlying idea is that people are prepared to accept that internal logic is a reasonable requirement for joint exploration. Common ground can be built on the general acceptance that stories that lack internal consistency are not worth pursuing.

One requirement which can sometimes be relaxed in exploratory scenarios is that the client organisation should avoid playing a role in its own scenarios. As the exploratory scenarios are specifically not being developed as a testbed in a decision making process this discipline is less important. In such cases it is acceptable to divert to normative (good/bad) scenarios. The idea that the group could come closer together on what is considered "good" and "bad" is often one of the objectives aimed for.

In this situation it is worthwhile to consider from whose point of view this judgement is made. For any consensus to emerge there must be a common underlying world view that the group can appeal to in order to come to agreement. So for example, if a group of public sector organisations are fighting over a housing strategy, strenuously defending their own turf, appeal can be made to general societal values. Even if the housing department is at loggerheads with the social benefits department, they may eventually agree that it would be worthwhile if something constructive could be done to relieve deprivation in the inner city. Therefore the norm implicit in the normative scenarios must be aimed at this level of shared world view. A normative scenario project can bring this out, and demonstrate that there is this deep shared vision among the political combatants.

However, if this proves difficult, in a politically highly charged situation, it may be advisable to stay away from the client's own strategy, to avoid charging the scenarios with political value which may irretrievably divide the participants.

Morale building projects

Scenarios are sometimes used as organisational "cognitive behaviour therapy". In organisations that have gone through traumatic experiences, such as severe and ongoing downsizing, morale often has to be rebuilt. A typical indication of a "worried organisation" are people talking among themselves interminably about problems or unpleasant events in the past or anticipated in the future. The worrying group will in their conversation move from one calamity to another in a never ending procession, with a lot of repetition. The process is difficult to stop, the group is its own prisoner. They are motivated to continue this conversation, based on people's belief that rehearsing scenarios makes them more resilient to possible dangers. Conditioning takes place, as the worst scenarios imagined do not happen, so the worrying seems to pay off.

A powerful remedy is to "give permission" to problems and dangers without translating these in interminable internal dialogue. One way of doing this is for management to suggest that people engage in facilitated scenario discussions, which provide plenty of room for the pessimistic futures, but which are structured such that more positive outcomes also have a chance. With some more positive scenarios becoming part of the shared futures people will gradually start seeing events and signals indicating more positive developments.

Chapter Eleven

Option Planning

The learning loop is not closed until we have addressed the need to translate new insights into actions. Actions result from decisions taken by the people with the power to act. We need to consider how decision making takes place in the context of a scenario planning approach.

DEVELOPING STRATEGIC DIRECTION

Scenarios can address the basics of strategy through two categories of questions:

- The internal perspective, is our organisation equipped to survive and flourish in any of the multiple equally plausible future environments we may be facing (organisational capability)?
- The external perspective, are we developing our business(es) in the right direction, considering the sort of organisation we are and the environment we may encounter (business portfolio)?

The direct application of scenarios for strategy design addresses these questions in four steps:

- Capability review.
- Portfolio review.
- Strategic option generation.
- Strategic option testing.

The dialogue in all these steps is essentially about the ability of the organisation to survive and grow. The issue raised at this point addresses the question whether this organisation is wellprepared to face the uncertainties of the future as portrayed in the completed set of scenarios. Scenarios as a representation of the outside world need to be confronted with an equivalent representation of the organisation itself, out of which strategic conclusions emerge. The strategic dialogue requires a language, in which the essence of organisational capability and success can be expressed. As we have seen, the concept of the Business Idea serves this purpose. The Business Idea expresses the basis of the organisation's overall competitive strength and growth principle.

In the chapter Articulation of the Business Idea (page 159) we have described how a Business Idea can be developed in a management team, and we have seen how the contextual environment scenarios provide a testbed on which it can be tested. Opportunities and threats can come from many directions, including societal trends, technological development, political developments, economics, environmental concerns, etc. They can also arise from competitive imitation. Significant potential developments in these areas need to be reflected in the scenarios. Having used the current Business Idea in the scenario agenda setting exercise will ensure relevance, as its most important aspects will have been consciously addressed in the scenarios.

By running the Business Idea through multiple futures the team discusses whether it will stand up across the range of what might happen and in this way acquires a comprehensive overview of potential threats against it. Testing the Business Idea against the various scenarios involves the team in considering the performance outlook for the Business Idea in each of the scenarios in turn. The team mentally walks through each scenario one by one and decides in each case:

- The extent to which the Business Idea continues to create customer value/cost leadership.
- The competitive threat to the system of Distinctive Competencies identified.

Specifically the following questions should be raised:

- Will our system of Distinctive Competencies continue to be socially efficient? Will there be continuing demand for our current offerings, and for any new offerings we are planning to introduce. Will we be able to continue to exploit the competitive advantage we derive from our system of Distinctive Competencies?

- Will our system of Distinctive Competencies continue to be defensible against competitive onslaught? How can we continue to protect its systemic uniqueness? What are the continuing barriers to entry in this future?

Having considered these questions for each scenario the management team will develop a view on the overall strength of the organisation, and a conclusion will emerge on the resilience of the Business Idea against the uncertain future.

The discussion then moves to the options this opens to the organisation. If the conclusion is that the Business Idea is weak the team needs to turn its attention to the question of how to make it stronger. This leads to a discussion around the capabilities of the organisation, resulting in the generation of Capability Options. If the conclusion is that the Business Idea is robust and will stand up under a range of futures, the primary task becomes finding ways of extending the range of its exploitation. This leads to the generation of Business Portfolio Options.

A more detailed discussion of important points in these stages of the strategic conversation follows.

BUSINESS ACTIVITY PORTFOLIO

The review of the Business Idea against the scenarios may bring the client team to the conclusion that it is strong and will stand up robustly against the whole range of futures as we can see them.

If the conclusion is positive the basic question then becomes how we can exploit the Business Idea and its positive feedback loop in the future business worlds as portrayed. This requires the development of a portfolio of businesses realising the Business Idea in the real world. Before discussing potential new additions to the business portfolio in the light of the scenarios the management team needs to review its existing business portfolio along the following guidelines:

1. If a business unit is directly related to the overall Business Idea it needs to be justified through
   - identification and confirmation of its embedded Distinctive Competencies, and
   - synergy with the rest of the business.
2. If a business unit is unrelated to the overall Business Idea it needs

to be justified on the basis that

- it is successful in its own right, and
- it offers opportunities for Distinctive Competencies to be integrated at some future time.

If these conditions are not fulfilled, the business under consideration has no relation to the Business Idea and is an isolated activity to be judged on its own merits. It does not form part of this analysis.

The next step is to consider new options. This can be attempted in a management team brainstorming session, but experience has shown that this tends to produce a somewhat disappointing result. It is normally more productive to assign the job of trawling for portfolio options to one of the managers. If the organisation has a Business Development manager (s)he is the logical candidate to co-ordinate this job. Otherwise the team needs to appoint one of the managers to carry out this task. The facilitator (as we will designate this person) needs to go around the organisation having in depth interviews with the business managers to explore ways in which the Business Idea can be exploited. This discussion can be based on the current portfolio as a starting point. From there the organisation has the following generic options to increase the portfolio through internal development, joint venture, acquisition or merger:

1. Inside-out focus (investments in organic growth):
   - Concentrated growth (expansion into similar markets adjacent to those already served).
   - Market development (investments in expansion of market share).
   - Product development (spreading the Business Idea across a wider range of products).
2. Outside-in focus (investments in growth through partnerships, joint ventures, mergers and acquisition):
   - Horizontal integration (expand into adjacent similar markets by mergers and acquisitions).
   - Concentric diversification (expand into different, but closely related markets by mergers and acquisitions).

It is useful to circulate this list of generic option categories to the interviewees in advance, to trigger thinking and help them to articulate any ideas that they may be able to raise. The list also serves as a trigger during the interview itself. Going around the organisation the facilitator gradually develops a list of potential business options. Recall that the management team had decided that the Business Idea was strong. It therefore will not be too difficult to find options for expansion.

Having gone through the organisation, and having checked back with each interviewee on "second thoughts", the facilitator writes an overview of the options available to the organisation, for feedback to the management team.

ORGANISATIONAL CAPABILITY REVIEW

The strength of Business Ideas deteriorates over time with the depreciation of their Distinctive Competencies. If the management team decides that the current Business Idea is less than robust it will discuss what needs to be done to protect it against serious threats, while, if possible, maintaining its upward potential. Through this discussion the management team may start to realise the fundamental weakness of the Business Idea, and the conclusion may be that changes are desirable. This raises the general question of what sort of actions management can take to develop an existing Business Idea. In thinking about this the notion of leveraging is useful. As we saw in the chapter "Building for the future", page 110, the important point to make here is that future distinctiveness cannot be bought, it can only be either:

- invented (discovered by luck?), or
- developed by leveraging existing distinctiveness.

Most management teams will be reluctant to plan only on the basis of serendipity. The leveraging concept therefore is clearly important. It is at this point that Capability Options become extremely important. These are options to develop the capabilities of the organisation, by leveraging Distinctive Competencies the organisation already possesses. One way of articulating these is by brainstorming in the team, but as we discussed earlier this tends to produce less than satisfactory results. People seem to need more time to think these issues through. Therefore, as discussed under Portfolio Options, it is advisable for a facilitator to discuss people's ideas one-to-one in individual interviews. The following generic categorisation of Capability Options can be used to trigger the thoughts of the business managers:

1. Inside-out focus (investments in organic growth):
    - Market development (developing new relational Distinctive

Competencies in the market).

- Product development (developing new generational Distinctive Competencies, leading to new product ideas).
- Innovation (Applying new combinations of Distinctive Competencies, changing the "rules of the commercial game").

2. Outside-in focus (investments in partnerships, joint ventures, mergers and acquisitions):
   - Vertical integration (buying competencies that leverage the existing Business Idea upstream or downstream of current activity).
   - Conglomerate diversification (buying competencies that leverage the Business Idea in new business areas).

The facilitator collects all relevant ideas from the managers and prepares a comprehensive report listing all Capability Options that seem open to the organisation. This is fed back to the management team for discussion.

Having decided on the various ways how the Business Idea might be modified to enhance the chance of success in the future, the modified versions are run again through all scenarios to consider whether a more robust situation has been obtained. The process is essentially iterative and continues until a satisfactory result emerges.

It may not always be possible to come up with ideas to redesign the Business Idea towards increased robustness. The conclusion may be that the Business Idea is weak, and that it will be difficult to strengthen it through development of new capabilities. In that case the conclusion may be reached that the portfolio may need to be reduced, and the following options considered:

- Reformulating of existing businesses.
- Concentration, through consolidation, divestment or abandonment.
- Liquidation.

OPTION GENERATION

The management team may find it desirable to meet to discuss potential Portfolio and/or Capability Options. Properly developed scenarios prove to be potentially useful triggers to generate ideas in such a meeting. The process requires the client team to imagine itself living in each of the scenarios in turn, and asking the question: "What would we want to do if this was how the real world would be developing, what would seem good business opportunities?". As we saw above (see page 124) the process cannot be rushed. This exercise requires a number of discussions in the management team, possibly organised as a series of workshops. Members need to prepare themselves by becoming familiar with the thinking embedded in the scenarios and with the ideas generated by the facilitator trawling throughout the organisation. Chances of success are improved if the meeting is well-prepared and facilitated, including capturing of the discussion on flip chart.

It has proven useful to organise the discussion at three levels in turn:

1. *At the level of societal value*, addressing the question of what the world at large, and specifically the organisation's stakeholders (including existing and new customers, competitors, employees, shareholders) will need in this specific scenario. Specify for each stakeholder what value changes are involved in the scenario. What are the new bottlenecks in the system? Who is getting squeezed? And what will they want to do about it? Identify for each value change the associated business opportunity. This discussion is crucial to set the appropriate context for option generation, and should not be skipped.

2. *At the level of strategic implications for the organisation.* Useful questions to assist this part of the discussion:
   - What is the degree of overlap between each of the identified opportunities and the Business Idea?
   - What are good things to have
   - What happens if the organisation does nothing
   - What happens if the organisation reacts optimally
   - What can be done now to be prepared

3. *At the level of strategic options.* As we saw (page 225) these come in two varieties:
   - Opportunities that can be readily exploited, portfolio options
   - Opportunities for further development of the Business Idea, capability options

One source of ideas are the scenarios themselves, but these are by no means the only source. Original ideas often come from elsewhere. It needs to be recognised that very few of the strategic options pursued by organisations are normally generated in formal management meetings. Specific ideas for Portfolio or Capability Options are continuously created throughout the organisation. The word "option surfacing" often better indicates what management needs to aim for at this stage than "option generation". Most ideas for options grow out of the general formal and informal strategic conversation that takes place in the organisation, both in meeting rooms but also in the corridors and over the lunch table. Scenarios come into their own if they can penetrate this conversation and help in giving it direction. A process is needed that can bring the discussion deep into the organisation. We discuss the institutional aspects further in Part Four of this book.

With options surfacing from many different sources the resulting overall list will contain ideas over a wide range of conceptualisation, from major restructuring to relatively modest actions to address hygiene factors. Before moving on to option evaluation, the management team will want to reformulate possible action options to a manageable number of genuine strategic options of appropriate weight. This can be achieved by clustering ideas together. The approach is similar to the clustering of ideas generated in interviews, see page 152. The clustering criterion is that two ideas belong together, if pursuing one logically requires serious consideration of the other. Each cluster represents a strategic option and should be given a suitable indicative name, under which it will be evaluated.

Having generated a set of ideas for enhancement of the business, and having reached diminishing returns in the creation/surfacing activity, management now needs to start thinking about making choices. Apart from triggering ideas scenarios also provide conditions under which these can be tested.

OPTION EVALUATION

The notion of option evaluation evokes fairly clear-cut schemas in the minds of most managers. This will include at least a financial assessment of the value of the option, possibly in terms of "pay-out time" or Net Present Value. One of the many plausible futures, somewhere in the centre of the field, will be chosen as a "base case". This single line future will be used as the input for the calculation of the future cash flow of the option under consideration. The option with the highest

Net Present Value, or the shortest pay-out time prima facie seems to be the one to be preferred.

In fact most managers would consider this approach somewhat simplistic, and would be looking for additional dimensions in which the options could be compared. The more thoughtful manager normally looks at least at four criteria for strategic choice:

- Financial performance.
- Risk across the range of uncertainty, i.e. evaluation across the full scenario set.
- Strategic fit, i.e. fit with the Business Idea.
- Organisational fit, which takes account of organisational and cultural factors.

However, this approach to strategic evaluation expresses a rationalistic decision making frame of mind. The more processually thinking scenario planner will think not only in terms of "choice", but will always be on the look-out for using the evaluation process to improve the set of options on the table. Whilst commitments have to be made from time to time, many parameters in the situation will remain open to further enhancement, until closure becomes advantageous at some future moment in time. The instinct of the scenario planner is improvement of options rather than closure of alternatives, until choice is absolutely inevitable.

Therefore scenario based decision making is philosophically different from traditional "rationalistic" decision theory/decision analysis. The latter aims to reason to a point where a proposal can be characterised as either acceptable or unacceptable. The assumption is that there is one ultimate right answer, and the purpose of the analytical work is to get as close as possible to that. The scenario approach is based on the assumption that every proposal has attractive and unattractive aspects, and that there are no absolute criteria to weigh one side against the other. The premise is that the future is uncertain in a fundamental way, and that beyond a certain point no amount of additional analysis will throw any further light on what might be happening. One needs to consider multiple futures, and one needs to consider these equally plausible. And in some futures the proposal may work better than in others. Decisions therefore always are compromises, capable of being improved upon at anytime.

Whilst ideas for specific options are generated by specific scenarios, the evaluation of each option needs to be done against the full scenario set. When this evaluation is made management does not know which of the multiple equally plausible futures will develop. The evaluation of options against multiple futures is known as "windtunnelling" of strategic options. The metaphor tries to put across the idea of the scenarios being used as test conditions for the assessment of the value of options. No design will be satisfactorily tested until the full range of conditions (the full range of scenarios) has been applied, see Figure 24, page 170. To ensure that option evaluation will be done against the full range of possible futures it is useful to draw up a matrix in which columns designate scenarios, and rows designate options, and intersection fields are used to score each option against each scenario (see Figure 32, scenario/option matrix.).

Most work associated with strategic decisions is concerned with redesigning proposals and options such that the upsides are maximised and the downsides are minimised. In the metaphor of the windtunnel, scenarios are the test conditions which bring out the strong and weak points of a proposed design. Possible strategies and business policies are the model to be tested. The purpose is to assess a proposal under a range of conditions which are representative of what could happen. The purpose is not primarily to decide between acceptance or rejection, but to work towards improving the proposal, such that

	Ostrich	Lame duck	Icarus	Flamingoes	
Withdraw	+		-	--	
Continue as is					
Short-term investments	-		++	+	
Long-term investments	---	--		+++	

Figure 32. *Scenario/option matrix.*

outcomes are as robust as possible over a range of possible futures. This is why it is important for the scenario planner to see all scenarios as equally likely, and equally valuable as test conditions. On the other hand test conditions must be appropriate for the model to be tested and modified. Therefore scenario projects are always customised.

A useful device in the "windtunnelling" exercise is the scenario-option matrix, with columns representing scenarios and rows representing options. Each of the options under consideration is evaluated for each scenario, and appropriate annotations are made in the boxes in the matrix showing the attractiveness of the option under those scenario conditions. Only a crude distinction is made in the table, by using evaluative words, colour codes, shades of grey, or symbols ranging from $+++$ through 0 to $---$. The matrix provides a quick overview of the degree of robustness of the options as they are formulated at that point in time. The main purpose of the scenario/option matrix is to instil a discipline to consider options across all scenarios. An example is shown in Figure 32. It is good practice to include the "zero" option in the table against which the other options are evaluated. In the example the zero line is the "continue as is" option.

STAKEHOLDER TESTING OF OPTIONS

A final check evaluates the strategies emerging from this process against the most important stakeholders and actors involved in it. In the same way as options were reviewed across the scenarios a similar exercise is now done across actors/stakeholders.

The matrix in Figure 31 categorises the main actors and stakeholders around a strategic issue. In the testing of strategic options we are particularly interested in the category of actors called "players". As shown in Figure 31 they are characterised as having both interest and power. The most obvious example are direct competitors. They are directly interested in the Business Idea of our organisation, and will consider the possibility of emulation if it proves successful. Options need to be evaluated against the possibility that the Business Idea might become ineffective through imitation by competitors. We discussed this earlier as the Devil's Advocate question. But other potential claimants have to be considered as well. These may include suppliers,

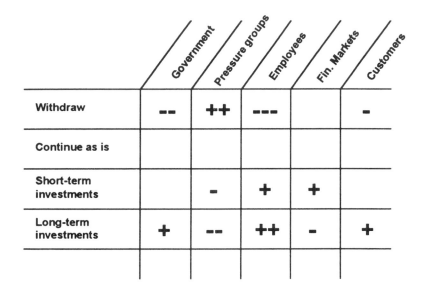

Figure 33. *Stakeholder-Option matrix.*

customers, new entrants etc. which need to be specifically identified. Will they act deliberately to sabotage or support the strategies the organisation seeks to play out? Once again it is useful to adopt a matrix approach like the evaluation of options against scenarios, in this case showing the options against stakeholders, with intersection fields used to indicate the reaction to be expected from the stakeholders concerned. Figure 33 is an example.

Once again the objective is primarily to attempt to improve the options considered, by making them more robust against possible onslaught of adversarial stakeholders.

In preparation for a discussion in the management team the options/ stakeholders matrix needs to be prepared by the facilitator, listing the real and potential players in the situation associated with each option. These have to be ranked in terms of their potential influence on the organisation. The facilitator needs to concentrate on the most powerful in the list.

The team discussion can be structured by going systematically through the option/stakeholder matrix, evaluating each intersection. For each option/player combination the potential reaction of the players is evaluated, and indicated on a scale from adversarial to supportive. In this way an overview is obtained of the area where further thinking and development is required. The facilitator then addresses the question whether the options which do not seem robust can be made stronger. Once again taking account of the whole portfolio of options while studying the possible improvement of one will help building the list of options gradually into one overall strategic approach.

INTEGRATION OF STRATEGY

The scenario planner thinking in terms of option development and improvement aims towards the development of one overall strategy out of all options on the table. The scenario-option and the stakeholder-option matrices help in guiding this activity. The main purpose of the matrix is not to make a decision on which option is preferred, but to obtain an impression of where work is still required in option development. For example, in Figure 32 a composite option which seems risky in one of the scenarios may do better overall if it is broken down in a number of steps, and only the first step committed to at this stage. A similar line of thinking is triggered by the options/stakeholder matrix. In this way the scenario planner works through the list until not much further improvement can be made. Some options will prove attractive across all scenarios, some will be less attractive in one, but at an acceptable risk, and some will show an unacceptable risk in one or more of the scenarios.

Once the scenario planner starts working on improving the downsides of the options on the table these often start to converge, and eventually many can be combined into a small number of more generically strategic options, or strategic directions. The process needs to continue until a small number of fundamentally different strategic directions are left to choose from. The scenario planner using the scenarios in the windtunnelling mode will find that strategy no longer constitutes "lists of things", but has grown into one holistic concept of "direction".

Part Four

Institutionalising Scenario Planning

OVERVIEW

So far we have discussed scenario planning and organisational learning as largely rational conversational processes in the management team. In this part we will discuss the institutional aspects of scenario planning. We will argue that the full benefits of scenario planning can only be realised in an organisation that has adopted scenario thinking as the dominant strategic thinking style. It has to become a cultural phenomenon that co-evolves with the quality of the decision making and institutional action.

Management can influence this, through a process that we will call the "management of change". The literature of change management has interesting things to say to the manager or management team wishing to introduce scenario thinking in the organisation.

Cultural processes depend on communication and networking. Attention needs to be paid to both the formal and the informal communication processes in the organisation. Culture often depends more on the latter. In the context of scenario planning we are particularly interested in the formal and informal "strategic conversation". It is the general conversational process by which people influence each other, the decision taking and the longer term pattern in institutional action and behaviour.

As we are discussing cultural processes, the introduction of scenario thinking is not something that can be "plugged in" overnight. It is only over a period of time that people start to realise that without it they are becoming more and more handicapped playing in the organisational game. Getting to this stage requires persistence and consistency on the part of management.

The introduction of scenario planning and thinking is a long-term project, not just a decision.

Chapter Twelve

The Management of Change

SCENARIO PLANNING AN INSTITUTIONAL PROCESS

So far we have discussed scenario planning as if it were an individual or small team activity. As Lindblom pointed out (as early as 1959) institutional decision making is a polycentric process. Significant decisions relating to strategy normally emerge from contributions from and interaction between many people. Even if the formal power to act is in the hands of one individual or management team the actual decision itself will have been influenced by many others, both inside and outside the organisation. Some of these contributions are formal activities, for example the preparation of a case for or against a decision option, but many more influence the outcome by participating in the ongoing strategic conversation in the organisation.

The theory of the learning cycle (see Part One) suggests that scenario planning can only lead to institutional learning if it affects institutional action. Institutional action requires a critical mass of consensus compromise on what to do. Scenario planning affects institutional action by contributing to this process of alignment of ideas. Only if it becomes a process in the organisation of sufficient significance to affect mental models will it play a role in the institutional learning loop and thereby make the organisation a more effective adaptive player in its ever-changing environment.

Many management teams initially engage in a scenario planning process in order to conceptualise and clarify for themselves an otherwise unstructured area of concern about developments in the outside world. Management Teams that take scenario planning seriously can widen their range of vision in this way. However, things normally don't stop at that point. Often the scenario planner will find that the management team, having spent time and resources on the development of a set of scenarios, will want to take these further into, firstly, a consideration of strategy and if successful, secondly, a process of institutional development. This can be done on an ad hoc basis or it can be formally tackled in the organisation. This requires embedding scenario planning in a formal process of strategy development, by making it the basis of the corporate planning cycle. When this is done effectively scenario planning will influence strategy in the formal decision making process, but also in a less formal way by becoming part of the general conversation about strategy in the organisation. Views will be heard which otherwise would remain in the background. Weak signals of impending change, which would otherwise go unnoticed will be picked up and considered. New questions will be asked, triggering new thinking. There will be increased confidence that the organisation is capable of dealing with change. Change and uncertainty are no longer threatening but are understood in context, and therefore experienced as manageable opportunities for growth and development.

Effective institutionalisation will lift scenario planning from an intellectual exercise by individuals, following the rationalistic paradigm of strategy, to a capability for organisational learning, in line with the processual view of strategic management. In this context we can speak of scenario planning opening up the organisational mind to the many different possible futures that could arise, and in that way developing a more skilful response.

PLANNING FOR ACTION

Planning for action consists of four steps:

- Specification of the present situation.
- Specification of the desired future, which needs to be clearly stated as one choice among many within an environment which becomes more and more uncertain the further out we look.
- Clarification of the gap to be bridged.
- Development of detailed plans to make the transistion (Figure 34).

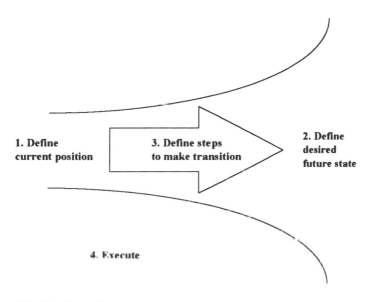

Figure 34. *Creating action.*

From this four-stage process plans will emerge to gradually move the corporation from the present to the desirable future. This will have to be done within resource constraints experienced by the corporation. Therefore choices have to be made. Clear objectives for the desired future help management in clarifying priorities.

Once the objectives have been set plans to bridge the gap can be made and actions will be undertaken by the organisation. But even the best-laid plans meet unexpected obstacles. Management need to appraise progress on a continuous basis, and exercise control action if unexpected deviations occur. For this reason objectives need to be set to measure progress against and to indicate whether progress is on course. This means that what is included in, and what is excluded from, the set of objectives will influence where action will be focused, "what is measured is what you get". It is therefore crucially important that objectives include all areas where strategic initiatives are important. The discussion of the Business Idea (and hygiene factors, see page 143, if applicable) shows management where to look beyond obvious financial targets.

"Making it happen" is not a trivial matter. Many management teams have experienced what is known as the "implementation" problem, i.e. the problem of realising a strategic vision in real terms by creating the appropriate organisational action. The problem is closely linked up with the rationalistic paradigm, in which thinking and action are seen as different consecutive activities. The processual view sees thinking and action as interwoven activities, and explains "implementation problems" as the result of the inability to take that into account. Learning from experience is a fundamental aspect of the processual perspective, and the organisation's ability to acknowledge, assess and deal with deviations of experience from intentions are seen as directly driving the organisation's learning and adaptation. An organisation's skill in this respect depends on the skills of the individuals in it and the degree to which the culture allows ideas to be exchanged and aligned. The skill of an organisation to adapt will depend on the degree to which deviations are discussible. In a political "blaming" culture, where deviations are interpreted as "error", defensive routines will throw up barriers to exchanging of views. It will take longer for experience to be reflected in corporate action. The more open culture in which deviation from plan is seen as a way of life will perceive weak signals earlier and react quicker.

CONDITIONS FOR SUCCESSFUL CHANGE MANAGEMENT

The formal planning process cannot in itself produce change. More is required. However sophisticated the formal planning processes most of the decision making takes place through informal contacts in which most of the strategic conversation takes place. Skilful scenario planners will take account of this and attempt to influence action through these channels. In order to study how this can be achieved we need to consider the processes leading to change in organisations.

One perspective on this is based on research by Pettigrew, who identified five conditions required for any planned change and adaptation to take place (Pettigrew & Whipp 1991):

- Exercise of leadership to put the "change project" on the agenda, and keep it there.
- Active recognition that people are the asset through which change is created.

- Awareness in the organisation of the business imperative for change.
- Expression of the strategy in operational and actionable terms.
- Coherence of action among all members of management.

This model shows that scenario planning can be a major factor for change. It makes a contribution to the operationalisation of most of these factors at the institutional cognitive level. For example, it can:

- Enlist the people in the organisation with the power to act.
- Create wide awareness of external imperatives for change.
- Guide formulation of operational plans.
- Create coherence in management action through development of consensus in the management team.

In addition it can make a contribution at the leadership level, through the defusing of political tension around strategic issues in the organisation.

In Part Three we discussed development of strategy. In Part Four we discuss both formal and informal aspects of the institutional process that makes strategy happen. We will briefly touch on the important phases of the planning cycle and strategic interventions in the strategic conversation, which turn the thinking phase into learning and adaptation in the organisation. In particular we will discuss the contribution of scenario planning in all of these areas. At various points we will revisit Pettigrew's criteria for successful change management and relate these to the contribution made by scenario planning.

Chapter Thirteen

Planning Process

THE PLANNING CYCLE

Most organisations in their approach to planning institutionalise a form of the Learning Cycle (Part One, page 37). Consider a budget system, which looks one year ahead against which actual performance is compared as results come in during the year. Management tries to make sense of events by discussing the reasons for these differences. This can be compared with the reflection and theory building phases of the Learning Cycle. On the basis of the explanation of differences from the budget new predictions are made for the coming year and the budget is adjusted. This can be compared with the "planning new steps" stage of the Learning Cycle. This leads to new actions by the organisation. Results deviating from plan constitute the new experience on which new organisational learning is based.

The formal planning activity is often financially oriented. Money is the prime common measure of performance in organisations. But there are points in the planning cycle where a more fundamental view needs to be taken of what is being done. Most management teams feel the need to base their budgets and plans on a strategy. This is caused by the awareness that there are many more things an organisation could undertake than it has capacity to carry out, and choices have to be made. The discussion about these alternatives is often somewhat informal and many choices are made intuitively. This means that they are not very well explained to others in the organisation, leading to tacit, but significant, differences of view, in the management team and beyond. If these are not resolved the team starts to fragment, resulting in mixed signals to the organisation. As we saw in the previous chapter mixed signals from the top is one of the five conditions that frustrate planned change. Most teams therefore feel the need to take off time to think together about the future. In Part Three we discussed ways to improve the quality of this discussion. The next step is to bring this thinking into the rest of the organisation. Particularly when the conclusion is that significant change has to be created this is an important part of the management process.

The learning cycle view of organisational learning emphasises the importance of the link to action in the cognitive processes underlying organisational behaviour. So far we have discussed processes which help thinking in the management group. How does the link to action take place?

HYGIENE FACTORS

Managers are people with institutional "power-to-act". Triggers to action originate in strategic objectives or the need to apply accepted principles of "good practice". The latter are sometimes referred to as hygiene factors, activities which are generally seen as necessary for the proper conduct of organisational and business affairs (see page 143). For example an organisation requires a good bookkeeping system. Commercial organisations need proper marketing skills. Management needs a system to control expenditure. A minimum of internal communications is required. And so on. These are the principles of good management practice that need to be in place if the organisation is to survive at all.

Hygiene factors should be considered under two categories:

- Maintaining sound and efficient relationships with all stakeholders.
- Ensuring sound and efficient business processes.

Stakeholders have expectations and the challenge is not only to identify these, but also to find a balance in terms of what can be delivered. Sound and efficient business processes will establish the company as an efficient going concern.

Knowledge about management hygiene factors is readily available to every manager, codified and documented in text books, and taught through management courses. This is not repeated here, I refer the reader to the management literature. Professional managers are expected to be aware of these hygiene factors, and non-performance in these areas is accepted ground for disqualification. They are necessary minimum conditions to play the game. Organisations that find that they lack the necessary hygiene factors have to address these deficiencies immediately, and raise projects to repair the situation as soon as possible. This book is in the first place about strategy. Strategic management as a discipline assumes that the necessary hygiene factors are in place. If this is not so, then management is well advised to concentrate on establishing these minimum conditions first. You cannot win the race if you haven't got to the starting line first.

FIVE LEVELS OF PLANNING IN A PLANNING CYCLE, OVERVIEW

We can distinguish five stages in the organisational planning cycle, namely strategic planning, masterplanning, project planning, budget planning, and appraisal, see Figure 35.

At the top we find strategic planning, which incorporates the activities as described in Part Three of this book. It involves exploring

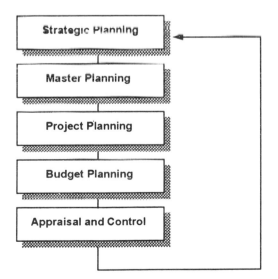

Figure 35. *The five levels of business planning.*

the future and defining and developing it in the form of a Business Idea of the organisation, and testing this against multiple futures as these may unfold. As we saw strategic planning can take place at the business and the corporate level. These two levels of strategic planning affect each other. The corporate Business Idea describes competencies the corporate level contributes to the businesses. On the other hand the corporate competencies do not exist in isolation but are to a considerable extent embedded in the businesses. When starting the strategic planning phase from scratch the preferred order is to develop the Business Ideas of the businesses before tackling the corporate level. Being able to put the businesses next to each other and identify commonalties in Distinctive Competencies provides a strong steer towards the shape of the corporate Business Idea.

A useful output of the strategic planning phase is the definition of a set of strategic objectives, defining the main elements of the state of affairs the organisation hopes to achieve over time between now and the horizon year. Strategic objectives will give a broad indication of the result of the consideration of Portfolio and Capability options in the management team, and the conclusions reached on which direction to adopt. A strategic objectives statement is always simple, as it has been derived from a Business Idea for the future, describing the distinctiveness of the organisation in not more than some seven to ten Distinctive Competencies (see page 77).

Actions can range from taking small incremental steps to undertaking major projects. Any operational plan intended to result in action is a project to be undertaken. Some projects are undertaken by individuals of their own accord, some by groups of people who join forces for the purpose of bringing a bigger strategic project to fruition. In order to organise their actions project managers engage in project planning, intended to convert strategy into action. It concerns the detailed operational planning of the steps in such terms that they are immediately indicative of what individuals need to do.

Very few projects can be planned entirely in isolation. Organisations operate an "infrastructure" which benefits more than one project. Most projects contain elements of planned activities of an infrastructural nature which need to be put together with related actions planned in other projects to create a coherent overall plan that deals with it across the organisation. For this reason organisations, especially large ones, need to engage in "masterplanning", through which the overall coherence of the totality of all project plans is ensured. For example personnel requirements will need to be aggregated across the organisation in order to create an overall recruitment/training plan. Masterplanning typically results in an overall plan which addresses the total cost/benefit performance of the combined project plans. Specifically it considers allocation of corporate resources across the whole of the organisation.

Some masterplans may develop into significant projects in their own right. Others may be developed informally, e.g. in a series of meetings between the various project champions involved. Masterplanning is carried out in conjunction with project planning. It can only be done in direct co-operation with project planners, who will be the ultimate users of the outcomes of masterplans.

Having developed the various plans the next task is to express these in a detailed budget. This includes targets for income and expenditure, based on performance assumptions which take account of the projects and masterplans which are being undertaken. The targets are the basis against which actual performance will be measured and assessed later.

In summary, the planning cycle involves the development of strategy (as discussed in Part Three of this book), masterplanning (involving the translation of this into a description of the cross-functional overall business plan), project planning (involving the translation of the strategy into business projects and action steps), budget planning (involving the overall quantification and the setting of targets), and appraisal (looking at actual performance in the light of what was intended in the plans). Ultimately the purpose of all this is to learn from experience such that the organisation becomes more skilful in dealing with change in the business environment.

Having overviewed the whole process we will now revisit the various aspects of the corporate planning cycle and consider these in the context of the approach to strategy discussed here, involving scenario planning of the Business Idea.

STRATEGIC PLANNING

In Part Three we considered the intellectual processes a management team invokes to develop strategy for the organisation. By considering the fit between the Business Idea and scenarios of the future business environment an agenda of change was developed under two categories:

1. Capability options (development of Distinctive Competencies), for example:
   - Physical assets
   - Legal position
   - Reputation and brand image
   - Human resource
   - Knowledge
   - Process
   - Culture
2. Portfolio options (development of business areas), for example:
   - Markets
   - Channels
   - New product development
   - Pricing
   - Promotion

As we saw management will consider the options in the context of two questions:

- How to improve the fit between the Business Idea and future environments that could develop?
- How to exploit the strength of a powerful Business Idea across a wider area of future activities?

This discussion takes place against the background of limitations and scarce resources. Management need to consider constraints in various categories of resources, including:

- Financial assets
- Physical assets
- Human resources
- Managerial attention.

It is because of these constraints that choices have to be made. These decisions are particularly difficult in the absence of a strong Business Idea, when the ongoing activities do not throw off a big surplus. Management will not normally want to make these decisions in isolation, but want to mobilise the knowledge of the whole organisation. The main purpose of a creating a planning system in the organisation is to create a conversational process around these issues, mobilising the totality of the organisational knowledge towards an emerging solution to this complex optimisation problem.

Management will need to set the process in motion by sharing the conclusions of their strategic thinking with the rest of the organisation. They will need to indicate whether the prime strategic thrust is in exploitation of the Business Idea or in the development of it. They will have to indicate in which direction they see these developments taking place in order to maintain overall coherence between the Business Idea and the business environment outlook. A useful way of summarising this is through the formulation of strategic objectives, shared by all members of the management team. This sharing is important. As we saw from Pettigrew's research, one of the main reasons why change programmes derail is lack of coherence resulting from mixed signals from the top.

STRATEGIC OBJECTIVES

All change programmes depend on the human resource for their execution. The organisation needs a set of unified and relatively stable plans of action that can be articulated, communicated, discussed and agreed such that all can subscribe to them. These plans will exist at various levels in the corporation, linking strategic purpose with details of operation. Corporate management face a formidable task in maintaining coherence across the whole front. The specification of shared and agreed corporate objectives is the first crucial step in this process.

The two sources of corporate objectives are hygiene factors ("getting to the starting line in a fit state to play"), and the corporate Business Idea ("winning the race").

As we saw hygiene factors belong to two categories:

1. Maintaining sound and efficient relationships with all stakeholders.
2. Ensuring sound and efficient business processes.

But for competitive success a unique factor needs to be added, which sets this company apart from any other player in the market place. The Business Idea for the future (Strategic Vision) and its associated Distinctive Competencies express how management intend to establish this. In terms of objectives there are two elements in this:

3. The Distinctive Competencies intended to establish unique competitive advantage.

4. The level of profitability aimed for to keep the Business Idea loop robustly in the growth spiral.

A comprehensive set of corporate objectives addresses all four categories. Developing a set of objectives therefore requires consideration in all four areas:

- Who are our key stakeholders, and how do we need to perform on the interfaces with them to maintain optimal relationships?
- What are our most important business processes? Where is our performance less than what may be expected from a professional company? What needs to be done about repairing the situation?
- What are the Distinctive Competencies we intend to rely on for our future success? How will we know that they are in place?
- What level of profitability will be manifestation of our competitive success, and what will be required to exploit the growth opportunities the Business Idea will open up for us?

How many objectives should a company pursue? If objectives are to lead to action and results, the set as a whole should become a holistic source of inspiration in the organisation. This requires that the whole set can be seen as one image of the organisation in the future. As with the number of elements in the Business Idea it is important to remember that a holistic overview is lost if the number of objectives exceeds around seven to ten. If an organisation has more than this number of "corporate objectives" it is losing the potential enlisting power of this management instrument.

The four questions above can be used as the basis for developing specific corporate objectives. In each of the four categories management needs to consider how performance will be measured, what will be considered a satisfactory state of affairs to be reached in the future. The Devil's Advocate question here might be: "If, in ten years' time, the organisation has been a roaring success, how will we know? What are the very few necessary *and* sufficient markers of success?"

In principle four tasks are involved:

Step 1. Identifying objectives

The management team will first of all think about what is required in each of the four areas and try to discover the implicit objectives. A useful way to think about what is required is to consider why the absence of each objective could not be tolerated. What would we expect to happen if the objective was not met, and how would this undermine the whole operation.

Step 2. Quantifying objectives

The next question to address is how management will know that objectives have been reached. This will require the objective to be expressed in measurable terms. Each qualitative objective may find expression in one or more quantitative targets to be reached.

Quantitative objectives come in two forms:

- Static targets to be achieved independent of time. For example, a management team may aim to maintain a market share of at least 25 per cent.
- Dynamic targets to be reached at a specific point in time. For example, management may specify that logistics costs should have become competitive within one year. Time dependent objectives are sometimes called "milestones".

Most strategic objectives are difficult to quantify. And they are also the most important. Distinctive Competencies may be especially hard to express in numbers, as they are often culture-related. For example the Business Idea may identify the area of customer orientation as an opportunity to develop unique capabilities (an example of this is British Airways' well-known "Putting People First" policy and programmes). In such cases, objectives may have to express derived activities, such as number of employees trained. However, managers should try to express the basic competitive aims of an objective as closely as possible, to ensure that no false impressions are created, based more on hope than reality. Measuring the wrong thing may cause a false mood of complacency, which could be even more dangerous than not having the policy in the first place.

The final test that the right measures have been found is whether measuring reality in these terms will indicate to management whether and to what extent the objectives are met.

Step 3. Considering appropriateness

Following the quantification of the objectives management needs to consider whether the quantified objectives are appropriate. The ultimate test is whether by achieving the objectives the company will achieve success as envisaged in the Business Idea for the future. The following questions may help management in considering this point:

- Is the objective realistic, and within the means available or attainable?
- Is the objective stretching?

Both criteria are important. An unrealistic target will be ignored in the organisation and become ineffective. On the other hand the target must be stretching if it is to lead to competitive improvement. Care should be taken to find the right balance between the two. Erring on either side would make the exercise less than effective as an institutional device.

Step 4. Assigning responsibility

Finally each of the corporate objectives should become the explicit responsibility of one of the members of the management team. Responsibility involves:

- Ensuring that one or multiple programmes are in place to bridge the gap between the present state of affairs and where we aim to end up.
- Ensuring that aims are communicated down the line, discussed and modified, until full buy-in has been achieved.
- Ensuring that objectives are translated into action projects, assigned to individuals or teams.
- Ensuring that resources are made available at the appropriate place and time.
- Measuring progress against target, and taking control action if progress is unsatisfactory.
- Informing the management team if achieving the objective is becoming less than likely.

DEVELOPING OBJECTIVES IN A MANAGEMENT TEAM

Although the above four tasks can be executed by an individual manager, the resulting set of objectives will need to be discussed in the team, where agreement and "buy-in" needs to occur. Also the result of appraisal activities will need to be considered, before management finalise the set of objectives.

The development of objectives is not a once-and-for-all exercise, but needs to iterate with the development of feasible action plans and the allocation of resources. Initial ideas about objectives may prove unrealistic, or the resources needed to do everything that the management team might find desirable may not be available.

Specifically it is desirable that objectives are developed in conjunction with a first specification of masterplans. This will result in a robust set which carries a realistic relationship to action plans in the company.

MASTERPLANNING

Masterplanning is closely connected with the economic purpose of organisations, which is to bring activities together to exploit economies of scale and scope. Masterplanning is the process of thinking about this, planning it and ultimately exploiting it to the maximum.

Because the Business Idea runs across the whole organisation many of the ideas for change involve various functions and departments in the organisation. Some will have repercussions for the infrastructural needs in the organisation as a whole and meet resource constraints. As we saw earlier, constraints are normally encountered in infrastructural resources, such as:

- Financial assets
- Physical assets
- Human resources
- Managerial attention.

The organisation needs to establish which resource limitations constrain further development. These limiting resources need to be considered on potential scope for expansion. But expanding a scarce resource requires the investment of resources, often of the same resource. For example the expansion of the human resource requires recruitment and training which will temporarily reduce the availability of the human resource for other business in the immediate future. Therefore such constraints require making choices and priority setting. Development needs to be carefully planned. And limitations in scope for expansion has repercussions for the overall concept of the organisation. All this is co-ordinated across the organisation by means of masterplanning. Masterplans deal with scarce corporate resources required by projects. Interfunctional co-ordination involves two tasks:

- Allocation of the scarce resource across individual projects.
- Planning of expansion of the resource, in a way that balances costs and benefits.

Both aspects involve the individual project planners, who have to be able to make their case in the allocation process, and who have to develop the benefit side of the cost benefit equation.

Generally a masterplan is a description of the future generation and disposition of a scarce central resource, and a plan to reach this future state by deliberate action. It describes the physical state of affairs as it is intended to develop over time in terms of assets, people and resources for the activity concerned with implications across the whole organisation (and beyond). Typical examples include a computer/information systems masterplan, a production/factory masterplan, a human resource masterplan (including recruitment, career development, succession plans and so on), a management development masterplan, etc. Financing needs can only be dealt with at the aggregated level and needs a masterplan. Offices and buildings need to be planned across the departments. The factory lay-out will depend on more than one project. Relations with suppliers involve overall purchasing considerations, but also logistics, including warehousing, working capital and so on. "Softer" masterplans address less tangible assets, such as creating desirable cultural characteristics across the organisation, in line with the Business Idea.

Some of these responsibilities naturally fit in the mandate of specific departments, and these are the logical candidates to champion the development of the appropriate masterplans. Other masterplans may not be the subject of departmental responsibility and these need special attention from the management team. Departments responsible for physical facilities will often already be familiar with the concept of a masterplan. Laying out a factory for example cannot be done in a step by step fashion, but must be approached top down from the perspective of a future integrated state of affairs. Thought will have to be given to future expansion and space, and capacity will have to be reserved for that. Most factory managers will have experienced that without enough topdown facilities planning work-flow will gradually become unwieldy and work efficiency will be lost. The same applies to departments responsible for logistics, computing and communications, facilities management etc.

While using the Business Idea/scenario approach described here management will become more skilful in articulating change in terms of less tangible resources of the organisation such as its people skills and culture, brand name, information flows etc. Many of these invisible assets are of an infrastructural nature, involving people and behaviour across the organisation. They often require long lead times to plan. If these are the basic drivers of the Business Idea for the future they will require their own masterplans as much as the more tangible physical manifestations of the organisation.

Therefore masterplans can be characterised as follows:

- They are blueprints describing the future manifestations of a specific shared scarce resource, showing actions designed to develop the resource.
- They can cover both tangible and intangible assets.
- They tend to take a longer term view of the future, related to the life span of the resources considered.

Good masterplanning will manifest the following characteristics:

- It may be triggered by the need to protect a specific hygiene factor, or to build a specific Distinctive Competence, as specified in the Business Idea of the organisation.
- It identifies key decision points, and key "milestones" to be reached at specific times in the future.
- It allows communication both vertically and horizontally in the organisation.
- It is a vehicle for delegation from the top.
- It ensures compatibility between the long and the short term.
- It ensures consistency between functional and departmental plans.
- It provides data for budget and cash flow planning purposes.

Masterplans help the organisation in the management of change:

- Comparison with the current state of affairs will provide an overview of additional resources required. Aggregation allows management an overall view of the needs resulting from the totality of the projects under consideration, as a result of which control action can be taken.

- An important aspect of the masterplan is the overview it provides of the way that projects link areas of responsibility across the organisation, allowing people not directly involved in its conception to study and comment. In this way masterplans are a powerful integrating mechanism in the organisation.

Drawing up masterplans can be organised in various different ways. Management can appoint ad hoc teams to draw up these plans. Alternatively existing organisational units can be asked to take on the task. Some masterplans can be farmed out, particularly those relating to the maintenance of hygiene factors in the organisation. However, masterplans for the development of Distinctive Competence by their nature cannot be left to anyone other than the organisation itself.

Development of Distinctive Competencies will often be allocated to functional units while development of business areas will be considered by business units. However, the masterplan does not only involve this co-ordinating unit. It will be their task to ensure that others involved are consulted and that the final plan has the support of everyone with an interest across the whole organisation.

The project planning and masterplanning activities need to take place in conjunction with each other. A process of iteration is required, in which project plans inform the masterplans, and the other way around. This requires a deliberate approach towards the planning activity. It is normal practice in most organisations to make someone responsible for the overall co-ordination of the total planning activity, which includes ensuring that all appropriate masterplans are considered. If the process is suitably co-ordinated it will be possible to aggregate plans into an overall business plan, as input for discussions with stakeholders.

SCENARIOS AND MASTERPLANNING

Scenario planning can play an important direct role in masterplanning. As masterplans tend to be of a long term nature there will be a lot of uncertainty to be considered in their development. The masterplanner can improve his/her understanding of the potential and risk involved by developing a number of suitably focused scenarios through which masterplans can be tested.

PROJECT PLANNING

Experience has shown that "making it happen" requires the allocation of specific responsibility to teams and individuals. The overall strategy and masterplan needs to be translated in terms of team and individual projects that people can take away and implement. As we saw earlier one of the five essential conditions for change is the linkage of strategy with operations, and the translation of strategy into actionable operational plans. Managers need to be proactive in this area. Developing the strategy is not enough, there should be conscious activity in the organisation to start things moving by operationalising strategy. A useful intervention at this stage is engaging the organisation in conversation about implementation of plans through "implementation workshops". There are many ways of conducting these. Below we discuss one model (based on the model of Figure 34, page 243) which can be used at various levels in the organisation and which has proven productive in practice.

It is assumed that through strategic planning and masterplanning an overview has been obtained of what needs to be done. The manager responsible needs to take the lead by bringing together a team of implementers in a workshop. It normally helps to appoint a facilitator, who is not directly involved in the project. A suitable process for defining and breaking down the projects required would involve the following steps:

Step 1. Introduction of the workshop

A workshop requires some way of settling down. This is provided by creating an initial "database" shared by the group. It has proven important that participants early on get as clear a picture as possible of what is to be expected from the workshop. Operational teams are often not used to discussing strategic issues formally and in depth. Therefore the manager starts the meeting by explaining the objectives, namely:

- To discuss strategic issues as specified by the Management Team, and options for addressing these.
- To review masterplans in which this group is involved.
- To develop detailed project objectives and action project commitments.

The manager needs to set the scene by making the link with the Business Idea, the strategic objectives developed and the masterplans being prepared. In addition some participants may be asked to prepare presentations on the detail of new masterplans which involve this group.

It is often useful to give 10 minutes' air time to all participants to allow them to indicate what issues, from their perspective, they see emerging. Participants should be left free (apart from time) to decide what they wish to bring up.

This process helps in starting the conversation on implementation. The manager can also observe to what extent the issues are shared among the members of the team.

Step 2. Project objectives and key implementation domains

The facilitator then invites the group to discuss the objectives which they as a project group need to pursue. (S)he needs to be somewhat proactive in this, to avoid vague, not actionable formulation, which would derail the workshop. The facilitator must prove tough in insisting that any objectives are quantified and implementable. The best way of going about this is to start with a free brainstorm on what might have to be included in the list. At this stage no rules apply, and anything goes. The facilitator records on a flip chart. Not only physical and operational, but also financial and human resource objectives are included.

When this activity reaches diminishing returns the facilitator changes tack. (S)he raises specific corporate strategic objectives and masterplans and discusses the question where this group needs to make a contribution. From this the group will generate further ideas on project objectives for them. These are added to the flip chart record.

When no further ideas come forward the facilitator goes back to each stated objective and insists that the following questions are addressed:

- Is the objective realistic?
- What are the criteria for success, how and when will we know that the objective is fully met?
- Why is *not* meeting this objective unsatisfactory. What would happen if the objective is not met?

- How will we measure that satisfactory progress is being made on the way?
- Who in the group is primarily responsible for ensuring that this objective is reached?

The facilitator needs to keep this process moving, prevarication in the light of uncertainty is the big danger here. Initially this may require that some arbitrary decisions are made. Later on the list will be revisited and further iterations will be made. Participants must be kept fully aware that opportunities will arise later on to have another go at this.

The next step is to brainstorm, and then cluster the various activities, required to realise the project. The purpose of clustering here is to come up with implementation domains in which activity can be organised. Implementation domains largely overlap with organisational units, but new projects often require the identification of domains which are not (yet) the subject of a formal organisational responsibility. The question of in which domains implementation plans are required is answered by reference to the objectives formulated. Typical exempts of implementation domains are:

- Relations with authorities
- Relations with customers
- Retail
- Brand development
- Competition
- Facilities management
- Cost reduction
- Plant optimisation
- Human resources development
- Management processes
- Information and information systems.

Developing a list of implementation domains during the workshop is essentially a brainstorming process, with subsequent clustering until a reasonably practical number is achieved (practical in the context of what follows).

Step 3. Gap analysis

The next step may take place in sub-groups. Each syndicate is allocated one or a few implementation domains, and the job is to develop an understanding of the gap between "where we are" and "where we need to end up".

Composition of the syndicates is worth some thought. In principle members are those with some organisational responsibility for the domain activities. However, it often proves productive to include in each syndicate a person from a different part of the organisation, to perform the function of devil's advocate.

The steps covered in the groups are the following:

- Project objectives revisited.
- Present domain position articulated.
- Critical success factors articulated.
- Strengths/weaknesses analysed.

First of all project objectives developed in the workshop earlier are made specific for the domain. The question addressed here is: "What domain objectives do we need in order to realise the overall objectives?" The domain objectives must be quite down-to-earth, and none should be included that cannot be quantified.

These are then compared to "where we are at the moment". This leads to understanding of the gap to be bridged, in quantified terms, against the objectives.

In order to understand what is involved in bridging the gap, some further thinking is required. Therefore the following two questions are addressed:

1. What are the critical success factors (CSFs), of an external or an internal nature, that will determine our ability to bridge the gap? This stage concerns the few developments that must go well. Typically the group is looking for around five CSFs. A typical list of CSFs:
   - Externally: Demand for the product
     Attitude by the authorities
   - Internally: Distribution skills
     Motivated people
     Information system
2. Having thought through what needs to happen the question is: Where does the organisation stand in terms of its ability to deliver? This can be addressed through an analysis of its strengths and weaknesses in the CSF areas.

Both of these questions are addressed in brainstorming mode. In this way the gap is not only determined in its quantifiable aspects, but also in terms of the organisation's chances and ability to bridge the gap at some appropriate time.

Following this step it is advisable to review the overall objectives in plenary. At this point the participants have given thought to what is involved in getting there, and this may throw a new and different light on the objective as formulated earlier. For example second thoughts will have come up on the feasibility of some of the objectives. Or new ideas may have come up. A discussion in plenary is useful at this stage to ensure that the set of overall project objectives remains the property of the entire group. The facilitator brings everyone together, and leads a discussion on how the list of overall objectives needs to be modified.

Step 4. Development of action items

Having formulated the revised organisational objectives the syndicates review their earlier work and redefine the gap. The next step is to define what needs to be done to bridge the gap. The following steps are involved:

- A list of actions is developed by systematically thinking through how the gap will be bridged. This results in a list (on flip chart) of actions per identified gap (objective/present reality).
- It has proven useful to remind syndicates specifically to include actions for building organisational capabilities, related to the development of Distinctive Competencies, as these are often overlooked.
- Actions then need to be ordered in terms of priority.
- Syndicates are then required to indicate who is the responsible party for each action.

Finally syndicates summarise their findings under the following headings for each implementation domain:

- Domain objectives.
- Present position.
- Critical success factors.
- Actions per objective, including capability actions.
- Relative priorities and approximate timing.
- Responsible party per action.

The facilitator collects this from all syndicates for subsequent editing and amalgamation in a report. The workshop breaks up at this point to allow the report to be prepared. The number of domains can be large, each addressing a number of objectives, which in turn each produce a list of actions. Therefore the resulting overview can be substantial and good editing is essential for the next step to progress smoothly.

Step 5. Development of action programme

As soon as the report is available it is circulated to all participants. This is the first time that people see how other syndicates have translated organisational objectives into actions. Following this the workshop reconvenes to discuss the amalgamated result.

First syndicates meet separately to discuss and comment on the actions developed in the other syndicates. Following this the comments are presented in plenary. The resulting discussion can be time consuming. Many alterations are proposed and adopted or rejected. At the end of this discussion the meeting needs to agree on the final set of organisational objectives. This step is crucial for ownership of the whole programme and therefore should not be rushed. The facilitator must ensure there is at least half a day available for this last meeting.

When reasonable agreement has been reached the actions, expressed as action sub-projects, are written on cards. Each card contains a short title with a verb describing the essence of the action sub-project, the approximate timing, together with the party, team or individual, responsible for its execution. It is useful to use different colours for different action parties. Each action item is individually vetted by the action party indicated. These cards are then displayed on a white-board in time order.

It is to be expected at this stage that too many action items end up for immediate execution, beyond the capacity of the organisation to cope. The colours show clearly who is overloaded, and how projects can be reallocated over people and over time. The final step is then to move action projects along the time axis until the total programme seems manageable. The new target times are copied on to the action cards.

Step 6. Reporting

The final step is for the facilitator to document the result obtained, indicating who is responsible for which project step, when progress is expected and what are the relative priorities. This final report subsequently becomes the basis for regular project appraisal meetings to assess progress in each sub-project, and to adjust in the face of unexpected deviations.

SCENARIOS AND PROJECT PLANNING

As in masterplanning, scenarios can play an important part in the development of a project. Large projects need to be considered against the longer term future, and there will be considerable uncertainty around many key variables. The assessment of profitability against multiple equally likely futures will allow the assessment of the risk involved in the many aspects of the project. By looking at the range of possible outcomes across a range of possible futures an indication is obtained of the robustness of the profitability assessment. Large projects which involve the organisation in commitments which are significant in comparison to its overall operation should always be assessed against multiple futures.

PROJECT DEVELOPMENT AND EVALUATION

One of the results of the implementation discussions may be the definition of other projects to be developed further into detailed proposals by identified action parties. The job may involve the further definition of the scope of those projects, design, negotiation with potential partners, costing, profitability assessment and so on.

BUDGET PLANNING

Once the organisation has, through masterplanning and project planning, obtained an idea of what it can reasonably hope to achieve it will want to create an overview of what the total plan looks like. There are a number of reasons why a management might want to develop an overall quantified business plan:

- Management will want to satisfy itself that resources are available for the plans formulated, and specifically they will want to make sure that cash resources are sufficient.
- Management may also want to compile an overall business plan for presentation to outside stakeholders, including shareholders, financiers or funding agencies.
- Another purpose of developing the overall business plan is to define budgets for control purposes across the organisation.

The activity is co-ordinated by the planning co-ordinator and often delegated to the finance/controller function, which collects the results of the deliberations and compiles the overall financial overview.

The activity can be particularly useful if it is part of the overall iterative planning process. The first results may not be quite acceptable to management, if these indicate that the total commitment would stretch the resources beyond what is considered prudent financial policy. In that case management may want to reconsider and postpone some projects which are now seen to be beyond its financial capability. Most budget planning takes place as part of an annual cycle, if only to set budgets and targets for the following year. In such a cyclical process the strategic and implementation planning do not start from scratch and planning often boils down to adjusting last year's plans to take account of new developments and information. Therefore the overall plan normally is not too much of a surprise, and iteration proves to be a manageable activity.

APPRAISAL

In the introduction, the planning cycle was compared with the learning cycle, discussed in Part One. We compared strategic planning with the "building of mental models" stage, and masterplanning and project planning with the "planning new steps" stage. The learning loop is completed by reflection on the experience obtained as a result of the actions undertaken. In the planning cycle this is embodied in the appraisal of the actual performance. This may result in control action to bring things back on track, as articulated in the Business Idea. This is known as single loop learning. Or appraisal may give rise to an awareness that the situation has changed enough to make the basic concept of the organisation (its Business Idea) invalid. In this case the whole strategy concept has to be rethought. This is known as double loop learning.

Although appraisal goes on constantly at many different levels in the organisation (most intra-organisational interactions imply some level of informal appraisal at a person-to-person level), most organisations also operate a formal institutionalised system of appraisal of business and/or business units, and of individual performance appraisal. Actual performance as expressed in measured performance data, mostly generated by the accounts function, is compared with the budget for the same variables. If a significant difference opens up this is an indication that things are not working out as anticipated. An attempt is made to try to explain this difference, and control action may be undertaken, adjusting activity to achieve actuals closer to what was planned.

Appraisal processes are often compared with control feedback loops, where the state of the system is compared with a desired state and control action undertaken if the two deviate. There are a number of problems with this representation:

- In reality there are multiple decision centres deciding on goals. Several feedback loops interact, and sometimes counteract. And actions often are only a weak reflection of collective goal decisions by such decision centres, reflecting more the uncoordinated private goals down the line.
- In organisations that are not strongly centrally planned, interpretation and prioritising of goals is ambiguous. In such systems authorities often set goals that are expressions of values, without concrete criteria for error or success.
- Measuring the actual state of affairs is problematic too. Financial and economic variables can be quantitatively measured, but we often lack the conceptual tools to appraise the more value- and culture-based goals set to the organisation.

How can these problems be addressed in the world of management?

THE DILEMMA BETWEEN JOINT LEARNING AND ACCOUNTABILITY

Target setting and appraisal of actuals against these are essential parts of the managerial control function. There are two categories of reasons for doing this:

- Hierarchical, making people accountable for their actions.

- Organic, creating organisational learning from experience.

In the accountability mode management looks back and requires people to account for their stewardship of the assets which have been entrusted to their care. Performance assessment takes place on the basis of predetermined appraisal categories. It is essentially an individual motivational activity, often officially linked to reward/penalty systems. In this context the relationship between the management and the appraisees is a political one, involving the exercise of power of one over the other. It is done to create and encourage accountability and commitment to the plan, to exercise shareholder responsibility and to inform parties of possible changes in the plans. It is related to solving problems, demonstrating realism in objectives and supporting credibility of the planning process. It is the exercise of single loop learning, and aims to keep things on a predetermined track. The danger of an accountability emphasis is that the track may have become inappropriate.

Appraisal as part of organisational learning is sometimes called strategic evaluation. It is double-loop learning, guiding the strategic thinking process. It involves a fundamentally different relationship, in which both parties attempt to reflect on and understand deviations, and to adjust mental models accordingly, as a basis of future planning. This can only be successfully done in an atmosphere of openness, in which knowledge about the situation is freely exchanged.

The appraisal activity puts management in a dilemma, between on the one hand emphasising accountability and on the other double loop learning. Like many other managerial dilemmas this needs to be carefully managed.

To consider how this can be approached it is useful to go back to the concept of the learning loop. The driving forces behind the learning loop are three-fold (see Part One, page 39):

- The need to adjust the system's behaviour to deal with external contingencies.
- The need to direct the system towards more favourable environments.
- The need to reorganise the system itself to make it more effective in these functions.

The appraiser is not required to motivate organisational units to pursue these goals on their own accord. There is no pleasure for an organisational unit in under-performing or being pushed about by the competition. System theory suggests that the involvement of the higher hierarchical level is concerned with imposing constraints on the behaviour of the lower level to the extent required to create the desirable emergent behaviour of the whole. Creating synergy is the only substantive justification for a higher level imposing itself on the affairs of the units in the organisation. This requires behavioural adjustments on the part of the members of the organisation and to bring this about is the concern of the appraisers.

A legitimate appraisal system requires a clear-cut understanding and expression of the sources of synergy in the company. Unless the appraiser is specific in its concept and related instructions, there will be uncertainty about a demonstrable contribution to the appraisal by the appraisers.

An organisation's appraisal system needs to start with consideration of the question of what constitutes the extra value of the overall organisation, over and above what its separate units operating independently would create. Examples of corporate synergy include:

- The central know-how pool, constituting the institutionalised memory of business experience.
- The identity of the organisation, associated with emergent behaviour of the whole.
- Reputation, based on history, size and scope.
- Portfolio management and overall optimisation through allocation of scarce resources, such as management, expertise, talent, capital.
- Cohesion and internal trust, leading to commitment.
- Development of "requisite variety" in thinking, to enable the organisation to broaden its perception of the business environment.

There are many synergy issues to be considered when discussing subsidiary behaviour. The underlying common element is to decide in what way belonging to the overall organisation will assist the subsidiary unit driving its own learning cycle, including:

- Dealing better with disturbances in its business environment.
- Finding its "high ground".
- Organising itself more effectively for survival and success.

We seem to have returned to the question of the definition of the

Business Idea of the organisation as a whole, describing this role. It seems that appraisal effectiveness requires clear-cut answers to the Business Idea question. Unless the overall Business Idea is fully understood it is not possible to define the appropriate appraisal criteria which steer units towards the desired overall behaviour. Unless the organisation has a clear and shared understanding of the Business Idea it is probably better to de-emphasise the accountability aspect of appraisal, and stress the joint learning and problem solving aspect. In the absence of a clear explicit understanding of what units should be accountable for, a general discussion is to be preferred, which leaves room for people's intuition to consider the whole terrain.

Chapter Fourteen

Guiding the Strategic Conversation

So far we have discussed the elements of the formal planning activities in an organisation and the contribution made by scenario planning and the Business Idea to strategy design. However, in many organisations the formal decision making processes contribute only little to what is ultimately decided. Often much more important is the informal "learning" activity, consisting of unscheduled discussions, debate and conversation about strategic questions that goes on continuously at all levels in the organisation.

Embedded scenario thinking is like a culture. It cannot be a "plug and play" decision by top management. It can work only provided that the organisation has achieved the necessary level of sophistication in thinking that is compatible with the sophistication of the tool. Scenario planning co-evolves with the quality of strategic thinking in the organisation. This is the basis of its competitive advantage. Like most other cultural characteristics of organisations it can be a true Distinctive Competence, not easily emulated by competitors.

For these reasons introducing scenario planning in an organisation involves more than just introducing a new planning system. It also involves affecting the general ad hoc conversation about strategy that takes place in the corridors and canteens among groups of cognitively "networked" people.

Weick (1969) has argued that organisations are primarily systems of such cognitive loops. These constitute the underpinning tacit infrastructure of thought, created through the interactions of members, which can become rigid and/or fragmented. As Bougon points out Weick created in this way a dynamic theory of organisational change

(Bougon & Komocar 1990). Most theories around organisation are of a static nature, based on hierarchy and sources of influence. Change is replacing one steady state with another. For example in order to implant a new strategic direction the CEO is replaced. However, such change projects are often unsuccessful, organisational behaviour often persists, notwithstanding the hierarchical changes made. It is clear that loops of influence are a lot more complex than the hierarchical structure might imply.

Organisational structure exists in action and interaction. The interaction takes place through conversation, some formal but most of it informal. Conversations lead to action, illustrated in the learning loop, as discussed in Part One of this book. Such systems of interactive loops behave rather differently than static models based on hierarchical structure would imply. Because of the dynamic nature of systems of loops organisations are systems of change. The situation is dynamic, not static. Organisations consist in conversations, which lead to action which evolves the organisation, and the associated conversation in an ongoing loop. Figure 36 summarises this diagramatically. To intervene in organisations is to intervene in these conversational/influence loops.

Successful organisations contain within their system of loops at least

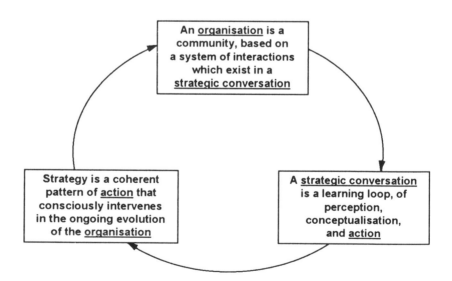

Figure 36. *The art of strategic conversation.*

one positive feedback loop, driving growth. We have called this the Business Idea. Many of the other loops take the form of negative feedback loops, which attempt to keep disturbances outside the system, in order not to interfere with the growth loop. If this has been operating successfully for some time the defence loops may become strongly entrenched. This often leads to the denial of signals of change, disabling the organisation from perceiving threats to its successful Business Idea. As we quoted Miller in the introduction, "nothing fails like success". It is in recognition of this danger that management may wish to broaden the field of vision of the organisation, by introducing scenario planning. A project of this nature requires dealing with the dynamic system of loops, involving both formal and informal processes of strategic conversation.

SCENARIOS AND THE INFORMAL EXCHANGE OF VIEWS

So what can management do to develop the level of sophistication of the strategic thinking culture?

First of all the formal part of the strategic conversation can be mapped out, and should include such activities as:

* Processes, systems, methods.
* Explicit and implicit processes and topics.
* Key meetings, decision points.
* Budgeting, project evaluation.
* Strategy reviews.
* Cost-cutting exercises.
* Product, capital, market decision points.

Normally it is within management's power to ensure that scenario thinking is introduced in each of these activities and events. In any of these management can demand that considerations take account of a scenario way of considering the business environment. In this way the organisation will become used to thinking in terms of multiple equally plausible futures, and incorporate scenarios in the day-to-day conversation, as a shorthand to convey different business futures.

With scenarios introduced at appropriate points in the ongoing strategic conversation, they will gradually start to serve the following functions:

- Strategic conversation tools
- Awareness raisers
- Question raisers
- Conceptualisation tools and elements of language.

SCENARIOS AND THE CORPORATE LANGUAGE

If a set of scenarios are widely disseminated in an organisation they tend to become part of the corporate language. A well-chosen name becomes the shorthand for communicating a complex image of a complex specific future. In the conversation there is no need to go into detail, the other party knows what the scenario name stands for. This process can be assisted by the choice of effective names which need to be at the same time:

- Short (not more than two or three words).
- Descriptive of the essence of the scenario.
- Memorable.

A good example of effective scenario names are the "flying" or "bird" names of the Mont Fleur scenarios mentioned in Part Three (page 200). "Ostrich", "Lame Duck", "Icarus" and "Flight of the Flamingoes" call up images which clearly and efficiently characterise the nature of the story line involved. Experienced scenario planners devote a lot of attention to the choice of good scenario names.

Once the scenarios have entered the corporate language they start having a major influence on corporate strategic thinking by triggering multiple equally plausible futures in conversations about strategy. This constitutes a major evolution in the thinking process in the organisation, from an episodic activity of trying to find the "one right answer" to an ever ongoing activity of trying to craft strategy by moulding and building on strategic options to gradually move the organisation closer to a robust "high ground", which will make the organisation less vulnerable to whatever business environment future comes about.

One of the main effects of this is that organisational perception of the environment has strengthened. Scenario story lines have proven to be one of the most effective devices for mentally organising a large area of seemingly unrelated data. A set of corporate scenarios make people in the organisation share a wider set of models with which events can be interpreted. This means that a wider range of events will be seen. An example is the way various groups in Shell reacted to the energy crisis, as described in Part Two. The manufacturing group which had exercised with the scenarios could fit events in a pattern, and saw the underlying forces which were playing out. The Marine group could not, and therefore ignored for a much longer time the fundamental importance of what was happening.

An organisation that has reached this stage will see focused scenario projects emerge throughout the organisation, whenever a group of people are confronting a difficult or puzzling situation. In addition to top management project managers, people in charge of masterplans, even appraisers will reach for the scenario planning tool to enhance their effectiveness. It will become apparent that a useful scenario project can be executed in a matter of days, or even hours if necessary. Eventually scenario planning will pervade all five levels of planning. It will no longer be seen as a management technique, it will become a natural way of thinking about the future.

INSTITUTIONALISATION

Good scenarios can provide new interpretations of what is going on in the environment, open new perspectives, and help the conversation as memorable thinking aids. And by developing understanding they will reduce anxiety about the future. But in order to function in this way they need to be introduced in the organisation, scenario planning needs to be institutionalised. The degree of institutionalisation will be highly contingent on the situation in the organisation, its structure, its culture, and its experience with the scenario planning methodology. Various models can be distinguished:

- Scenario planning by planners on behalf of a management team.
- Scenario planning as a tool for management team discussion on corporate development.
- Scenarios as a tool used by management to influence the organisational agenda.
- Scenarios as a language to facilitate institutional discussion on corporate development.

Scenario planning typically starts in the management team as an aid to thinking and strategy development, as described in Part Three. If they become instrumental in the design of strategy, they will quickly prove to be powerful tools communicating strategic direction and objectives down the line. In a scenario planning culture it is impossible to discuss strategy without bringing in the various futures this has been based on.

Initially scenarios will be passed on to the organisation in presentations, and in written form. Scenario presentation, by top managers or their planners, is an important part of most scenario planning processes, and the next chapter discusses some aspects of this. The transfer of scenarios into the organisation can be improved by engaging teams down the line in strategic workshops in which they consider the strategic implications for them of the set of scenarios as developed by top management. Examples of such workshops are discussed below. Although it is somewhat unlikely that an incidental workshop of this type will produce surprises in terms of new strategies, the workshop format has proven to be a more effective transfer device than presentations to a passive audience.

The final proof that scenario planning has arrived is when acceptance is such that corporate management incorporates it in the formal communication processes about strategy. Ultimately the most effective way to ensure institutional effectiveness of the scenario process is for management to make the scenarios part of the ongoing formal decision making process. If this is not done scenario planning remains a take-it-or-leave-it activity that some may opt out of, often for political reasons. Experience has shown that this can be overcome if scenario planning is made an integral part of the formal management processes. An example is given on page 20 where management required any project submitted for approval to be evaluated and justified on the basis of the going set of scenarios. It is a powerful way to ensure that everyone pays attention to what is in the scenarios. The locking-in of scenario planning is completed when management realise the extent to which scenarios have come to influence decision making across the organisation, and consequently become deeply interested in their content. Once this state of affairs has been reached management will find that the organisation has acquired a powerful new management tool, as through shaping the content of the scenario agenda, they can ensure that important topics are on the agenda, whenever important decisions are made down the line in the organisation. A simple "rule of the game" of this nature firmly seals the scenarios in the strategic conversation, and it assures that both management and organisation can no longer take a hands-off attitude.

SCENARIO PRESENTATIONS

To become fully effective scenarios must become part of the language used in the organisation for discussing strategic questions. Depending on how far scenario planning has been embedded in the organisation the scenario team needs to undertake institutional tasks:

- Quantification of the scenarios to make them useful down the line, e.g. as input to project appraisal (experience has shown that quantification can be an efficient method of ensuring internal consistency in the scenarios, independent of whether the organisation requires quantification).
- Development of presentation, e.g. development in audio/visual media, writing a scenario book, etc. This is greatly helped if the scenarios have provocative and memorable names. Time and effort are required to publicise the scenarios in the organisation effectively.
- Organising the institutional discussion process, through meetings, workshops, documentation, etc.
- Institutionalising scenarios in the "rules of the game" of the formal decision making process.

There are many ways in which scenarios can be publicised in the organisation. Modern technology provides new options in the form of video, multimedia etc. in addition to personal presentation. However, there are a number of points of "good practice" in presenting scenarios, whatever mode is used, which are worth keeping in mind.

Listening to and absorbing a number of different stories in a row is cognitively a demanding task. If the scenario presenter wants the audience to internalise a set of scenarios it is important that a cognitive framework is provided first, such that the listener can "place" each scenario and avoid confusion between one and the other. A number of examples for such frameworks were discussed in Part Three, page 202. A popular approach places the scenarios in a 2 × 2 matrix, in which the scenarios are distinguished by reference to the two most impactful dimensions used to delineate the story lines. Following from this the

scenario presenter may want to consider providing further help for the
audience, including:

- Providing an overview of all scenarios and their differences as a
  road map for the audience.
- Explaining the logic of branching points, i.e. why these scenarios
  and not others.
- Showing logical cause-and-effect development from history to
  the present and on into each scenario story, rooting each story in
  history.
- Highlighting the driving forces behind each scenario, in their
  systemic interaction.
- Summarising cause/effect logic of each scenario in simple logic
  diagrams.
- Selecting effective names for all scenarios.
- Minimising the use of text, and maximising the use of images, to
  emphasise the holistic character of the scenarios.

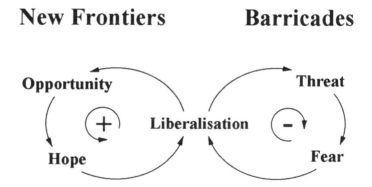

Figure 37. *Two scenarios about societal development.*

An interesting example of effective scenario presentation was
developed by a scenario team who considered the driving forces of
liberalisation and cohesion/fragmentation in society. Figure 37 shows
the way in which the two scenarios were summarised in one diagram.
This showed in one simple context the most crucial elements of the
analysis by the scenario team:

- The central role of liberalisation.
- The distinguishing contrasts of opportunity/threat and
  hope/fear.

- The distinguishing contrast between a positive feedback (growth) and negative feedback (stabilising) dynamics in the system studied.
- All this illustrated in the two evocative scenario names, New Frontiers and Barricades.

Having been internalised, this representation of the scenario structure is not easily forgotten.

The initial task is to embed the scenarios in the memories of the members of the organisation. The question is how complex stories can be most effectively be presented in media such that they stick in the mind of the audience. A few approaches that scenario presenters have found useful over the years include:

- *Metaphors*. Compare the scenario story to a generally known phenomenon, if possible found in nature. Scenario names often are metaphoric, and this can obviously be exploited in the presentation.
- *Anecdotes*. Any logic structure can be humanised and personalised. Think like a novelist, i.e. what the story is. *Not* the issue; the story. Use narrative flow. Issues come later.
- *Repetition*. Tell essentially the same story again. Change the characters and the dialogue; change the setting; change the bells and whistles. But tell the same story.
- *Aphorisms*. Make up a few quotable sentences per scenario. Say them frequently.

SCENARIO WORKSHOPS

However professionally the presentation of the scenarios is approached there is a limit to what a passive audience can absorb in a lecture–type presentation. For a more effective process of transfer it is preferable to get the audience actively involved.

Scenarios can be highly effective as a basis for running strategy workshops. A typical model brings a team of managers together for a 24-hour period for a facilitated discussion. The discussion starts over dinner, with a short presentation of the scenarios and a free-ranging discussion of strategic implications. The following day the team meets to work this out more formally. This can be done by creating a situation in which they are made to retrace some of the steps in the thinking process of the scenario team. Alternatively the audience can be invited to work through each scenario by considering strategic implications.

RETRACING THE SCENARIO BUILDING PROCESS

The challenge here is to make the audience build their own scenarios, but at the same time make sure that they do this in the context of the conclusions reached by the management team. The essence of the thinking of management has to be transferred, but there must be enough room for the workshop audience to experiment themselves. An effective way to do this is by using the "event card" methodology developed by David Mason (page 196). In preparation the scenario team develops each scenario story line into a series of illustrative events. The next step is to transfer each event on to a card, giving a short description of the event and the timing in the scenario story. Typically one scenario might be reasonably represented by a series of 20 to 30 event cards. Altogether a scenario set might produce some 100 cards. The presenter hands over the cards in one pile in random order to the workshop audience. The task is to lay out the cards along a time line, so as to create a number of logical scenarios. The workshop should be provided with plenty of empty event cards, and the audience should be invited to produce their own, as required to complete the story lines. They should be specifically encouraged to fill in local detail by creating events that make the scenarios particularly relevant to their own specific business situation.

In order to create a well-rounded workshop it is advisable to divide the group into a number of syndicates, and ask each to perform the task separately. When finished they are invited to present their results to each other. To round off the occasion the scenario presenter then explains how the management team organised the events in scenarios, and shows how this represents current understanding of driving force dynamics. The work in the syndicates will have prepared the audience and created a "need to know" which makes the final presentation a more effective transfer of knowledge. Having struggled with the events themselves the audience will be particularly interested in the way simple causal loop models can be brought to bear to organise events into storylines. Experience has shown that this is a powerful methodology to make scenario stories stick in the mind of the audience.

IMPLICATIONS WORKSHOP

This type of workshop is modelled on the option planning activity as explained in Part Three, page 225. Here the scenario presentation takes place in the conventional lecture style, but the audience is invited afterwards to consider strategic implications by articulating strategic options that are indicated by the developments as discussed in the scenarios. This activity again best takes place in small syndicates, and is organised in two steps:

Step 1: Option generation by scenario

Each of the syndicates is allocated one of the scenarios. The task is to think through strategic options indicated by the developments in the scenario. This is in itself a two-step activity, in which the group first translates the scenario into terms that are relevant to their own specific business situation, and then consider how they would wish to react to such a train of events.

Step 2: Option evaluation across all scenarios

Following this the syndicates meet in plenary to create an overall list of strategic options generated by all syndicates. The next step is to cluster these options using Post-its in the by now familiar way, and to create a small number of strategic options to be carried further. Each syndicate is allocated one or two of these, and the task is to evaluate the optional strategy across the scenarios. The first task is to consider the performance of the optional strategy in each of the scenarios. This is followed by a discussion of how the strategy could be made more robust across all futures considered. One way to achieve that is by breaking the strategy up in a series of separate strategic projects over time and committing only part of the way at this point in time, by building in optional decision points in the future.

The last part of the task is to consider what signals should be followed in the environment to ensure that when the time for subsequent decisions arrives a better idea has been developed on where the business environment world is heading.

One should not have exaggerated expectations of the capability of these type of workshops to develop new strategy. This is not their primary objective, which remains to transfer the scenarios as effectively as possible. The discussion on strategic options is intended to focus the attention on the scenario futures, and to make the audience actively involved in them. It is important that the scenario presenter explains this sufficiently up front, such that expectations for the workshop are realistic.

TREATING ORGANISATIONAL LEARNING PROBLEMS

An organisation that has culturally embedded scenario planning in its strategic conversation has developed a learning capability, in terms of the learning loop model as discussed in Part One. Specifically it has developed the following institutional capabilities:

- Increased its institutional environmental perception and awareness through an increased arsenal of shared scenarios, functioning as institutional "memories of the future".
- Enriched its differentiated set of models, enabling it to make sense of a wider range of events.
- Acquired a rich language in which views can be discussed, compared and integrated.
- Enhanced its action capability by addressing "management of change" issues (page 241).

As we saw in Part One (see Learning pathologies, page 47), the first task of managing organisational learning is to manage the dilemma between differentiation and integration, to avoid the dangers of the extremes of either fragmentation or group-think in the organisation. Like any genuine dilemma, it cannot be resolved, it requires constant management. What can management do if it comes to the conclusion that the situation is out of balance, and requires correction?

INCREASING INTEGRATION

Management may come to the conclusion that there is not enough integration in the organisation. Symptoms include a lack of strategic discussion in the management team, a lack of a shared sense of direction, a lack of co-ordination in decision making, too much "us and them" feeling among factions in the organisation, a lack of openness, a political orientation in the way groups interact, manifesting itself in defensive routines, strategic implementation problems, generally people or groups "doing their own thing" without taking account of others. Under these circumstances management needs first of all to increase the "quantity" of strategic conversation. This can be done by creating conversational events during which people are brought together and encouraged to discuss strategy. These can range from small ad hoc affairs to large well-prepared gatherings.

A distinction needs to made between top-down versus bottom-up information exchange. Both are important in the integration process. In the top-down mode management informs the organisation of the results of their strategic deliberations. An important vehicle for this can be the printed "mission statement", which management formulates to summarise conclusions reached as a result of the strategic thinking process they have gone through. A somewhat less formal way to achieve the same result is in the form of a letter by the CEO to the organisation. Documents of this nature are expressions of the strategic objectives management have formulated (see page 253).

On the other hand management may wish to communicate on strategic objectives in a two-way communication mode, in which the organisation is invited to participate in the development of the strategic objectives. Information meetings may be organised in which various levels of management interact with their reports on strategy and where dialogue is encouraged. Meetings of this sort are often organised as part of the planning cycle, for example as part of the strategic appraisal process.

Organising the bottom-up process is not a trivial matter. Because of hierarchical relationships good bottom-up strategic dialogue is not common. A special effort may be required from management to engage the organisation in such processes. An example of such a discussion is the Strategy Evaluation Session.

THE STRATEGIC EVALUATION SESSION

The Strategic Evaluation Session is a relatively modest effort, in which top management engages in a dialogue about specific businesses with the business managers involved. In order to minimise barriers in the conversation a number of "rules of the game" need to be agreed in advance:

- The meeting is basically an interaction between the CEO and the business manager, with intermediate levels present, if desired.
- Initiative for the meeting may come from either the CEO or the business manager.
- Length of the meeting is typically half a day.
- The meeting is focused, avoiding wide-ranging discussions.
- The business manager refrains from advocating preferred lines of action, projects or expenditures.
- The CEO refrains from making decisions or suggesting particular lines of action.
- An initial presentation is made by the business manager, not by intermediate management layers.
- There are no formal minutes, only copies of OHP viewgraphs are distributed.
- The participating group is kept small, maximum say ten people.

The agenda of the meeting would typically include items under the following headings:

- The business environment scenarios
- The competitive position
- The Business Idea
- Optional strategies open to the business.

The purpose of the meeting is to increase understanding by the CEO of the business details, and by the business managers of overall strategy at the top. It is important that the process does not develop into a bureaucratic "rain dance". Documentation needs to be kept to a minimum, and any hand-out prepared by the business manager needs to be limited to one page only.

INCREASING DIFFERENTIATION

On the other hand, management may come to the conclusions that there is too much group-think, and not enough "requisite variety" in ideas in the organisation. As we saw this can be a particularly dangerous state of affairs, as it leads to the organisation closing its mind unwittingly to processes of change in the environment, and failing to adapt in time. In this case management may want to reduce the top-down part of the strategic dialogue, and let the bottom-up process dominate. It becomes important that the organisation starts putting increasing value on divergent views. An atmosphere needs to be created in which exploration and experimentation in the margin are encouraged. Clear signals are required from the top that the "maverick" view is rewarded. Tolerance for error needs to be increased, error should become a positive investment in the future, not a mistake to be punished.

In situations which are locked-in a clear signal from management may be required. This can take an organisational form, such as a reorganisation or reallocation of responsibilities. The purpose is to shake up the organisation and give a signal: "Things are changing, new ideas are rewarded".

Scenario planning can be particularly powerful in helping the organisation to increase its field of vision. In analogy with the model of "memories of the future" as developed by Ingvar (see page 116) management needs to increase the number of different futures which play an active role in the strategic conversation. Scenarios can be seen as the memories of the future of the organisation. Just as a wider range of memories of the future helps the individual to see and perceive more of what happens around him, so can the organisation use a wider range of shared images of the future to spread its attention wider.

This mode of scenario planning relies heavily on outside impulses. The main purpose is to get the organisation to move outside its shared thinking box, and this can only be triggered externally. In this case management will want to pay particular attention to the introduction of appropriate "remarkable persons" who have the capability to move the thinking on (see page 185). The introduction of these new ideas may be organised through a process known as Innovation Searches.

THE INNOVATION SEARCH

When a large number of people need to be involved in opening up the thinking, management can organise an Innovation Search. This workshop model was developed in the 1960s by Joe McPherson when he worked at SRI. These are events in which up to 50 people can participate. The purpose is to develop ideas for future development of the business. Events of this nature need to be carefully prepared. The first step is to decide a list of focus areas in which the group will brainstorm. The organisers need to search widely to come up with as many candidate focus areas as they can. In consultation with management this list is prioritised and the top-ranking four or five are selected. This is the maximum that one workshop can deal with.

Participants need to prepare themselves for such a meeting by pre-reading. A folder of "stretching" material is prepared, containing articles from the literature with innovative ideas, and sent around in advance for people to read. The purpose is to get the thinking away from the conventional. Organisers need not be too careful with the quantity of material included, there is an advantage in sending more material than people can be expected to absorb. A degree of information overload will help in getting out of traditional "thinking boxes".

The setting within which the meeting takes place is important. This will need to be away from the workplace so that interruptions are minimised. The environment presented by the meeting room needs to visibly indicate the purpose of the meeting which is to come up with innovative ideas. The seating arrangement in the room should be visibly different from a usual meeting room. The atmosphere is informal, dress is casual. Participants are permanently reminded of the discussion topics by means of posters on the wall summarising each topic area in some visible way. An overall facilitator reminds participants frequently why they are there, and encourages them to write down any idea that comes up on an idea sheet, blank copies of which are made available to participants in large quantities. To emphasise the importance of idea generation the idea sheets are given a distinct appearance, using pre-printing and colour.

During the meeting each of the focus areas are visited one by one. Approximately half a day is spent on each. The discussion is opened by a presentation discussing the relevance of the area to the organisation. This is done by someone from the organisation itself. This is followed with a presentation on how the topic area is seen from outside the organisation. This presentation needs to be prepared by an outside speaker, who is not part of the circle within which people in the organisation normally discuss the topic. Plenty of time needs to be allowed for discussion. The overall facilitator urges participants to continuously think about novel ways in which the organisation could improve and innovate its activities in the topic area. Breaks need to be scheduled frequently to allow participants to move around and discuss ideas with others one-to-one or in smaller groups of their choice. Participants are reminded to write down any ideas, however immature, on the idea sheets. These are collected frequently and the ideas are entered immediately into a computer database in the backroom. Print-outs are distributed at various times during the sessions to trigger further ideas. In true brainstorming style no quality judgements are made at this stage.

The meeting can be organised as an idea generation exercise only, as input to management consideration of strategy. It is important that participants are made aware of this in advance. People come to meetings expecting results or a "conclusion", and if instead the meeting ends without closure they will feel dissatisfied. In this case advance expectation management by the organisers is important to avoid disappointment and switch-off. In addition it is advisable to distribute a report after the meeting containing the ideas generated, hierarchically ordered in appropriate clusters, as a manifestation of what has been achieved.

If it is considered that the culture requires a more formal closure before the meeting breaks up participants may be asked to rank ideas. Usually a considerable number will have been generated and these need to be clustered first. Generally there is no time to cluster in plenary. Therefore clustering needs to be done in the backroom continuously as the ideas come in. Appropriate database software is a significant success factor in this process.

In a final step the facilitator may suggest that the group indicates action parties who will champion the specific innovation areas, at least until these have been incorporated as a strategic option in the company's strategy process.

PERSEVERANCE

We have been discussing a cultural phenomenon that cannot be implanted or turned around quickly. The scenario planning approach to institutional learning will stick in organisations if the requisite locking-in loops have been put in place among its networked people. In most cases for this to happen assumptions and values have to change. This takes time, and until this is the case management needs to continue to actively promote it. This is not a "get-rich quick" scheme for organisational development, effort must be sustained over time, if the full benefits are to emerge. Making an organisation adaptable requires perseverance. However, for organisations interested in survival and self-development the rewards are fundamental, including:

- An organisation aware of its purpose, business idea, strategy and objectives.
- An organisation alert to its business environment and capable of reading signals of structural change early.
- An organisation making sense of rapid change in its environment and its own relation to that, and thereby being confident enough to look at the future in terms of opportunities rather than threats.
- An organisation coming to timely conclusions on specific actions to take.
- An organisation adapting more quickly and effectively to a changing environment than its competitors.

As this culture pervades throughout the organisation it will affect and alter the nature of the many links in the organisational system of cognitive loops. It will become all-pervasive. The more skilful adaptive behaviour of the organisation will have become a systemic phenomenon, manifesting itself in all its strategy and decision making, independent of the particular individuals involved. For this reason it will be difficult to "prove" direct links between any specific scenario project and any specific strategy pursued. As André Bénard (Shell managing director) put it, "We are trying to make people think."

There is no other way to develop better strategy. As this involves organisational culture it cannot be easily copied, and for this reason will be the source of genuine competitive advantage and organisational success. Or to quote Arie de Geus (planning co-ordinator at Shell): "The ability to learn faster than your competitors may be the only sustainable advantage".

Conclusion

Organisations are systems of individuals linked together through a network of interconnections, largely based on conversation. Organisations can be interpreted as complex adaptive systems, existing in cognitive loops, internally and through its environment, therefore subject to continuous change. These loops over time develop more and more complex mediating processes that intervene between external forces and behaviour. At higher levels of complexity these mediating processes become more independent and autonomous and more determinative of behaviour. Most of our organisational models are quite inadequate to make any reliable predictions of this. Much of the pattern of reactions to events that organisations display can be interpreted only after the event, in terms of "emergent strategy".

Generally managers do not accept that all organisational behaviour is emergent, they tend to believe in investing energy in trying to make the organisation more skilful in reacting to environmental input. A useful way of thinking about organisational behaviour is by the notion of organisational learning. Not all organisational behaviour can be learned. In a competitive world the only thing needed is to be a little better at it than one's competitors. If the organisation can react a little faster than its competitors to environmental impulses, seeing dangers and opportunities a little earlier, then it has a preferential position in the battle for survival. This idea makes managers highly interested in the processes of decision making in their organisation.

The starting point of our study of organisational behaviour has been the network of interconnecting conversations that make up the organisation. The exchange of ideas between individuals about the organisation in its environment is expressed in language. And the language of organisations is rational. People try to explain their point of view in terms of a rational argument. A rational argument carries weight. This is why strategy is a discipline based on rationality. However, most managers realise that in an uncertain world skilful process is equally, if not more important. And having paid due attention to rationality and process they realise that what happens nevertheless often feels like the "throw of the dice", and that one requires a lot of luck for survival. We have paid attention to all these perspectives on the managerial task. But the central theme throughout this book has been the importance of the strategic conversation, as the underlying mechanism in which organisations come into being.

We have suggested that the strategic conversation is based on a major and fundamental distinction between the environment and the organisational self. Organisational learning is interpreted as the attempt to improve the fit between these two. The quality of the conversation can be improved if the available language includes simple and ready concepts in which the self and the environment can be expressed in its essence. So we have spent time trying to consider such concepts. As we are ultimately considering questions of survival we have interpreted the notion of the organisational self as its "success formula". We have considered what elements need to be included in corporate success. This has led us to the concept of the Business Idea as a valid and sufficient characterisation of the organisation in the conversation about fit with the environment. An important aspect in this is the notion of uniqueness vis-à-vis competitors. We have discussed how a management team could go about articulating the Business Idea for their own organisation.

We have then moved to the question of the characterisation of the environment. We have considered that this needs to look into the future which has led us to the question of how to deal with uncertainty. We have concluded that if there is uncertainty there is more than one feasible future, and we have introduced scenario planning, based on a set of different but equally plausible futures, as a suitable way to characterise the environment and understand the uncertainty. We have discussed practical ways in which the environment can be captured in a set of scenarios.

This has led us to the problem of organisational perception. So far the discussion has been entirely based on rationality. If rationality was all that was involved one sufficiently intelligent and knowledgeable person could do the thinking on behalf of the entire organisation. However, no person (or organisation) can see everything, therefore we have considered mechanisms by which organisations filter events in or out. This has led us to consideration of organisational cognitive processes, and how the organisational learning takes place. We have identified two requirements which are to some extent contradictory. First of all the organisation needs differentiation, it needs to incorporate a wide range of different views to perceive, make sense of and react to what is happening over a wide range in the environment. But organisational learning also requires joint experiences which can only derive from joint action. Joint action requires integration of views. Here we have entered the realm of organisational process. The individual, however, intelligent and knowledgeable, can no longer do all the thinking. The organisation needs to consider the contribution of all individuals in it, and the effect of their interactions on strategy.

The first concern of management is to manage the dilemma between differentiation and integration in the organisation. At both sides of this continuum lurk pathologies, in the form of either organisational fragmentation or group-think, that threaten survival. True dilemmas cannot be resolved, they need continuous management. This is the first task of a management who want to make their organisation more skilful in organisational learning.

The institutional discipline of Scenario Planning provides the organisation with concepts such as the Business Idea and the environmental scenarios, which become powerful elements in the organisational learning process. They become institutional concepts and language objects, used by the members of the organisation to make their strategic conversation more skilful and meaningful. In this way they enter institutional memory, and make the organisation more aware of what is going on outside, in a way that allows it to understand the meaning of signals and impulses. Shared concepts and stories then allow it to come to shared conclusions, and therefore react, faster. This richer arsenal of shared concepts becomes embedded in the language and culture, and in this way influences and mobilises the learning skills of the organisation as a whole.

This cultural element suggests that creating a learning organisation is not "plug in and play", but requires a high degree of perseverance on the part of management and the organisation. The various practical implementation tools discussed in this book are not difficult; what is difficult and takes time, energy and persistence is to stick with them until they have become part of the corporate culture, as part of the "way we do things over here". This is only to be expected. "Cheap and easy" success is a contradiction in terms. A simple formula which would seem to work quickly would be copied by everyone, become a hygiene factor and lose its competitive power. If learning faster than your competitor is the only sustainable competitive advantage it cannot come cheap and easy. At the end of this discourse it has become clear why this is. We are dealing with a complex cultural phenomenon which can be turned around only slowly with a lot of perseverance and tenacity. However, anything less may be not be enough in times of accelerated environmental change.

References

Amara, R. & Lipinsky, A.J. (1983), *Business Planning for an Uncertain Future, Scenarios and Strategies,* Pergamon Press, New York

Argyrus, C. & Schon, D. (1978), *Organizational Learning: A Theory of Action Perspective,* Addison Wesley, Reading, MA

Ashby, W.R. (1983), Self-regulation and requisite variety, in Emery, F.E. (ed) *Systems Thinking,* Penguin, New York

Bateson, G.W. (1967), *Mind and Nature,* Dutton, New York

Bateson, G.W. (1972), *Steps to an Ecology of Mind,* Ballantine, New York

Bénard, A. (1980), World oil and cold reality, *Harvard Business Review,* Nov–Dec 1980, 91–101

Bougon, M.G. (1992), Congregate cognitive maps: a unified dynamic theory of organization and strategy, *Journal of Management Studies,* vol 29, 369–389

Bougon, M.G. & Komocar, J.M. (1990), Directing strategic change, a dynamic holistic approach, in Huff, A.S. (ed) *Mapping Strategic Thought,* Wiley, Chichester

BP Statistical Review, The British Petroleum Company Plc, Britannic House, 1 Finsbury Circus, London EC2M 7BA

Brand, S. (1994), *How Buildings Learn,* Viking, New York

Checkland, P. (1981), *Systems Thinking, Systems Practice,* Wiley, Chichester

De Geus, A.P. (1988), Planning as learning, *Harvard Business Review,* vol 66, no 2, 70–74

De Geus, A.P. (1997), *The Living Company,* in preparation.

Douglas, M. (1986), *How Institutions Think,* Syracuse University Press, New York

Eden, C. (1987), Problem solving/finishing, in Jackson, M. & Keys, P. (eds), *New Direction in Management Sciences,* Gower, Aldershot

Eden, C. (1992), Strategic management as a social process, *Journal of Management Studies,* vol 29, 799–811

Einhorn, H.J & Hogarth, R.M. (1982), Prediction, diagnosis and causal thinking in forecasting, *Journal of Forecasting,* 22–36

Emery, F.E. & Trist, E.L. (1965), The causal texture of organisational environments, *Human Relations,* vol 18, 21–32

Freeman, S. (1984), *Strategic Management,* Pitman, London

Galer, G. & van der Heijden, K. (1992), The learning organisation, how planners create organisational learning, *Information Systems for Strategic Advantage,* vol 10, no 6, 5–12

Goold, M., Campbell, A. & Alexander, M. (1994), *Corporate Level Strategy, Creating Value in the Multi-business Company,* Wiley, New York

Goold, M. & Quinn, J.J. (1990), *Strategic Control, Milestones for Long Term Performance,* Hutchinson, London

Grant, R.M. (1991), The resource-based theory of competitive advantage, implications for strategy formulation, *California Management Review,* vol 23, Spring 1991, 114–135

Hart, S. & Banbury, C. (1994), How strategy-making processes can make a difference, *Strategic Management Journal,* vol 15, 251–269

Ingvar, D. (1985), Memories of the future, an essay on the temporal organisation of conscious awareness, *Human Neuro-biology,* 1985/4, 127–136

Kahane, A. (1992a), Scenarios for energy, sustainable world versus global mercantilism, *Long Range Planning,* vol 25, no 4, 38–46

Kahane, A. (1992b), The Mont Fleur scenarios, *Weekly Mail* and *The Guardian Weekly* Bellville, SA

Kahn, H. & Wiener, A. (1967), *The Year 2000,* Macmillan, New York

Kay, J. (1993), The structure of strategy, *Business Strategy Review,* vol 4, no 2, 17–37

Kelly, K. (1994), *Out of Control, the Rise of Neo-biological Civilization,* Addison Wesley, Reading, MA

Kemeny, J., Goodman, M. & Karash, R. (1994), Starting with storytelling, in Senge P. et al (eds), *The Fifth Discipline Fieldbook,* Doubleday Currency, New York.

Kirkland, R.I. (1987), L.C. van Wachem, Royal Dutch/Shell, *Fortune,* 3 August 1987, vol 116, p 28

Kleiner, A. (1996), *The Age of Heretics,* Currency Doubleday, New York

Kolb, D. & Rubin, I.M. (1991), *Organizational Behavior, an Experiential Approach,* Prentice Hall, Englewood Cliffs, NJ

Lindblom, C.E. (1959), The science of muddling through, *Public Administration Review,* vol 19, 79–88

Lorenz, C. (1993), Avoiding the IBM trap, *Financial Times,* 15 October 1993, p 18.

Marsh, B. & van der Heijden, K. (1993), System Thinking and Business Strategy, *Systems Thinking in Action Conferences,* 8 Nov 1993, Boston MA

Michael, D.N. (1973), *On Learning to Plan – and Planning to Learn,* Jossey-Bass, San Francisco, CA

Miller, D. (1993), The architecture of simplicity, *Academy of Management Review,* vol 18, no 1, 116–138

Miller, G.A. (1956), The magical number seven, plus or minus two, some limits on our capacity for processing information, *Psychological Review,* vol 63, no 2, 81–96

Mintzberg, H. & Waters, J. (1985), Of strategies, deliberate and emergent, *Strategic Management Journal,* vol 6, 257–272

Mintzberg, H. (1990), The design school, reconsidering the basic premises of strategic management, *Strategic Management Journal,* vol 11, 171–195

Mintzberg, H. (1994), *The Rise and Fall of Strategic Planning,* Prentice Hall, Hemel Hempstead

Norman, R. (1973), *Management for Growth,* Wiley, Chichester

Normann, R. (1984), *Service Management, Strategy and Leadership in Service Businesses,* Wiley, Chichester

Normann, R. & Ramirez, R. (1994), *From Value Chain to Value Constellation, Designing Interactive Strategy,* Wiley, Chichester

Pettigrew, A. & Whipp, R. (1991), *Managing Change for Competitive Success,* Blackwell, Oxford

Porter, M.E. (1980), *Competitive Strategy, Techniques for Analyzing Industries and Competitors,* The Free Press, New York

Porter, M.E. (1985), *Competitive Advantage, Creating and Sustaining Superior Performance,* The Free Press, New York

Quinn, J.B. (1980), *Strategies for Change, Logical Incrementalism,* Irwin, Homewood, IL

Quinn, J.L. & Mason, D. H. (1994), How Digital uses scenarios to rethink the present, *Planning Review,* vol 22, no 6, 14–17

Rosell, S.A. (1995), *Changing Maps, Governing in a World of Rapid Change,* Carleton University Press, Ottawa

Rumelhart, D.E. (1980), Schemata, the building blocks of cognitions, in Spiro, R.J. Bruce, B.C. & Rewer, W.F. (eds), *Theoretical Issues in Reading Comprehension,* Erlbaum, Hillsdale, NJ

Rumelt, R.P., Schendel, D. & Teece, D.J. (1991), Strategic management and economics, *Strategic Management Journal,* vol 12, 5–29

Rumelt, R.P. (1987), Theory, strategy and entrepreneurship, in Teece, D. J. (ed), *The Competitive Challenge,* Ballinger, Cambridge, MA

Schein, E. (1992), *Organizational Culture and Leadership,* 2nd edition, Jossey Bass, San Fransisco, CA

Schoemaker, P. (1992), How to link strategic vision to core capabilities, *Sloan Management Review,* vol 34, no 1, 67–81

Schoemaker, P. & van der Heijden, K. (1992), Integrating scenarios into strategic planning at Royal Dutch/Shell, *Planning Review,* vol 20, no 3

Schwartz, P. (1991), *The Art of the Long View,* Doubleday Currency, New York

Schwartz, P. (1992), Composing a plot for your scenario, *Planning Review,* vol 20, no 3, 4–9

Selznick, P. (1957), *Leadership in Administration,* Harper and Row, re-issued in 1984 by University of California Press, Berkeley, CA

Senge, P. (1990), *The Fifth Discipline,* Doubleday, New York

Smith, G.N. & Brown, P.B. (1986), *Sweat Equity, What It Really Takes to Build America's Best Small Companies – By The Guys Who Did It,* Simon and Schuster, New York

Stern, W. (1906), *Person und Sache,* Verlag von Johann Ambrosius Barth, Leipzig

Teece, D.J. (1986), Firm boundaries, technological innovation and strategic management, in Thomas, L.G. (ed) *The Economics of Strategic Planning,* Lexington Books, Lexington, MA

van der Heijden, K. (1993), Strategic vision at work, discussing strategic vision in management teams, in Hendry, J. & Johnson, G. (eds) *Strategic Thinking, Leadership and the Management of Change,* Wiley, Chichester

van der Heijden, K. (1994), Probabilistic planning and scenario planning, in Wright, G. & Ayton, P. (ed) *Subjective Probability,* Wiley, Chichester

Vygotsky, L.S. (1986), *Thought and Language,* MIT Press, MA

Wack, P. (1985a), Scenarios, uncharted waters ahead, *Harvard Business Review,* Sep–Oct 1985, 73–90

Wack, P. (1985b), Scenarios, shooting the rapids, *Harvard Business Review,* Nov–Dec 1985, 131–142

Weick, K.E. (1979), *The Social Psychology of Organizing,* Addison Wesley, Reading, MA

Weick, K.E. (1990), Cartographic myths in organizations, in Huff, A. S. (ed) *Mapping Strategic Thought,* Wiley, Chichester

Whittington, R. (1993), *What Is Strategy and Does It Matter?* Routledge, London

Index

Index compiled by Mary Kirkness